G.E. MOORE: SELECTED WRITINGS

'Moore was extremely clever. . . . That alone does not make him unique among twentieth-century philosophers. But other qualities do. First, he took extraordinary pains to say, or write, exactly what he meant, neither more nor less. Second, he utterly eschewed pseudo-profundity and flashiness of any kind. He wrote plain English with a minimum of technical language. He never dealt with trivial issues, but only with matters of central philosophical importance. He never wrote for effect; he never tried to dazzle; his only concern was with the truth. . . . Baldwin's selection of writings seems to me admirable. They include many of his best and most characteristic things.'

Sir Peter Strawson

'This is a well-chosen selection of the writings of a great philosopher of commonsense. His defense of commonsense was a twentieth-century development of the tradition of John Locke and Thomas Reid. Moore added a dimension of analytical acuteness and precision to the defense, however, that was previously unknown and remains unexcelled. His clear and profound analyses are a monument to the power of the human mind to understand itself, the external world, and the relation of one to the other. As we turn to a new century, we may observe the philosophical pretensions of our time and turn to commonsense, to Moore, to free us from them, just as he freed us in this century from the errors of the last. We may thus freed find the way to the truth.'

Keith Lehrer, Professor of Philosophy, University of Arizona

The classic essays included, 'A Defence of Common Sense', 'Certainty', 'Sense-Data', 'External and Internal Relations', Hume's Theory Examined', 'Is Existence a Predicate', and 'Proof of an External World', are crucial to major philosophical debates that still resonate today. In addition, this collection also contains the key early papers in which Moore signals his break with idealism, and three important previously unpublished papers from his later work which illustrate his relationship with Wittgenstein.

Thomas Baldwin is a lecturer at Cambridge University and a Fellow of Clare College.

International Library of Philosophy

Edited by Timothy Crane and Jonathan Wolff,
University College London

The history of the International Library of Philosophy can be traced back to the 1920s, when C.K. Ogden launched the series with G.E. Moore's *Philosphical Papers* and soon after published Ludwig Wittgenstein's *Tractatus Logico-Philosophicus*. Since its auspicious start, it has published the finest work in philosophy under the successive editorships of A.J. Ayer, Bernard Williams and Ted Honderich. Now jointly edited by Tim Crane and Jonathan Wolff the I.L.P. will continue to publish work at the forefront of philosophical research.

G.E. MOORE: SELECTED WRITINGS

Edited by Thomas Baldwin

London and New York

First published 1993
by Routledge
2 Park Square, Milton Park, Abingdon, Oxon, OX14 4RN (UK)

Simultaneously published in the USA and Canada
by Routledge
711 Third Avenue, New York, NY 10017 (US)

First issued in paperback 2013

Routledge is an imprint of the Taylor & Francis Group, an informa business

Typeset in 10/12pt Palatino
Florencetype Ltd, Kewstoke, Avon

British Library Cataloguing in Publication Data
A catalogue record for this book is available from the British Library

Library of Congress Cataloging in Publication Data
Moore, G.E. (George Edward), 1873–1958.
[Selections. 1993]
Selected writings / G.E. Moore: edited by Thomas Baldwin.
p.   cm. — (International library of philosophy)
Includes bibliographical references and index.
Contents: The nature of judgment – Truth and Falsity – The refutation
of idealism – Sense-data – Hume's theory examined – External and
internal relations – A defence of common sense – Is existence a predicate?
– Proof of an external world – Certainty – Being certain that one is in
pain – Moore's paradox – Letter to Norman Malcolm.
1. Philosophy. I. Baldwin, Thomas. II. Title. III. Series.
B1647.M71   1993
192 — dc20   93–16366

ISBN 0–415–09853–X
ISBN 978-0-415-86229-5 (Paperback)

CONTENTS

INTRODUCTION

G.E. Moore (1873–1958) was one of the most important philosophers of the century. After studying classics and philosophy at Cambridge, he won a prize fellowship in 1898 at Trinity College, Cambridge, on the basis of a dissertation entitled, somewhat misleadingly, 'The Metaphysical Basis of Ethics'. In this dissertation, and other writings of this period, he formulated lines of argument which helped to bring about the 'revolution in philosophy' through which the idealist philosophy of F.H. Bradley and others was replaced by the analytic approach which is still dominant within the English-speaking world. At much the same time, he composed his ethical treatise *Principia Ethica* (1903). In this book he set the scene for subsequent debates among philosophers concerning the foundations of ethics by declaring that all previous ethical theories were guilty of a major fallacy – the 'naturalistic fallacy' of attempting to define values in non-ethical terms. In addition, by affirming the supreme value of art and friendship, Moore's text provided a manifesto for the ideals characteristic of the Bloomsbury Group, several of whom had studied with him.[1]

In 1904 Moore left Cambridge and lived for some time in Edinburgh. While there he studied the writings of the great Scottish philosophers David Hume and Thomas Reid and, perhaps partly under their influence, he turned his attention to questions concerning the nature of perception and the grounds for our knowledge of the external world, as is shown in the excerpts here from his London lectures of 1910–11 (on 'Some Main Problems of Philosophy'). Throughout his life he returned again and again to these perennial questions of philosophy. In 1911 Moore moved back to Cambridge as a lecturer, and remained there for the rest of his subsequent career (apart from an extended visit to the United States during the Second World War when he enormously impressed his American hosts).[2] At Cambridge Moore quickly consolidated his reputation, so much so that J.M. McTaggart (who had taught Moore and sharply disagreed with him on most philosophical issues) wrote in 1920 that 'I have no hesitation in saying that I regard Dr G.E. Moore as unsurpassed in ability by any British philosopher now living'.[3] From 1921 until 1947 Moore was Editor of *Mind* (the pre-eminent British philosophy journal) and from 1925 until 1938 he was Professor of Philosophy at Cambridge. During this period Cambridge was the most important centre of philosophy in the world, thanks to the presence there of Frank Ramsey, Ludwig Wittgenstein and (occasionally) Bertrand Russell, as well as Moore himself. Moore's role during this great period of creative activity was partly personal; there are many testimonies to the Socratic impact of his interventions in philosophical discussion.[4] But Moore also provided many of the central themes of these discussions, and his influence is well attested by a remark of Austin Duncan-Jones that Moore's practice of philosophical analysis of common sense formed 'the intellectual background of many of us in recent years'.[5]

The writings included in this volume span the whole of Moore's career. His early paper, 'The Nature of Judgment', is a chapter from his 1898 Fellowship dissertation; Moore is here extricating himself from Bradley's idealist conception of judgment and developing in its place an alternative realist conception which is more clearly set out in the brief piece on 'Truth and Falsity' which Moore wrote in 1899 for J.M. Baldwin's *Dictionary of Philosophy and Psychology*. Moore's early critique of idealism is summed up in his famous polemical piece, 'The Refutation of Idealism' (1903). In thinking about this paper one should, however, bear in mind that when Moore republished it in his *Philosophical Studies* (1922) he remarked that 'This paper now appears to me to be very confused, as well as to embody a good many down-right mistakes'. Perhaps for this reason Moore continued to refine his criticisms of idealism in later writings, most notably his paper 'External and Internal Relations' (1919) in which he criticises the idealist thesis that all relations are internal. It is worth noting how, in comparison with his earlier writings, Moore has here become much more sophisticated concerning issues of logical theory (for example, Moore here introduces the concept of entailment). As Moore acknowledged, his logical sophistication owed much to the work of Bertrand Russell. Yet Moore was no passive expositor of Russell's logical theories; and in his later essay, 'Is Existence a Predicate?' (1936), he subjects Russell's treatment of the logic of existence to a decisive critical examination.

As I have already mentioned, Moore's attention turned to questions concerning perception and knowledge during his absence from Cambridge and the London lectures included here from this period – 'Sense-Data' and 'Hume's Theory Examined' – show him embarking on lines of argument which he was to pursue for the rest of his life. In his famous paper, 'A Defence of Common Sense' (1925), we see Moore, at the height of his powers, employing his analytic and dialectical skills to articulate and defend the 'common sense view of the world' while making it clear that such a position does not prejudge philosophical debates as to what this view amounts to. In his later paper, 'Proof of an External World' (1939), Moore, in effect, employs an appeal to common sense (though he does not actually use the phrase) in order to provide a refutation of idealist doubts about the existence of the external world. In 'Certainty' (1941) Moore turns to confront sceptical arguments which cast doubt on our knowledge of the external world; it is notable that his approach here (unlike that of 'Hume's Theory Examined') does not involve anything like an appeal to common sense. Instead he seeks to identify fallacies, inconsistencies, and *non-sequiturs* in the sceptical arguments. It is not clear whether, by the end of the paper, he takes himself to have altogether succeeded in this task: when the paper was originally published Moore himself expressed dissatisfaction with the closing paragraphs. For this reason I have taken the opportunity to add, as a footnote to the end of the paper, some paragraphs he deleted at a late stage which seem to me to make the conclusion of the paper more intelligible.

Moore's ethical writings are an important omission from this collection. This does not signify any devaluation of these writings on my part: it is, rather, a result of the fact that a new edition of *Principia Ethica* is currently in preparation and this will also include the best of Moore's other ethical writings.[6] So it seemed best to plan these volumes in such a way that overlap between them is avoided. By way of compensation for the omission I have included in this collection some previously unpublished late pieces by Moore. Most of these (including the alternative ending to 'Certainty' mentioned above) come from the collection of his papers which was recently given to the University Library, Cambridge, by his son Timothy Moore. In selecting any of them for publication I am conscious that I am taking the liberty of imposing my judgment concerning their merits in the face of Moore's presumed disagreement (since he did not attempt to prepare them for publication); I hope that readers of this volume will agree that they do indeed merit publication. One of these is a discussion of the paradox which has come to bear his name ('Moore's Paradox'); although Moore's published writings contain some discussion of this, they are very brief, and the paper published here shows that Moore had a much broader understanding of the phenomenon than one might otherwise have supposed. Another is a paper ('Being Certain that One is in Pain') in which Moore discusses the view that the certainty of first-person ascriptions of sensations arises from the fact that 'it makes no sense' to say that such ascriptions might be incorrect. Although Moore refers to a paper by John Wisdom,[7] the position under discussion had been advanced by Wittgenstein (as Wisdom himself makes clear) and, as with the discussion of his paradox, part of the interest of these two late pieces is that they show (as Moore's published writings do not) something of the intellectual relationship in the 1930s and 1940s between Moore and Wittgenstein. The theme is continued, again indirectly, in the long letter from Moore to Malcolm in which Moore responds to Malcolm's paper, 'Defending Common Sense'.[8] As Malcolm later explained,[9] he discussed both his paper and Moore's letter with Wittgenstein, who happened to be staying with him at the time, and these discussions provided Wittgenstein with the starting-point for the reflections later published as *On Certainty*.[10] So Moore's letter forms part of the context of that work, in which Wittgenstein explicitly discusses some of Moore's own writings (especially 'A Defence of Common Sense').

In preparing this collection I am indebted to Timothy Moore for permission to reprint, or publish here for the first time, his father's writings. I am also grateful to Adrian Driscoll of

Routledge, who first had the idea of putting together a selection of Moore's writings and then encouraged me to include previously unpublished material.

NOTES

1 The Bloomsbury Group was a group of writers and artists who lived in or near Gordon Square, London, at the start of this century. Virginia Woolf and her sister Vanessa Bell were at the centre of this group and both their husbands, Leonard Woolf and Clive Bell, had studied under Moore, as had Lytton Strachey and Maynard Keynes who were also members of the group.
2 Cf. M. White, 'Memories of G.E. Moore', *Journal of Philosophy* 57 (1960) pp.805–10.
3 This comes from a reference, preserved among Moore's papers in Cambridge, which McTaggart wrote for Moore when he was applying (unsuccessfully) for a Professorship.
4 G. Ryle, 'G.E. Moore' in his *Collected Papers* vol. 1 (Hutchinson, London: 1971), pp.268–71. R.B. Braithwaite, 'George Edward Moore: 1873–1958' in *G.E. Moore: Essays in Retrospect*, eds A. Ambrose and M. Lazerowitz (George Allen & Unwin, London: 1970), pp.17–33.
5 A. Duncan-Jones, 'Does Philosophy Analyse Common Sense?', *Aristotelian Society Supplementary Volume* 37 (1937), p.147.
6 The new edition of *Principia Ethica*, to be published by Cambridge University Press in 1993, will include a previously unpublished Preface which Moore wrote for a projected second edition of the book in 1922. In the event the project was abandoned, probably because Moore did not complete the Preface; nonetheless the part which survives casts important new light on Moore's later attitude to *Principia Ethica*.
7 J. Wisdom, 'Philosophical Perplexity', *Proceedings of the Aristotelian Society* 37 (1936–7) pp.71–88.
8 N. Malcolm, 'Defending Common Sense', *Philosophical Review* 58 (1949) pp.201–20.
9 N. Malcolm, 'Moore and Wittgenstein on the Sense of "I Know"' in *Thought and Knowledge* (Cornell University Press, Ithaca NY: 1977), pp.170–98.
10 *On Certainty*, eds G.E.M. Anscombe and G.H. von Wright, transl. D. Paul and G.E.M. Anscombe (Blackwell, Oxford: 1969).

1

THE NATURE OF JUDGMENT

'Truth and falsehood', says Mr Bradley[1] 'depend on the relation of our ideas to reality'. And he immediately goes on to explain that, in this statement, 'ideas' must not be understood to mean mere 'states of my mind'. The ideas, he says, on the relation of which to reality truth depends, are '*mere* ideas, signs of an existence other than themselves', and this aspect of them must not be confused either with their existence in my mind or with their particular character as so existent, which may be called their content. 'For logic, at least', he says, 'all ideas are signs' (p.5); and 'A sign is any fact that has a meaning', while 'meaning consists of a part of the content (original or acquired) cut off, fixed by the mind, and considered apart from the existence of the sign' (p.4).

But Mr Bradley himself does not remain true to this conception of the logical idea as the idea *of* something. As such, indeed, it *is* only the psychological idea, related, indeed, to that which it signifies, but only related to it. Hence he finds it necessary, later, to use 'idea', not of the symbol, but of the symbolised. Ideas, as *meanings*, not as 'facts, which have a meaning', 'are', he says (p.8), 'the ideas we spoke of, when we said "Without ideas no judgment"'. And he proceeds to show that 'in predication we do not *use* the mental fact, but only the meaning'; although, where he did say 'Without ideas no judgment', his words were 'we cannot judge until we use ideas *as* ideas. We must have become aware that they are not realities, that they are *mere* ideas, signs of an existence other than themselves'. It

Read before the Aristotelian Society. Originally published in *Mind* n.5. 8 (1899), pp. 176–93.

would seem plain, then, that there his doctrine was that we do, in predication, use the mental fact, though only as a sign; whereas here his doctrine is that we do not use the mental fact, even as a sign, but only that which it signifies. This important transition he slurs over with the phrase: 'But it is better to say the idea *is* the meaning'. The question is surely not of which is 'better to say', but which is true.

Now to Mr Bradley's argument that 'the idea in judgment is the universal meaning' I have nothing to add. It appears to me conclusive, as against those, of whom there have been too many, who have treated the idea as a mental state. But he seems to me to be infected by the same error as theirs, alike in his preliminary failure to distinguish clearly whether it is the symbol or the symbolised of which he is speaking, and in his final description of the 'idea, as meaning', when he has definitely decided in its favour. 'A meaning', he says, as we saw above, 'consists of a part of the content (original or acquired) cut off, fixed by the mind, and considered apart from the existence of the sign'. And again, 'an idea, if we use idea of the meaning, is neither given nor presented, but is taken' (p.8). If indeed 'the universal meaning' were thus simply a part of the content of our own ideas, as mental states, and that, too, a part 'cut off' by our own minds, it would be intelligible that 'truth and falsehood' should still be said to 'depend on the relation of our ideas to reality'. It will be our endeavour to show, on the contrary, that the 'idea used in judgment' is not a part of the content of our ideas, nor produced by any action of our minds, and that hence truth and falsehood are not dependent on the relation of *our* ideas to reality.

I shall in future use the term 'concept' for what Mr Bradley calls a 'universal meaning'; since the term 'idea' is plainly full of ambiguities, whereas 'concept' and its German equivalent *'Begriff'* have been more nearly appropriated to the use in question. There is, indeed, a great similarity between Kant's description of his *'Begriff'*, and Mr Bradley's of his 'logical idea'. For Kant, too, it is the 'analytical unity of consciousness' which *makes* a *'Vorstellung'* or 'idea' into a *'conceptus communis'* or *'gemeinsamer Begriff'* [B133n].[2]

It is our object to protest against this description of a concept as an 'abstraction' from ideas.

Mr Bradley's doctrine, as above sketched, presupposes that,

when I have an idea (*Vorstellung*) of something, that something is itself part of the content of my idea. This doctrine, for the present, I am ready to admit; my question now is whether, when I have an idea of something, that something must not *also* be regarded as something other than part of the content of my idea. The content of an idea is, Mr Bradley tells us, what the idea is; it is 'a character which is different or distinguishable from that of other' ideas, treated as mental facts. Now, before I can judge at all on Mr Bradley's theory, a part of this character must have been 'cut off and fixed by the mind'. But my question is, whether we can thus cut off a part of the character of our ideas, and attribute that part to something else, unless we already know, in part at least, what is the character of the idea from which we are to cut off the part in question. If not, then we have already made a judgment with regard to the character of our idea. But this judgment, again, requires, on Mr Bradley's theory, that I should have had an idea of my idea, and should have already cut off a part of the content of that secondary idea, in order that I may make a judgment with regard to the character of the primary idea that is in question. And similarly it is quite impossible that I should know what the content of my secondary idea is, until I have made it in its turn the object of a third idea, by taking part of this tertiary content. And so on *ad infinitum*. The theory would therefore seem to demand the completion of an infinite number of psychological judgments before any judgment can be made at all. But such a completion is impossible; and therefore all judgment is likewise impossible. It follows, therefore, if we are to avoid this absurdity, that the 'idea used in judgment' must be something other than a part of the content of any idea of mine. Mr Bradley's theory presupposes that I may have two ideas, that have a part of their content in common; but he would at the same time compel us to describe this common part of content as part of the content of some third idea. But what is gained by such a description? If the part of content of this third idea is a part only in the same sense, as the common part of the other two is a part of each, then I am offering an explanation which presupposes that which was to be explained. Whereas if the part, which is used in explanation, is a part in the only sense which will make my explanation significant, i.e., an existent part, then it is difficult to see how that which belongs to one idea can also come to belong to other ideas and yet remain one and the same. In short, the idea used in judgment is indeed a 'universal meaning'; but it cannot, for that very reason, be described as part of the content of any psychological idea whatever.

These difficulties, which are of the same nature as the famous τρίτος ἄνθρωπος urged against the hypostasised Platonic ideas,[3] inevitably proceed from trying to explain the concept in terms of some existent fact, whether mental or of any other nature. All such explanations do in fact presuppose the nature of the concept, as a *genus per se*, irreducible to anything else. The concept is not a mental fact, nor any part of a mental fact. Identity of content is presupposed in any reasoning; and to explain the identity of content between two facts by supposing that content to be a part of the content of some third fact, must involve a vicious circle. For in order that the content of the third fact may perform this office, it must already be supposed like the contents of the other two, i.e., having something in common with them, and this community of content is exactly what it was proposed to explain.

When, therefore, I say 'This rose is red', I am not attributing part of the content of my idea to the rose, nor yet attributing parts of the content of my ideas of rose and red together to some third subject. What I am asserting is a specific connexion of certain concepts forming the total concept 'rose' with the concepts 'this' and 'now' and 'red'; and the judgment is true if such a connexion is existent. Similarly when I say 'The chimera has three heads', the chimera is not an idea in my mind, nor any part of such idea. What I mean to assert is nothing about my mental states, but a specific connexion of concepts. If the judgment is false, that is not because my *ideas* do not correspond to reality, but because such a conjunction of concepts is not to be found among existents.

With this, then, we have approached the nature of a proposition or judgment. A proposition is composed not of words, nor yet of thoughts, but of concepts. Concepts are possible objects of thought; but that is no definition of them. It merely states that they may come into relation with a thinker; and in order that they *may* do anything, they must already *be* something. It is indifferent to their nature whether anybody thinks them or not. They are incapable of change; and the relation into which they enter with the knowing subject implies no action or

4

reaction. It is a unique relation which can begin or cease with a change in the subject; but the concept is neither cause nor effect of such a change. The occurrence of the relation has, no doubt, its causes and effects, but these are to be found only in the subject.

It is of such entities as these that a proposition is composed. In it certain concepts stand in specific relations with one another. And our question now is, wherein a proposition differs from a concept, that it may be either true or false.

It is at first sight tempting to say that the truth of a proposition depends on its relation to reality; that any proposition is true which consists of a combination of concepts that is actually to be found among existents. This explanation was indeed actually used above (p.4), as a preliminary explanation. And it may be admitted that propositions with which this is the case are true. But if this constituted the truth of a proposition, concepts too might in themselves be true. Red would be a true concept, because there actually are red things; and conversely a chimera would be a false concept, because no such combination either has been, is, or will be (so far as we know) among existent things. But the theory must be rejected as an ultimate one, because not all true propositions have this relation to reality. For example, $2 + 2 = 4$ is true, whether there exist two things or not. Moreover it may be doubted here whether even the concepts of which the proposition consists, can ever be said to exist. We should have to stretch our notion of existence beyond intelligibility, to suppose that 2 ever has been, is, or will be an existent.

It would seem, in fact, from this example, that a proposition is nothing other than a complex concept. The difference between a concept and a proposition, in virtue of which the latter alone can be called true or false, would seem to lie merely in the simplicity of the former. A proposition is a synthesis of concepts; and, just as concepts are themselves immutably what they are, so they stand in infinite relations to one another equally immutable. A proposition is constituted by any number of concepts, together with a specific relation between them; and according to the nature of this relation the proposition may be either true or false. What kind of relation makes a proposition true, what false, cannot be further defined, but must be immediately recognised.

And this description will also apply to those cases where there appears to be a reference to existence. Existence is itself a concept; it is something which we mean; and the great body of propositions, in which existence is joined to other concepts or syntheses of concepts, are simply true or false according to the relation in which it stands to them. It is not denied that this is a peculiarly important concept; that we are peculiarly anxious to know what exists. It is only maintained that existence is logically subordinate to truth; that truth cannot be defined by a reference to existence, but existence only by a reference to truth. When I say 'This paper exists', I must require that this proposition be true. If it is not true, it is unimportant, and I can have no interest in it. But if it is true, it means only that the concepts, which are combined in specific relations in the concept of this paper, are also combined in a specific manner with the concept of existence. That specific manner is something immediately known, like red or two. It is highly important, because we set such value upon it; but it is itself a concept. All that exists is thus composed of concepts necessarily related to one another in specific manners, and likewise to the concept of existence.

I am fully aware how paradoxical this theory must appear, and even how contemptible. But it seems to me to follow from premises generally admitted, and to have been avoided only by lack of logical consistency. I assume Mr Bradley's proof that the concept is necessary to truth and falsehood. I endeavour to show, what I must own appears to me perfectly obvious, that the concept can consistently be described neither as an existent, nor as part of an existent, since it is presupposed in the conception of an existent. It is similarly impossible that truth should depend on a relation to existents or to an existent, since the proposition by which it is so defined must itself be true, and the truth of this can certainly not be established, without a vicious circle, by exhibiting its dependence on an existent. Truth, however, would certainly seem to involve at least two terms, and some relation between them; falsehood involves the same; and hence it would seem to remain, that we regard truth and falsehood as properties of certain concepts, together with their relations – a whole to which we give the name of proposition.

I have appealed throughout to the rules of logic; nor, if any one rejects these, should I have much to fear from his arguments. An appeal to the facts is useless. For, in order that a fact may be made the basis of an argument, it must first be put in the form of a proposition, and, moreover, this proposition must be supposed true; and then there must recur the dilemma, whether rules of logic are to be accepted or rejected. And these rules once accepted, would seem themselves to offer a confirmation of our theory. For all true inference must be inference from a true proposition; and that the conclusion follows from the premiss must again be a true proposition: so that here also it would appear that the nature of a true proposition is the ultimate *datum*. Nor is an appeal to the 'matter' of the proposition more useful than the former appeal to the facts. It may be true that this matter is given in sensation, or in any other conceivable way. We are not concerned with its origin, but with its nature; and its nature, if it is to enter into a true proposition, must, we agree with Mr Bradley, be the nature of a concept and no other: and then the old conclusions follow. Nor, finally, is a vicious circle involved in our own attempt to establish conclusions with regard to truth, by rules of logic in which that conception is presupposed. For our conclusion is that truth is itself a simple concept; that it is logically prior to any proposition. But a vicious circle occurs only where a proposition is taken as prior to a concept, or a more complex proposition (one involving more concepts) as prior to one which is more simple. Valid logical processes would seem to be of two kinds. It is possible to start from a complex proposition and to consider what propositions are involved in it. In this case the latter must always be more simple than the former; and they may be true, although the former is false. Or it is possible to start from a more simple proposition and to deduce one that is more complex, by success-ive additions of concepts; which is the properly deductive pro-cedure exhibited in the propositions of Euclid: and in this case the premiss must be true, if the conclusion is so. It may be well to state that both procedures are synthetic, in the sense that the results arrived at are different from the premisses, and merely related to them. In a vicious circle, on the other hand, the two procedures are confused. A result arrived at by the former of the two processes just described, is regarded as involving the truth of its premiss. Thus, when we say that the conceptual nature of truth is involved in logical procedure, no vicious circle is com-mitted, since we do not thereby presuppose the truth of logical procedure. But when an existent is said to be involved in truth, a vicious circle is committed, since the proposition 'Something is true', in which 'Something exists' is supposed to be involved, must itself be true, if the latter is to be so.

It seems necessary, then, to regard the world as formed of concepts. These are the only objects of knowledge. They cannot be regarded fundamentally as abstractions either from things or from ideas; since both alike can, if anything is to be true of them, be composed of nothing but concepts. A thing becomes intelligible first when it is analysed into its constituent concepts. The material diversity of things, which is generally taken as starting-point, is only derived; and the identity of the concept, in several different things, which appears on that assumption as the problem of philosophy, will now, if it instead be taken as the starting-point, render the derivation easy. Two things are then seen to be differentiated by the different relations in which their common concepts stand to other concepts. The opposition of concepts to existents disappears, since an existent is seen to be nothing but a concept or complex of concepts standing in a unique relation to the concept of existence. Even the description of an existent as a proposition (a true existential proposition) seems to lose its strangeness, when it is remembered that a proposition is here to be understood, not as anything subjective – an assertion or affirmation of something – but as the combination of concepts which is affirmed. For we are familiar with the idea of affirming or 'positing' an existent, of knowing objects as well as propositions; and the difficulty hitherto has been to discover wherein the two processes were akin. It now appears that perception is to be regarded philosophically as the cognition of an existential proposition; and it is thus apparent how it can furnish a basis for inference, which uniformly exhibits the connexion between propositions. Conversely light is thrown on the nature of inference. For, whereas it could not be maintained that the conclusion was only connected with the premises in my thoughts, and that an inference was nothing, if nobody was making it, great difficulty was felt as to the kind of objectivity that belonged to the terms and their relation, since existence was taken as the type of objectivity. This difficulty is removed, when it is acknowledged that the relation of premises to conclusion is an objective relation, in the same sense as the relation of existence to what exists is objective. It is no longer necessary to hold that logical connexions must, in some obscure sense, exist, since to exist is merely to stand in a certain logical connexion.

It will be apparent how much this theory has in common with Kant's theory of perception. It differs chiefly in substituting for sensations, as the data of knowledge, concepts; and in refusing to regard the relations in which they stand as, in some obscure sense, the work of the mind. It rejects the attempt to explain 'the possibility of knowledge', accepting the cognitive relation as an ultimate *datum* or presupposition; since it maintains the objections which Kant himself urged against an explanation by causality, and recognises no other kind of explanation than that by way of logical connexion with other concepts. It thus renounces the supposed unity of conception guaranteed by Idealism even in the Kantian form, and still more the boasted reduction of all differences to the harmony of 'Absolute Spirit', which marks the Hegelian development. But it is important to point out that it retains the doctrine of Transcendentalism. For Kant's Transcendentalism rests on the distinction between empirical and *a priori* propositions. This is a distinction which offers a striking correspondence to that between the categorical and hypothetical judgments; and since one object of this paper is to combat the view which inclines to take the categorical judgment as the typical form, and attempts in consequence to reduce the hypothetical judgment to it, it will not be out of place to discuss Kant's distinction at some length.

Kant himself offers us two marks by which an *a priori* judgment may be distinguished. 'A proposition', he says, 'which is thought along with its necessity is an *a priori* judgment' [B3]. And it is absolutely *a priori* only if it be not deduced from any proposition, that is not itself a necessary proposition. The second mark of the *a priori* is strict universality. But unfortunately Kant himself seems to admit the invalidity of this as a mark; since he immediately proceeds to state that an empirical universality may hold in all cases (for example, in the proposition: 'All bodies are heavy') and hence be strictly universal [B4].

It is true Kant states that this empirical universality is merely arbitrary. We ought, he says, to express our proposition in the form: 'So far as we have yet observed, there is no exception from' [B3–4] the rule that all bodies are heavy. But it would seem that such a qualification can only affect the truth of our proposition and not its content. It may be questioned whether we have a right to assert universality, but it is universality which we assert. The limitations which Kant points out as belonging to the proposition, can properly be expressed only in the doubt whether we have found a rule at all, not in a doubt whether there are exceptions to it. It may not be true that all bodies are heavy; but whether true or not, it is a universal proposition. There is no difference between this proposition and such as are *a priori*, in respect of universality. And Kant could hardly wish to assert that the difference lay in its truth. For this proposition, he would admit, may be true; and, if so, then it would be *a priori*. But he would not admit the suggestion that it *may* be *a priori*: he asserts that it is not so. The difference between the empirical and the *a priori*, if there is a difference, must therefore be in some other mark than in this universality, which Kant nevertheless asserts to be 'by itself an infallible criterion' [B4]. We may next consider whether such a mark is to be found in 'necessity'.

In this investigation, too, it may be well to examine his example 'All bodies are heavy', since this proposition might seem to have a claim to necessity also, just as it is undoubtedly universal. Kant speaks of it as 'a rule borrowed from experience' [B2]. By this language and by his use of 'Bodies are heavy' as convertible with it, he would seem to suggest that he would not base its empirical character solely on its extensional interpretation. If, as seems probable, he would allow 'Body is heavy' or 'Man is mortal', to be equally empirical propositions, then it is plain that what he calls empirical may involve necessity. It is certain, at all events, that if we are to understand by empirical propositions only such as experience can justify, such a proposition as 'All bodies are heavy' cannot be regarded as empirical. It is based on the proposition 'Body is heavy', with which, if it is to be used for purposes of inference, it must be regarded as convertible. I assume, therefore, that Kant would not have refused to regard 'Body is heavy' as an empirical proposition. It would seem certainly to come under his class of 'rules drawn from experience', whereas 'All bodies are heavy', regarded solely as extensional, cannot be called a rule. The use of this example would seem to lead to important results with regard to the true definition of empirical propositions.

But let us first return to 'All bodies are heavy'; since even this would seem to involve in its very meaning an assertion of necessity. If it be taken purely in extension, it must be resolved into 'This body, and that body, and that body, *ad infinitum*, are, have been and will be heavy'. It involves, therefore, the proposition 'This body is heavy'. But in any proposition of this simple categorical form the notion of substance and attribute is already involved [B6]. Wherever a predicate is asserted of a subject, it is implied that the subject is *a thing*; that it is something marked by the possession of certain attributes and capable of possessing others. 'This body is heavy' presupposes, therefore, 'Body is a thing, and heaviness is a mere attribute'. For we could not convert the proposition into 'Heaviness is corporeal'. But that 'Body is a thing', and that 'Heaviness is an attribute', would seem to be necessary propositions. We may indeed be mistaken in supposing that they are true; but if we were ever to find that heaviness was not an attribute, we should be bound to conclude that it never had been and never would be, not that it was so once but had ceased so to be. All such judgments are truly 'thought along with their necessity' [B3]. They are as necessary as that 2 + 2 = 4. The difference between the two forms of proposition lies not in that the former lacks necessity, nor even that it implies the proposition 'Heaviness exists', for even if heaviness did not exist, the proposition would be true. The proposition means that heaviness could not be other than an attribute; and hence, if Kant's words [B3] are to be taken strictly, it cannot be empirical. In this respect, therefore, it is quite on a level with '2 + 2 = 4'; which also would be true even if there were no two things. The difference seems to lie rather in the nature of the concepts of which the necessary relation is predicated. 'Heaviness' can exist; it is not meaningless to say 'Heaviness exists here and now'; whereas 'attribute', 'two', and other like conceptions can only claim a precarious sort of existence in so far as they are necessarily related to these other notions of which alone properly existential propositions can be made.

If, therefore, we wish to find propositions involving no necessity,* we must descend to purely existential propositions – propositions which do not involve the notions of substance and attribute. These alone can be truly taught us by experience, if experience 'cannot teach us that a thing could not be otherwise'

---

* Even these involve the necessary properties of time; but this point may be reserved for later consideration.

[B3]. And even these are free from necessity, only if they are understood to assert something with regard to an actual part of actual time. They must involve necessity as soon as the distinction between 'This is' and 'This was' is disregarded. It would seem, in fact, to be a mark of the sort of existence which they predicate that it is in time. They may affirm 'This exists', or 'This has existed', but if they take the general form 'This is', that must always be understood to mean no more than 'This always has been, is now, and always will be', and can be strictly analysed into as many different judgments as time is divisible into separate moments.

If, therefore, the difference between the empirical and *a priori* lay primarily, as Kant implies, in the nature of the judgment, not in that of the concept, only existential propositions could be empirical. In order to represent even 'This body is heavy' as an empirical proposition, it would be necessary to analyse it into the form 'Heaviness and the marks of body exist here and now'. But this is certainly not its whole meaning. We must, therefore, suppose that in order to obtain a clear definition of what Kant meant by empirical propositions, we must base it upon the nature of the concepts used in them. Empirical concepts are those which can exist in parts of time. This would seem to be the only manner of distinguishing them. And any proposition into which an empirical concept enters may be called empirical.

Kant himself does recognise the necessity involved in such a proposition as 'This body is heavy', although, for reasons which will appear hereafter, he states it in a somewhat different way. The main object of his 'Analytic' is to show that any such judgment involves a 'synthesis of the manifold of sense-intuition', which is 'necessary *a priori*' [B151]. But he regards this synthesis rather as necessary in order to bring mere perceptions into relation with the 'unity of apperception', than as directly involved in the empirical judgment. Moreover, in order to explain how the forms of synthesis can apply to the manifold, he introduces the inner sense as mediator, and describes the judgment as converting the psychical connexion of the presentations into an objective connexion rather than as applying the categories to a mere manifold, which cannot properly be described as psychical. Accordingly he gives as the ultimate empirical judgment, out of which the application of substance and attribute produces 'Bodies are heavy', the subjective judgment

'When I carry a body, I feel an impression of heaviness', instead of that given above 'Heaviness and the marks of body exist together' [B142].[4] He does not seem to see that his subjective judgment already fully involves the category in question. A statement about my feelings is just as 'objective', in the required sense, as a statement about what is conceived as in space.

With the above definition, therefore, it is obvious why 'Body is heavy' should be called empirical; whereas, if absence of necessity had been the mark required, it would have been difficult to find a reason. For this proposition does not only involve, like 'This body is heavy' or 'All bodies are heavy', the necessary judgments that body is a thing, and heaviness an attribute; it asserts a relation between a 'heaviness' and 'corporeity' such as no experience can prove or disprove. If we found a body which was not heavy, that would indeed lead us to deny the truth of the proposition; but it would also entitle us at once to the opposite necessary proposition 'Body cannot be heavy'. And this is just what holds of $2 + 2 = 4$. It is perhaps inconceivable to us now that two and two should not make four; but, when numbers were first discovered, it may well have been thought that two and two made three or five. Experience, no doubt, must have been the means of producing the conviction that this was not so, but that two and two made four. The necessity of a proposition, therefore, is not called in question by the fact that experience may lead you to think it true or untrue. The test of its necessity lies merely in the fact that it must be either true or untrue, and cannot be true now and untrue the next moment; whereas with an existential proposition it may be true that this exists now, and yet it will presently be untrue that it exists. The doubt about the truth of 'Body is heavy' would seem to proceed chiefly from our uncertainty as to what we mean by 'Body' and by 'heavy'. We cannot recognise instances of them with as great precision as we recognise instances of number; and hence we cannot be sure whether the truth of our proposition may not be overthrown. The proposition is arbitrary solely in this sense. There would seem no doubt that we mean by it to assert an absolute necessity; but between what precise concepts the necessary relation, of which we are certain, holds, we must leave to experience to discover.

From the foregoing analysis it would, therefore, appear that the true distinction upon which Kant's division of propositions into *a priori* and *a posteriori*, necessary and empirical, is based, is the distinction between concepts which can exist in parts of time and concepts which seem to be cut off from existence altogether, but which give rise to assertions of an absolutely necessary relation. Kant would seem to include among empirical propositions all those in which an empirical concept is used; whether the proposition asserts a necessary relation between an empirical and an *a priori* concept, or between two empirical concepts. What it is important to emphasise is that these two kinds of proposition are not distinguished by the absence of the marks which he gives for the *a priori*; they both include both necessity and strict universality. Empirical propositions would therefore include a wide range of propositions, differing very much in the meaning of their assertions. They seem to extend upwards from mere assertions of the existence of this or that, of the type 'Heaviness exists here and now'; through propositions of the usual categorical form 'This body is heavy', which include necessary propositions in their meaning, but at the same time imply an assertion of existence; to propositions which assert existence at every time, while still retaining the element of necessity included in the last, like 'All bodies are heavy'; and finally to those propositions, upon which alone the validity of the last class can be based – propositions which assert a necessary relation, without any implication of existence whatever, of the type 'Body is heavy'. The only common element in all these different classes would seem to be that they all make assertions with regard to some empirical concept, i.e., a concept which can exist in an actual part of time. The second and third classes are mixed and involve necessity, because there is also included in them an assertion with regard to an *a priori* concept. To all of them Kant would seem to oppose as purely *a priori* propositions, those which make an assertion solely with regard to *a priori* concepts and which for that reason can imply no assertion of existence, since an *a priori* concept is one which cannot exist in the limited sense above explained.

The line of division, therefore, upon which Kant's Transcendentalism is based, would seem to fall between propositions involving empirical concepts and those which involve none such; and an empirical concept is to be defined, not as a concept given by experience, since all concepts are so given, but as one which can exist in an actual part of time. This division is necessary in order to include all the various kinds of propositions which Kant includes under the term empirical, many of which involve *a priori* concepts. If the division were to be based on the nature of the propositions as such, as Kant pretends to base it, we saw that pure existential propositions alone could be thought to have a claim to form a class by themselves, as empirical propositions. These do indeed obviously form the basis of the other division; for a simple concept cannot be known as one which could exist in time, except on the ground that it has so existed, is existing, or will exist. But we have now to point out that even existential propositions have the essential mark which Kant assigns to *a priori* propositions – that they are absolutely necessary.

The distinction of time was said to be ultimate for an existential proposition. If this is so, it is obvious that necessary propositions, of the kind which Kant endeavours to establish in the Aesthetic, are involved in them. It was pointed out that a pure existential proposition could only assert the existence of a simple concept; all others involving the *a priori* concepts of substance and attribute. If now we take the existential proposition 'Red exists', we have an example of the type required. It is maintained that, when I say this, my meaning is that the concept 'red' and the concept 'existence' stand in a specific relation both to one another and to the concept of time. I mean that 'Red exists now', and thereby imply a distinction from its past and future existence. And this connexion of red and existence with the moment of time I mean by 'now', would seem to be as necessary as any other connexion whatever. If it is true, it is necessarily true, and if false, necessarily false. If it is true, its contradictory is as fully impossible as the contradictory of $2 + 2 = 4$.

But the necessity thus involved in existential propositions does not do away with the importance of Kant's distinction between the empirical and the *a priori*. So far as he attempts to base it upon the fact that what is empirical alone is 'given in experience' and may be referred to 'sense' [B2], it must indeed be given up; but as against the English philosophers, who held the same view about sense-knowledge, it retains its full weight. The Transcendental Deduction contains a perfectly valid answer to Hume's scepticism, and to empiricism in general. Philosophers of this school generally tend to deny the validity of any propositions except those about existents. Kant may be said to have pointed out that in any of these propositions, which the empiricists considered to be the ultimate, if not the only, data of knowledge, there was involved by the very same logic on which they relied to support their views, not only the uniform and necessary succession of time, and the geometrical properties of space, but also the principles of substance and causality. He does not, indeed, thereby prove the truth of the axioms and principles in question; but he shows that they are at least equally valid with, and more ultimate than, those upon which empiricism builds. Although, therefore, it seems no longer possible to hold, as Kant held, that a reference to existents is necessary to any proposition that is to claim the title of 'knowledge', and that the truth of such propositions can alone claim *immediate* certainty; although, on the contrary, it seems that existential propositions are only a particular class of necessary proposition: yet the Transcendental Deduction is still important. A deduction from the 'possibility of experience' does not indeed really represent the nature of Kant's argument. For the possibility of experience presupposes that we have experience, and this again means that certain existential propositions are true: but this does not involve the truth of any particular existential propositions; although its truth is involved in theirs. What Kant really shows is that space and time and the categories are involved in particular propositions; and this work is of greater value than a deduction from the possibility of experience would have been. He does not indeed recognise that the propositions from which he is deducing are themselves necessary, and that there may therefore be other necessary propositions, with a like claim to certainty, not to be deduced from them. He therefore imagines himself to have exhausted the field of knowledge; whereas in fact he has only shown certain logical connexions within that field. But it is not here proposed to dispute the truth of particular existential propositions; and though, unlike Kant, we admit them to be merely assumed, we may be thankful that he has shown us what can be inferred from them.

Moreover, Kant's distinction between space and time on the one hand, and the categories on the other, also retains its value, though we can no longer describe their general difference as he did. It seems rather to be this: That time alone is sufficient for some sort of experience, since it alone seems to be involved in the simplest kind of existential proposition, e.g., 'Pleasure exists'; and that again time and space together will suffice to account for the possibility of other pieces of knowledge, without the use of the categories. It is necessary to make a fresh assumption of propositions such as even Hume recognised, and such as are universal in physical science, in order to find the principles of substance and accident and causality implied. In all such propositions time and space are presupposed as well, but these categories are not implied in every proposition involving time and space.

The simplest existential propositions are then to be regarded as necessary propositions of a peculiar sort. In one kind the necessary properties of time are involved; in another those of space also. But though this fact, which Kant points out, is very important against empiricists, we cannot regard it with him as establishing the truth of geometry and of the corresponding propositions about time. For existential propositions which are false, as well as those which are true, involve the same propositions about space and time. No existential proposition of any sort seems discoverable, which might not thus be false; not even the famous 'Cogito' is indubitable. We cannot, therefore, take the 'possibility of experience' in any possible sense, as sufficient warrant for our knowledge of space and time; and we must regard the truths of geometry as independently known for true, just in the same way as some existential propositions are so known.

Similarly, those propositions which involve substance and attribute are not sufficient to establish the truth of the propositions thereby involved. The permanence of substance is indeed, Kant shows us, as certain as the empirical propositions which Hume took to be alone certain. But its truth must be known independently of these, since it is involved also in false propositions of this type. It would, in fact, be true, whether any such propositions were true or not. Kant has only taught us that, if any of them are true, it must be so likewise. He failed to see that its truth may be asserted immediately on the same ground as theirs; for he was misled by the previous course of philosophy to suppose that there was something more immediately indubitable in them. Their truth is, in fact, the last thing which common sense doubts, in spite of its familiarity with erroneous perceptions. Kant's merit was in pointing out, what he himself did not recognise, that their being undoubted does not prove them to be indubitable; or rather, that the doubt which is cast on some of them proves conclusively, what common sense, in its contentment with rules that have exceptions, does not perceive, that they are highly doubtful.

Our result then is as follows: That a judgment is universally a necessary combination of concepts, equally necessary whether it be true or false. That it must be either true or false, but that its truth or falsehood cannot depend on its relation to anything else whatever, reality, for instance, or the world in space and time. For both of these must be supposed to exist, in some sense, if the truth of our judgment is to depend upon them; and then it turns out that the truth of our judgment depends not on them, but on the judgment that they, being such and such, exist. But this judgment cannot, in its turn, depend on anything else, for its truth or falsehood: its truth or its falsehood must be immediate properties of its own, not dependent upon any relation it may have to something else. And, if this be so, we have removed all reason for the supposition that the truth and falsehood of other judgments are not equally independent. For the existential judgment, which is presupposed in Kant's reference to experience or in Mr Bradley's reference to reality, has turned out to be, as much as any other, merely a necessary combination of concepts, for the necessity of which we can seek no ground, and which cannot be explained as an attribution to 'the given'. A concept is not in any intelligible sense an 'adjective', as if there were something substantive, more ultimate than it. For we must, if we are to be consistent, describe what appears to be most substantive as no more than a collection of such supposed adjectives: and thus, in the end, the concept turns out to be the only substantive or subject, and no one concept either more or less an adjective than any other. From our description of a judgment, there must, then, disappear all reference either to our mind or to the world. Neither of these can furnish 'ground' for anything, save in so far as they are complex judgments. The nature of the judgment is more ultimate than either, and less ultimate only than the nature of its constituents – the nature of the concept or logical idea.

NOTES

1 F.H. Bradley, *The Principles of Logic* (Oxford University Press, London: 1883) p.2. All further references are to this edition.
2 Moore's paper includes references to G. Hartenstein's edition of Kant's *Kritik der reinen Vernunft* (Leopold Voss, Leipzig: 1867) which is based on Kant's second (B) edition. It is now standard practice to refer to the original page numbers of this edition itself and I have altered Moore's references accordingly. At the same time I have added some further references to passages which Moore cites without reference.
3 The 'third man (τρίτος ἄνθρωπος) argument' is alluded to by Aristotle in *Metaphysics* 990b17. It is generally supposed that the argument is a variant of that discussed by Plato in *Parmenides* 132a1–b2.
4 Moore adds here a further reference to p.54n of Kant's *Prolegomena* in G. Hartenstein's edition. This passage occurs on p.64n of the English translation by P. Lucas (Manchester University Press, Manchester: 1953).

2

TRUTH AND FALSITY

'Truth' and 'falsehood' are used in two main senses, according as (a) our belief in some proposition, (b) the proposition which we believe, is said to be true or false. True and false belief may be defined, respectively, as belief in propositions which are true or false: and *error* denotes false belief. Further, true and false propositions may be called, respectively, *truths* and *errors*. *Falsehood*, however, or falsity, and not error, is used to denote that property of a false proposition in virtue of possessing which it is called an error.

'True' and 'false', as applied to propositions, denote properties attaching to propositions which are related to one another in such a way that every proposition must be either true or false, and that to every true proposition there corresponds a false one, and to every false proposition a true one, differing from it only as being its negation. There are, properly speaking, no degrees of truth or falsehood, but one error may be said to be truer or more erroneous than another, according as a greater or smaller number of the propositions it implies are true.

The following proposed definitions call for notice, both because of their wide acceptance, and because a notice of them will serve to isolate the properties which the terms really denote.

(1) It is commonly supposed that the truth of a proposition consists in some relation which it bears to reality; and falsehood in the absence of this relation. The relation in question is generally called a 'correspondence' or 'agreement', and it seems to be

Originally published in the *Dictionary of Philosophy and Psychology*, ed. J. Baldwin (Macmillan, London: 1901–2), vol. 2 pp.716–18. Moore probably wrote it in 1899.

generally conceived as one of partial similarity; but it is to be noted that only propositions can be said to be true in virtue of their partial similarity to something else, and hence that it is essential to the theory that a truth should differ in some specific way from the reality, in relation to which its truth is to consist, in every case except that in which the reality is itself a proposition. It is the impossibility of finding any such difference between a truth and the reality to which it is supposed to correspond which refutes the theory. For:

(a) It is now generally agreed that the difference does not consist in the fact that the proposition is a mere grammatical sentence or collection of words; but that the popular sense, in which a *statement* may be said to be true or false, is merely derived from that in which what it signifies may be so.

(b) It is, however, generally held that the difference consists in the fact that the proposition is a *mental* copy of the reality, or an 'idea'. This view seems to be solely due to the almost universal error, whereby the *object* of a belief or idea is regarded as the attribute or content of such belief or idea; an error which is refuted by the fact that it denies the existence of that unique relation which we mean by knowing, and is therefore never consistently held: e.g., those who hold this view must, in consistency, deny any difference between those senses of truth in which it is applied to a belief and to the object of such belief – a difference which in practice they cannot fail to recognise; for no one ever consistently held that when two persons are said to know the same truth, all that can be meant is that their states of mind are similar.

(c) No other difference has ever been proposed; and, indeed, once it is definitely recognised that the proposition is to denote, not a belief or form of words, but an *object* of belief, it seems plain that a truth differs in no respect from the reality to which it was supposed merely to correspond: e.g., the truth that I exist differs in no respect from the corresponding reality – my existence. So far, indeed, from truth being defined by reference to reality, reality can only be defined by reference to truth: for truth denotes exactly that property of the complex formed by two entities and their relation, in virtue of which, if the entity predicated be existence, we call the complex real – the property, namely, expressed by saying that the relation in question does truly or really hold between the entities.

21

(2) It seems to be frequently implied that the truth of a proposition may consist in its relation to other propositions – in the fact that it 'fits into a system'. This view, however, simply neglects the admitted fact that any logical relations which hold between a set of true propositions will also hold between a set of false ones; i.e., that the only kind of system into which a true proposition will fit, and a false one will not, is a system of true propositions. The view derives its plausibility merely from the fact that the systems of propositions considered are ones to which we are so thoroughly accustomed that we are apt to regard their contradictories as not merely false but self-contradictory.

The Greek and Latin equivalents for 'true' and 'false' are respectively ἀληθής, *verus*; ψευδής, *falsus*. Error has the equivalents ἁμαρτία or ἁμάρτημα, and *error*; but 'falsehood' as distinguished from 'error', i.e., as denoting the property of a false proposition, has no corresponding abstract noun in Greek nor in classical Latin. There is, properly speaking, no history of the terms, since they have always been used in philosophy and always in very much the same senses. That truth consists in some relation of words to what they signify, or even to one another, has indeed been seriously held at various times; and the fact that it seems scarcely necessary any longer to discuss that view, perhaps marks some progress in the conception of the terms. The view that truth consists in relation to a system owes its vogue to Kant's theory of experience, which appears to make the objectivity of a judgment consist in the fact that its subject is related to other subjects, and does not clearly distinguish objectivity from truth. It should, perhaps, be noted that error or false belief has been frequently held to consist, not in consciousness of something different from the truth, but merely in the absence of consciousness of the truth or of the whole truth – a view which naturally follows as one of the alternative inferences from the premiss that false=not-true, and from the premiss that consciousness of the truth=true consciousness.

3

THE REFUTATION OF IDEALISM

Modern Idealism, if it asserts any general conclusion about the universe at all, asserts that it is *spiritual*. There are two points about this assertion to which I wish to call attention. These points are that, whatever be its exact meaning, it is certainly meant to assert (1) that the universe is very different indeed from what it seems, and (2) that it has quite a large number of properties which it does not seem to have. Chairs and tables and mountains *seem* to be very different from us; but, when the whole universe is declared to be spiritual, it is certainly meant to assert that they are far more like us than we think. The Idealist means to assert that they are *in some sense* neither lifeless nor unconscious, as they certainly seem to be; and I do not think his language is so grossly deceptive, but that we may assume him to believe that they really are very different indeed from what they seem. And secondly when he declares that they are *spiritual*, he means to include in that term quite a large number of different properties. When the whole universe is declared to be spiritual, it is meant not only that it is in some sense *conscious*, but that it has what we recognise in ourselves as the *higher* forms of consciousness. That it is intelligent; that it is purposeful; that it is not mechanical; all these different things are commonly asserted of it. In general, it may be said, this phrase 'reality is spiritual' excites and expresses the belief that the *whole* universe possesses *all the qualities* the possession of which is held to make us so superior to things which seem to be inanimate: at least, if it does not possess exactly those which we possess, it possesses not one only, but several others, which, by the same ethical standard,

Originally published in *Mind* n.s. 12 (1903), pp.433–53.

would be judged equal to or better than our own. When we say it is *spiritual* we mean to say that it has quite a number of excellent qualities, different from any which we commonly attribute either to stars or planets or to cups and saucers.

Now why I mention these two points is that when engaged in the intricacies of philosophic discussion, we are apt to overlook the vastness of the difference between this Idealistic view and the ordinary view of the world, and to overlook the number of *different* propositions which the Idealist must prove. It is, I think, owing to the vastness of this difference and owing to the number of different excellences which Idealists attribute to the universe, that it seems such an interesting and important question whether Idealism be true or not. But, when we begin to argue about it, I think we are apt to forget what a vast number of arguments this interesting question must involve: we are apt to assume, that if one or two points be made on either side, the whole case is won. I say this lest it should be thought that any of the arguments which will be advanced in this paper would be sufficient to disprove, or any refutation of them sufficient to prove, the truly interesting and important proposition that reality is spiritual. For my own part I wish it to be clearly understood that I do not suppose that anything I shall say has the smallest tendency to prove that reality is not spiritual: I do not believe it possible to refute a single one of the many important propositions contained in the assertion that it is so. Reality may be spiritual, for all I know; and I devoutly hope it is. But I take 'Idealism' to be a wide term and to include not only this interesting conclusion but a number of arguments which are supposed to be, if not sufficient, at least *necessary*, to prove it. Indeed I take it that modern Idealists are chiefly distinguished by certain arguments which they have in common. That reality is spiritual has, I believe, been the tenet of many theologians; and yet, for believing that alone, they should hardly be called Idealists. There are besides, I believe, many persons, not improperly called Idealists, who hold certain characteristic propositions, without venturing to think them quite sufficient to prove so grand a conclusion. It is, therefore, only with Idealistic *arguments* that I am concerned; and if any Idealist holds that *no* argument is necessary to prove that reality is spiritual, I shall certainly not have refuted him. I shall, however, attack at least one argument, which, to the best of my belief, is considered necessary to their position by *all* Idealists. And I wish to point out a certain advantage which this procedure gives me – an advantage which justifies the assertion that, if my arguments are sound, they will have refuted Idealism. If I can refute a single proposition which is a necessary and essential step in all Idealistic arguments, then, no matter how good the rest of these arguments may be, I shall have proved that Idealists have *no reason whatever* for their conclusion.

Suppose we have a chain of argument which takes the form: Since A is B, and B is C, and C is D, it follows A is D. In such an argument, though 'B is C' and 'C is D' may both be perfectly true, yet if 'A is B' be false, we have no more reason for asserting A is D than if all three were false. It does not, indeed, follow that A is D is false; nor does it follow that no other arguments would prove it to be true. But it docs follow that, so far as this argument goes, it is the barest supposition, without the least bit of evidence. I propose to attack a proposition which seems to me to stand in this relation to the conclusion 'Reality is spiritual'. I do not propose to dispute that 'Reality is spiritual'; I do not deny that there may be reasons for thinking that it is: but I do propose to show that one reason upon which, to the best of my judgment, all other arguments ever used by Idealists depend is *false*. These other arguments may, for all I shall say, be eminently ingenious and true; they are very many and various, and different Idealists use the most different arguments to prove the same most important conclusions. Some of these *may* be sufficient to prove that B is C and C is D; but if, as I shall try to show, their 'A is B' is false the conclusion A is D remains a pleasant supposition. I do not deny that to suggest pleasant and plausible suppositions may be the proper function of philosophy: but I am assuming that the name Idealism can only be properly applied where there is a certain amount of argument, intended to be cogent.

The subject of this paper is, therefore, quite uninteresting. Even if I prove my point, I shall have proved nothing about the Universe in general. Upon the important question whether Reality is or is not spiritual my argument will not have the remotest bearing. I shall only attempt to arrive at the truth about a matter, which is in itself quite trivial and insignificant, and from which, so far as I can see and certainly so far as I shall say, no conclusions can be drawn about any of the subjects about

which we most want to know. The only importance I can claim
for the subject I shall investigate is that it seems to me to be a
matter upon which not Idealists only, but all philosophers and
psychologists also, have been in error, and from their erroneous
view of which they have inferred (validly or invalidly) their most
striking and interesting conclusions. And that it has even this
importance I cannot hope to prove. If it has this importance, it
will indeed follow that all the most striking results of philosophy
– Sensationalism, Agnosticism and Idealism alike – have, for all
that has hitherto been urged in their favour, no more foundation
than the supposition that a chimera lives in the moon. It will
follow that, unless new reasons never urged hitherto can be
found, all the most important philosophic doctrines have as
little claim to assent as the most superstitious beliefs of the
lowest savages. Upon the question what we have *reason* to
believe in the most interesting matters, I do therefore think that
my results will have an important bearing; but I cannot too
clearly insist that upon the question whether these beliefs are
true they will have none whatever.

The trivial proposition which I propose to dispute is this: That
esse is *percipi*. This is a very ambiguous proposition, but, in some
sense or other, it has been very widely held. That it is, in some
sense, essential to Idealism, I must for the present merely
assume. What I propose to show is that, in all the senses ever
given to it, it is false.

But, first of all, it may be useful to point out briefly in what
relation I conceive it to stand to Idealistic arguments. That
wherever you can truly predicate *esse* you can truly predicate
percipi, in some sense or other, is, I take it, a necessary step in all
arguments, properly to be called Idealistic, and, what is more, in
all arguments hitherto offered for the Idealistic conclusion. If
esse is *percipi*, this is at once equivalent to saying that whatever
is, is experienced; and this, again, is equivalent, in a sense, to
saying that whatever is, is something mental. But this is not the
sense in which the Idealist *conclusion* must maintain that reality
is *mental*. The Idealist *conclusion* is that *esse* is *percipere*; and
hence, whether *esse* be *percipi* or not, a further and different
discussion is needed to show whether or not it is also *percipere*.
And again, even if *esse* be *percipere*, we need a vast quantity of
further argument to show that what has *esse* has also those
higher mental qualities which are denoted by spiritual. This is

why I said that the question I should discuss, namely, whether or not *esse* is *percipi*, must be utterly insufficient either to prove or to disprove that reality is spiritual. But, on the other hand, I believe that every argument ever used to show that reality is spiritual has inferred this (validly or invalidly) from *'esse* is *percipere'* as one of its premisses; and that this again has never been pretended to be proved except by use of the premiss that *esse* is *percipi*. The type of argument used for the latter purpose is familiar enough. It is said that since whatever is, is experienced, and since some things are which are not experienced by the individual, these must at least form part of some experience. Or again that, since an object necessarily implies a subject, and since the whole world must be an object, we must conceive it to belong to some subject or subjects, in the same sense in which whatever is the object of our experience belongs to us. Or again, that, since thought enters into the essence of all reality, we must conceive behind it, in it, or as its essence, a spirit akin to ours, who think: that 'spirit greets spirit' in its object. Into the validity of these inferences I do not propose to enter: they obviously require a great deal of discussion. I only desire to point out that, however correct they may be, yet if *esse* is not *percipi*, they leave us as far from a proof that reality is spiritual, as if they were all false too.

But now: Is *esse percipi*? There are three very ambiguous terms in this proposition, and I must begin by distinguishing the different things that may be meant by some of them.

And first with regard to *percipi*. This term need not trouble us long at present. It was, perhaps, originally used to mean 'sensation' only; but I am not going to be so unfair to modern Idealists – the only Idealists to whom the term should now be applied without qualification – as to hold that, if they say *esse* is *percipi*, they mean by *percipi* sensation only. On the contrary I quite agree with them that, if *esse* be *percipi* at all, *percipi* must be understood to include not sensation only, but that other type of mental fact, which is called 'thought'; and, whether *esse* be *percipi* or not, I consider it to be the main service of the philosophic school, to which modern Idealists belong, that they have insisted on distinguishing 'sensation' and 'thought' and on emphasising the importance of the latter. Against Sensationalism and Empiricism they have maintained the true view. But the distinction between sensation and thought need not detain us here. For, in whatever respects they differ, they have at least this in common, that they are both forms of consciousness or, to use a term that seems to be more in fashion just now, they are both ways of experiencing. Accordingly, whatever *esse* is *percipi* may mean, it does *at least* assert that whatever is, is *experienced*. And since what I wish to maintain is, that even this is untrue, the question whether it be experienced by way of sensation or thought or both is for my purpose quite irrelevant. If it be not experienced at all, it cannot be either an object of thought or an object of sense. It is only if being involves 'experience' that the question, whether it involves sensation or thought or both, becomes important. I beg, therefore, that *percipi* may be understood, in what follows, to refer merely to what is *common* to sensation and thought. A very recent article states the meaning of *esse* is *percipi* with all desirable clearness in so far as *percipi* is concerned. 'I will undertake to show', says Mr Taylor,* 'that what makes [any piece of fact] real can be nothing but its presence as an inseparable aspect of *a sentient experience*.' I am glad to think that Mr Taylor has been in time to supply me with so definite a statement that this is the ultimate premiss of Idealism. My paper will at least refute Mr Taylor's Idealism, if it refutes anything at all: for I *shall* undertake to show that what makes a thing real cannot possibly be its presence as an inseparable aspect of a sentient experience.

But Mr Taylor's statement though clear, I think, with regard to the meaning of *percipi* is highly ambiguous in other respects. I will leave it for the present to consider the next ambiguity in the statement: *Esse* is *percipi*. What does the copula mean? What can be meant by saying that Esse *is* percipi? There are just three meanings, one or other of which such a statement *must* have, if it is to be true; and of these there is only one which it can have, if it is to be important. (1) The statement may be meant to assert that the word '*esse*' is used to signify nothing either more or less than the word '*percipi*': that the two words are precise synonyms: that they are merely different names for one and the same thing: that what is meant by *esse* is absolutely identical with what is meant by *percipi*. I think I need not prove that the principle *esse* is *percipi* is *not* thus intended merely to define a word; nor yet that, if it were, it would be an extremely bad

* A.E. Taylor, *International Journal of Ethics* XIII (1902–3), p.58.

definition. But if it does *not* mean this, only two alternatives remain. The second is (2) that what is meant by *esse*, though not absolutely identical with what is meant by *percipi*, yet *includes* the latter as a *part* of its meaning. If this were the meaning of '*esse* is *percipi*', then to say that a thing was real would not be the same thing as to say that it was experienced. That it was *real* would mean that it was experienced and *something else besides*: 'being experienced' would be *analytically essential* to reality, but would not be the whole meaning of the term. From the fact that a thing was real we should be able to infer, by the law of contradiction, that it was experienced; since the latter would be *part* of what is meant by the former. But, on the other hand, from the fact a thing was experienced we should *not* be able to infer that it was real; since it would not follow from the fact that it had one of the attributes essential to reality, that it *also* had the other or others. Now, if we understand *esse* is *percipi* in this second sense, we must distinguish *three* different things which it asserts. First of all, it gives a definition of the word 'reality', asserting that word stands for a complex whole, of which what is meant by '*percipi*' forms a part. And secondly it asserts that 'being experienced' forms a part of a certain whole. Both these propositions may be true, and at all events I do not wish to dispute them. I do not, indeed, think that the word 'reality' is commonly used to include '*percipi*': but I do not wish to argue about the meaning of words. And that many things which are experienced are also something else – that to be experienced forms part of certain wholes, is, of course, indisputable. But what I wish to point out is, that neither of these propositions is of any importance, unless we add to them a *third*. That 'real' is a convenient name for a union of attributes which *sometimes* occurs, it could not be worth anyone's while to assert: no inferences of any importance could be drawn from such an assertion. Our principle could only mean that when a thing happens to have *percipi* as well as the other qualities included under *esse*, it has *percipi*: and we should never be able to *infer* that it was experienced, except from a proposition which already asserted that it was both experienced and something else. Accordingly, if the assertion that *percipi* forms part of the whole meant by reality is to have any importance, it must mean that the whole is organic, at least in this sense, that the other constituent or constituents of it *cannot* occur without *percipi*, even if *percipi* can occur without them. Let us call these other constituents *x*. The proposition that *esse* includes *percipi*, and that therefore from *esse percipi* can be inferred, can only be important if it is meant to assert that *percipi* can be inferred from *x*. The only importance of the question whether the whole *esse* includes the part *percipi* rests therefore on the question whether the part *x* is necessarily connected with the part *percipi*. And this is (3) the third possible meaning of the assertion *esse* is *percipi*: and, as we now see, the only important one. *Esse* is *percipi* asserts that wherever you have *x* you also have *percipi* that whatever has the property *x* also has the property that it is *experienced*. And this being so, it will be convenient if, for the future, I may be allowed to use the term '*esse*' to denote *x alone*. I do not wish thereby to beg the question whether what we commonly mean by the word 'real' does or does not include *percipi* as well as *x*. I am quite content that my definition of '*esse*' to denote *x*, should be regarded merely as an arbitrary verbal definition. Whether it is so or not, the only question of interest is whether from *x percipi* can be inferred, and I should prefer to be able to express this in the form: Can *percipi* be inferred from *esse*? Only let it be understood that when I say *esse*, that term will not for the future *include percipi*: it denotes only that *x*, which Idealists, perhaps rightly, include *along with percipi* under *their* term *esse*. That there is such an *x* they must admit on pain of making the proposition an *absolute* tautology; and that from this *x percipi* can be inferred they must admit, on pain of making it a perfectly barren analytic proposition. Whether *x* alone should or should not be called *esse* is not worth a dispute: what is worth dispute is whether *percipi* is necessarily connected with *x*.

We have therefore discovered the ambiguity of the copula in *esse* is *percipi*, so far as to see that this principle asserts two distinct terms to be so related, that whatever has the *one*, which I call *esse*, has *also* the property that it is experienced. It asserts a necessary connexion between *esse* on the one hand and *percipi* on the other; these two words denoting each a distinct term, and *esse* denoting a term in which that denoted by *percipi* is not included. We have, then in *esse* is *percipi*, a *necessary synthetic* proposition which I have undertaken to refute. And I may say at once that, understood as such, it cannot be refuted. If the Idealist chooses to assert that it is merely a self-evident truth, I have only to say that it does not appear to me to be so. But I believe that no Idealist ever has maintained it to be so. Although this – that two distinct terms are necessarily related – is the only sense which *'esse* is *percipi'* can have if it is to be true and important, it *can* have another sense, if it is to be an important falsehood. I believe that Idealists all hold this important falsehood. They do not perceive that *Esse* is *percipi* must, if true, be *merely* a self-evident synthetic truth: they either identify with it or give as a reason for it another proposition which must be false because it is self-contradictory. Unless they did so, they would have to admit that it was a perfectly unfounded assumption; and if they recognised that it was *unfounded*, I do not think they would maintain its truth to be evident. *Esse* is *percipi*, in the sense I have found for it, *may* indeed be true; I cannot refute it: but if this sense were clearly apprehended, no one, I think, would *believe* that it was true.

Idealists, we have seen, must assert that whatever is experienced, is *necessarily* so. And this doctrine they commonly express by saying that 'the object of experience is inconceivable apart from the subject'. I have hitherto been concerned with pointing out what meaning this assertion must have, if it is to be an important truth. I now propose to show that it may have an important meaning, which must be false, because it is self-contradictory.

It is a well-known fact in the history of philosophy that *necessary* truths in general, but especially those of which it is said that the opposite is inconceivable, have been commonly supposed to be *analytic*, in the sense that the proposition denying them was self-contradictory. It was in this way, commonly supposed, before Kant, that many truths could be proved by the law of contradiction alone. This is, therefore, a mistake which it is plainly easy for the best philosophers to make. Even since Kant many have continued to assert it; but I am aware that among those Idealists, who most properly deserve the name, it has become more fashionable to assert that truths are *both* analytic and synthetic. Now with many of their reasons for asserting this I am not concerned: it is possible that in some connexions the assertion may bear a useful and true sense. But if we understand 'analytic' in the sense just defined, namely, what is proved by the law of contradiction *alone*, it is plain that, if 'synthetic' means what is *not* proved by this alone, no truth can be both analytic and synthetic. Now it seems to me that those who do maintain truths to be both, do nevertheless maintain that they are so in this as well as in other senses. It is, indeed, extremely unlikely that so essential a part of the historical meaning of 'analytic' and 'synthetic' should have been entirely discarded, especially since we find no express recognition that it is discarded. In that case it is fair to suppose that modern Idealists have been influenced by the view that certain truths can be proved by the law of contradiction alone. I admit they also expressly declare that they can *not*: but this is by no means sufficient to prove that they do not also think they are; since it is very easy to hold two mutually contradictory opinions. What I suggest then is that Idealists hold the particular doctrine in question, concerning the relation of subject and object in experience, because they think it is an analytic truth in this restricted sense that it is proved by the law of contradiction alone.

I am suggesting that the Idealist maintains that object and subject are necessarily connected, mainly because he fails to see that they are *distinct*, that they are *two*, at all. When he thinks of 'yellow' and when he thinks of the 'sensation of yellow', he fails to see that there is anything whatever in the latter which is not in the former. This being so, to deny that yellow can ever *be* apart from the sensation of yellow is merely to deny that yellow can ever be other than it is; since yellow and the sensation of yellow are absolutely identical. To assert that yellow is necessarily an object of experience is to assert that yellow is necessarily yellow – a purely identical proposition, and therefore proved by the law of contradiction alone. Of course, the proposition also implies that experience is, after all, something distinct from yellow – else there would be no reason for insisting that yellow is a sensation: and that the argument thus both affirms and denies that yellow and sensation of yellow are distinct, is what sufficiently refutes it. But this contradiction can easily be overlooked, because though we are convinced, in other connexions, that 'experience' does mean something and something most important, yet we are never distinctly aware *what* it means, and thus in every particular case we do not notice its presence. The facts present themselves as a kind of antinomy: (1) Experience *is* something unique and different from anything else; (2) Experience of green is entirely indistinguishable from green; two propositions which cannot both be true. Idealists, holding both, can only take refuge in arguing from the one in some connexions and from the other in others.

But I am well aware that there are many Idealists who would repel it as an utterly unfounded charge that they fail to distinguish between a sensation or idea and what I will call its object. And there are, I admit, many who not only imply, as we all do, that green is distinct from the sensation of green, but expressly insist upon the distinction as an important part of their system. They would perhaps only assert that the two form an inseparable unity. But I wish to point out that many, who use this phrase, and who do admit the distinction, are not thereby absolved from the charge that they deny it. For there is a certain doctrine, very prevalent among philosophers nowadays, which by a very simple reduction may be seen to assert that two distinct things both are and are not distinct. A distinction is asserted; but it is *also* asserted that the things distinguished form an 'organic unity'. But, forming such a unity, it is held, each would not be what it is *apart from its relation to the other*. Hence to consider either by itself is to make an *illegitimate abstraction*. The recognition that there are 'organic unities' and 'illegitimate abstractions' in this sense is regarded as one of the chief conquests of modern philosophy. But what is the sense attached to these terms? An abstraction is illegitimate, when and only when we attempt to assert of *a part* – of something abstracted – that which is true only of the *whole* to which it belongs: and it may perhaps be useful to point out that this should not be done. But the application actually made of this principle, and what perhaps would be expressly acknowledged as its meaning, is something much the reverse of useful. The principle is used to assert that certain abstractions are *in all cases* illegitimate; that whenever you try to assert *anything whatever* of that which is *part* of an organic whole, what you assert can only be true of the whole. And this principle, so far from being a useful truth, is necessarily false. For if the whole can, nay *must*, be substituted for the part in all propositions and for all purposes, this can only be because the whole is absolutely identical with the part. When, therefore, we are told that green and the sensation of green are certainly distinct but yet are not separable, or that it is an illegitimate abstraction to consider the one apart from the other, what these provisos are used to assert is, that though the two things are distinct yet you not only can but must treat them as if they were not. Many philosophers, therefore, when they admit a distinction, yet (following the lead of Hegel) boldly assert their right, in a slightly more obscure form of words, *also* to deny it. The principle of organic unities, like that of combined analysis and synthesis, is mainly used to defend the practice of holding *both* of two contradictory propositions, wherever this may seem convenient. In this, as in other matters, Hegel's main service to philosophy has consisted in giving a name to and erecting into a principle, a type of fallacy to which experience had shown philosophers, along with the rest of mankind, to be addicted. No wonder that he has followers and admirers.

I have shown then, so far, that when the Idealist asserts the important principle '*Esse* is *percipi*' he must, if it is to be true, mean by this that: Whatever is experienced also *must* be experienced. And I have also shown that he *may* identify with, or give as a reason for, this proposition, one which must be false, because it is self-contradictory. But at this point I propose to make a complete break in my argument. '*Esse* is *percipi*', we have seen, asserts of two terms, as distinct from one another as 'green' and 'sweet', that whatever has the one has also the other: it asserts that 'being' and 'being experienced' are necessarily connected: that whatever *is* is *also* experienced. And this, I admit, cannot be directly refuted. But I believe it to be false; and I have asserted that anybody who saw that '*esse*' and '*percipi*' *were* as distinct as 'green' and 'sweet' would be no more ready to believe that whatever *is* is *also* experienced, than to believe that whatever is green is also sweet. I have asserted that no one would believe that '*esse* is *percipi*' if they saw how different *esse* is from *percipi*: but *this* I shall not try to prove. I have asserted that all who do believe that '*esse* is *percipi*' identify with it or take as a reason for it a self-contradictory proposition: but this I shall not try to prove. I shall only try to show that certain propositions which I assert to be believed, are false. That they are believed, and that without this belief '*esse* is *percipi*' would not be believed either, I must leave without a proof.

I pass, then, from the uninteresting question 'Is *esse percipi*?' to the still more uninteresting and apparently irrelevant question 'What is a sensation or idea?'

We all know that the sensation of blue differs from that of green. But it is plain that if both are *sensations* they also have some point in common. What is it that they have in common?

And how is this common element related to the points in which they differ?

I will call the common element 'consciousness' without yet attempting to say what the thing I so call *is*. We have then in every sensation two distinct terms, (1) 'consciousness', in respect of which all sensations are alike; and (2) something else, in respect of which one sensation differs from another. It will be convenient if I may be allowed to call this second term the 'object' of a sensation: this also without yet attempting to say what I mean by the word.

We have then in every sensation two distinct elements, one which I call consciousness, and another which I call the object of consciousness. This must be so if the sensation of blue and the sensation of green, though different in one respect, are alike in another: blue is one object of sensation and green is another, and consciousness, which both sensations have in common, is different from either.

But, further, sometimes the sensation of blue exists in my mind and sometimes it does not; and knowing, as we now do, that the sensation of blue includes two different elements, namely consciousness and blue, the question arises whether, when the sensation of blue exists, it is the consciousness which exists, or the blue which exists, or both. And one point at least is plain: namely that these three alternatives are all different from one another. So that, if any one tells us that to say 'Blue exists' is the *same* thing as to say that 'Both blue and consciousness exist', he makes a mistake and a self-contradictory mistake.

But another point is also plain, namely, that when the sensation exists, the consciousness, at least, certainly does exist; for when I say that the sensations of blue and of green both exist, I certainly mean that what is common to both and in virtue of which both are called sensations, exists in each case. The only alternative left, then, is that *either* both exist or the consciousness exists alone. If, therefore, anyone tells us that the existence of blue is the same thing as the existence of the sensation of blue he makes a mistake and a self-contradictory mistake, for he asserts *either* that blue is the same thing as blue together with consciousness, *or* that it is the same thing as consciousness alone.

Accordingly to identify either 'blue' or any other of what I have called *'objects'* of sensation, with the corresponding sensation

35

is in every case, a self-contradictory error. It is to identify a part either with the whole of which it is a part or else with the other part of the same whole. If we are told that the assertion 'Blue exists' is *meaningless* unless we mean by it that 'The sensation of blue exists', we are told what is certainly false and self-contradictory. If we are told that the existence of blue is inconceivable apart from the existence of the sensation, the speaker *probably* means to convey to us, by this ambiguous expression, what is a self-contradictory error. For we can and must conceive the existence of blue as something quite distinct from the existence of the sensation. We can and must conceive that blue might exist and yet the sensation of blue not exist. For my own part I not only conceive this, but conceive it to be true. Either therefore this terrific assertion of inconceivability means what is false and self-contradictory or else it means only that *as a matter of fact* blue never can exist unless the sensation of it exists also.

And at this point I need not conceal my opinion that no philosopher has ever yet succeeded in avoiding this self-contradictory error: that the most striking results both of Idealism and of Agnosticism are only obtained by identifying blue with the sensation of blue: that *esse* is held to be *percipi*, solely because *what is experienced* is held to be identical with *the experience of it*. That Berkeley and Mill committed this error will, perhaps, be granted: that modern Idealists make it will, I hope, appear more probable later. But that my opinion is plausible, I will now offer two pieces of evidence. The first is that language offers us no means of referring to such objects as 'blue', and 'green' and 'sweet', except by calling them sensations: it is an obvious violation of language to call them 'things' or 'objects' or 'terms'. And similarly we have no natural means of referring to such objects as 'causality' or 'likeness' or 'identity', except by calling them 'ideas' or 'notions' or 'conceptions'. But it is hardly likely that if philosophers had clearly distinguished in the past between a sensation or idea and what I have called its object, there should have been no separate name for the latter. They have always used the same name for these two different 'things' (if I may call them so): and hence there is some probability that they have supposed these 'things' *not* to be two and different, but one and the same. And, secondly, there is a very good reason why they should have supposed so, in the fact that when we refer to introspection and try to discover what the sensation of blue is, it is very easy to suppose that we have before us only a single term. The term 'blue' is easy enough to distinguish, but the other element which I have called 'consciousness' – that which sensation of blue has in common with sensation of green – is extremely difficult to fix. That many people fail to distinguish it at all is sufficiently shown by the fact that there are materialists. And, in general, that which makes the sensation of blue a mental fact seems to escape us: it seems, if I may use a metaphor, to be transparent – we look through it and see nothing but the blue; we may be convinced that there *is something* but *what* it is no philosopher, I think, has yet clearly recognised.

But this was a digression. The point I had established so far was that in every sensation or idea we must distinguish two elements, (1) the 'object', or that in which one differs from another; and (2) 'consciousness', or that which all have in common – that which makes them sensations or mental facts. This being so, it followed that when a sensation or idea exists, we have to choose between the alternatives that either object alone, or consciousness alone, or both, exist; and I showed that of these alternatives one, namely that the object only exists, is excluded by the fact that what we mean to assert is certainly the existence of a mental fact. There remains the question: Do both exist? Or does the consciousness alone? And to this question one answer has hitherto been given universally: That both exist.

This answer follows from the analysis hitherto accepted of the relation of what I have called 'object' to 'consciousness' in any sensation or idea. It is held that what I call the object is merely the 'content' of a sensation or idea. It is held that in each case we can distinguish two elements and two only, (1) the fact that there is feeling or experience, and (2) *what* is felt or experienced; the sensation or idea, it is said, forms a whole, in which we must distinguish two 'inseparable aspects', 'content' and 'existence'. I shall try to show that this analysis is false; and for that purpose I must ask what may seem an extraordinary question: namely what is meant by saying that one thing is 'content' of another? It is not usual to ask this question; the term is used as if everybody must understand it. But since I am going to maintain that 'blue' is *not* the content of the sensation of blue, and what is more important, that, even if it were this analysis would leave out the most important element in the sensation of blue, it is necessary that I should try to explain precisely what it is that I shall deny.

What then is meant by saying that one thing is the 'content' of another? First of all I wish to point out that 'blue' is rightly and properly said to be part of the content of a blue flower. If, therefore, we also assert that it is part of the content of the sensation of blue, we assert that it has to the other parts (if any) of this whole the same relation which it has to the other parts of a blue flower – and we assert only this: we cannot mean to assert that it has to the sensation of blue any relation which it does not have to the blue flower. And we have seen that the sensation of blue contains at least one other element beside blue – namely, what I call 'consciousness', which makes it a sensation. So far then as we assert that blue is the content of the sensation, we assert that it has to this 'consciousness' the same relation which it has to the other parts of a blue flower: we do assert this, and we assert no more than this. Into the question what exactly the relation is between blue and a blue flower in virtue of which we call the former part of its 'content' I do not propose to enter. It is sufficient for my purpose to point out that it is the general relation most commonly meant when we talk of a thing and its qualities; and that this relation is such that to say the thing exists implies that the qualities also exist. The *content* of the thing is *what* we assert to exist, when we assert *that* the thing exists.

When, therefore, blue is said to be part of the content of the 'sensation of blue', the latter is treated as if it were a whole constituted in exactly the same way as any other 'thing'. The 'sensation of blue', on this view, differs from a blue bead or a blue beard, in exactly the same way in which the two latter differ from one another: the blue bead differs from the blue beard, in that while the former contains glass, the latter contains hair; and the 'sensation of blue' differs from both in that, instead of glass or hair, it contains consciousness. The relation of the blue to the consciousness is conceived to be exactly the same as that of the blue to the glass or hair: it is in all three cases the *quality* of a *thing*.

But I said just now that the sensation of blue was analysed into 'content' and 'existence', and that blue was said to be *the* content of the idea of blue. There is an ambiguity in this and a possible error, which I must note in passing. The term 'content' may be used in two senses. If we use 'content' as equivalent to what Mr Bradley calls the '*what*' – if we mean by it the *whole* of what is said to exist, when the thing is said to exist, then blue is certainly not *the* content of the sensation of blue: part of the *content* of the sensation is, in this sense of the term, that other element which I have called consciousness. The analysis of this sensation into the 'content' 'blue', on the one hand, and mere existence on the other, is therefore certainly false; in it we have again the self-contradictory identification of 'Blue exists' with 'The sensation of blue exists'. But there is another sense in which 'blue' might properly be said to be *the* content of the sensation – namely, the sense in which 'content', like εἶδος, is opposed to 'substance' or 'matter'. For the element 'conscious-ness', being common to all sensations, may be and certainly is regarded as in some sense their 'substance', and by the 'content' of each is only meant that in respect of which one differs from another. In this sense then 'blue' might be said to be *the* content of the sensation; but, in that case, the analysis into 'content' and 'existence' is, at least, misleading, since under 'existence' must be included '*what* exists' in the sensation other than blue.

We have it, then, as a universally received opinion that blue is related to the sensation or idea of blue, as its *content*, and that this view, if it is to be true, must mean that blue is part of *what* is said to exist when we say that the sensation exists. To say that the sensation exists is to say both that blue exists and that 'consciousness', whether we call it the substance of which blue is *the* content or call it another part of the content, exists too. Any sensation or idea is a '*thing*', and what I have called its object is the quality of this thing. Such a 'thing' is what we think of when we think of a *mental image*. A mental image is conceived as if it were related to that of which it is the image (if there be any such thing) in exactly the same way as the image in a looking-glass is related to that of which it is the reflection; in both cases there is identity of content, and the image in the looking-glass differs from that in the mind solely in respect of the fact that in the one case the other constituent of the image is 'glass' and in the other case it is consciousness. If the image is of blue, it is not conceived that this 'content' has any relation to the consciousness but what it has to the glass: it is conceived *merely* to be its *content*. And owing to the fact that sensations and ideas are all considered to be *wholes* of this description – things in the mind – the question: What do we know? is considered to be identical with the question: What reason have we for supposing that there are things outside the mind *corresponding* to these that are inside it?

What I wish to point out is (1) that we have no reason for supposing that there are such things as mental images at all – for supposing that blue *is* part of the content of the sensation of blue, and (2) that even if there are mental images, no mental image and no sensation or idea is *merely* a thing of this kind: that 'blue', even if it is part of the content of the image or sensation or idea of blue, is always *also* related to it in quite another way, and that this other relation, omitted in the traditional analysis, is the *only* one which makes the sensation of blue a mental fact at all.

The true analysis of a sensation or idea is as follows. The element that is common to them all, and which I have called 'consciousness', really *is* consciousness. A sensation is, in reality, a case of 'knowing' or 'being aware of' or 'experiencing' something. When we know that the sensation of blue exists, the fact we know is that there exists an awareness of blue. And this awareness is not merely, as we have hitherto seen it must be, itself something distinct and unique, utterly different from blue: it also has a perfectly distinct and unique relation to blue, a relation which is *not* that of thing or substance to content, nor of one part of content to another part of content. This relation is just that which we mean in every case by 'knowing'. To have in your mind 'knowledge' of blue, is *not* to have in your mind a 'thing' or 'image' of which blue is the content. To be aware of the sensation of blue is *not* to be aware of a mental image – of a 'thing', of which 'blue' and some other element are constituent parts in the same sense in which blue and glass are constituents of a blue bead. It is to be aware of an awareness of blue; awareness being used, in both cases, in exactly the same sense. This element, we have seen, is certainly neglected by the 'content' theory: that theory entirely fails to express the fact that there is, in the sensation of blue, this unique relation between blue and the other constituent. And what I contend is that this omission is *not* mere negligence of expression, but is due to the fact that though philosophers have recognised that *something* distinct is meant by consciousness, they have never yet had a clear conception of *what* that something is. They have not been able to hold *it* and *blue* before their minds and to compare them, in the same way in which they can compare *blue* and *green*. And this for the reason I gave above: namely that the moment we try to fix our attention upon consciousness and to see *what*, distinctly, it is, it seems to vanish: it seems as if we had before us a mere emptiness. When we try to introspect the sensation of blue, all we can see is the blue: the other element is as if it were diaphanous. Yet it *can* be distinguished if we look attentively enough, and if we know that there is something to look for. My main object in this paragraph has been to try to make the reader *see* it; but I fear I shall have succeeded very ill.

It being the case, then, that the sensation of blue includes in its analysis, beside blue, *both* a unique element 'awareness' *and* a unique relation of this element to blue, I can make plain what I meant by asserting, as two distinct propositions, (1) that blue is probably not part of the content of the sensation at all, and (2) that, even it were, the sensation would nevertheless not be the sensation *of* blue, if blue had only this relation to it. The first hypothesis may now be expressed by saying that, if it were true, then, when the sensation of blue exists, there exists a *blue awareness*: offence may be taken at the expression, but yet it expresses just what should be and is meant by saying that blue is, in this case, a *content* of consciousness or experience. Whether or not, when I have the sensation of blue, my consciousness or awareness is thus blue, my introspection does not enable me to decide with certainty: I only see no reason for thinking that it is. But whether it is or not, the point is unimportant, for introspection *does* enable me to decide that something else is also true: namely that I am aware *of* blue, and by this I mean, that my awareness has to blue quite different and distinct relation. It is possible, I admit, that my awareness is blue *as well* as being *of* blue: but what I am quite sure of is that it is *of* blue; that it has to blue the simple and unique relation the existence of which alone justifies us in distinguishing knowledge of a thing from the thing known, indeed in distinguishing mind from matter. And this result I may express by saying that what is called the *content* of a sensation is in very truth what I originally called it – the sensation's *object*.

But, if all this be true, what follows?

Idealists admit that some things really exist of which they are not aware: there are some things, they hold, which are not inseparable aspects of *their* experience, even if they be inseparable aspects of some experience. They further hold that some of the things of which they are sometimes aware do really exist, even when they are not aware of them: they hold for instance that they are sometimes aware of other minds, which continue to exist even when they are not aware of them. They are, therefore, sometimes aware of something which is *not* an inseparable aspect of their own experience. They do *know some* things which are *not* a mere part or content of their experience. And what my analysis of sensation has been designed to show is, that whenever I have a mere sensation or idea, the fact is that I am then aware of something which is equally and in the same sense *not* an inseparable aspect of my experience. The awareness which I have maintained to be included in sensation is the very same unique fact which constitutes every kind of knowledge: 'blue' is as much an object, and as little a mere content, of my experience, when I experience it, as the most exalted and independent real thing of which I am ever aware. There is, therefore, no question of how we are to 'get outside the circle of our own ideas and sensations'. Merely to have a sensation is already to *be* outside that circle. It is to know something which is as truly and really *not* a part of *my* experience, as anything which I can ever know.

Now I think I am not mistaken in asserting that the reason why Idealists suppose that everything which *is* must be an inseparable aspect of some experience, is that they suppose some things, at least, to be inseparable aspects of *their* experience. And there is certainly nothing which they are so firmly convinced to be an inseparable aspect of their experience as what they call the *content* of their ideas and sensations. If, therefore, *this* turns out in every case, whether it be also the content or not, to be at least *not* an inseparable aspect of the experience of it, it will be readily admitted that nothing else which *we* experience ever is such an inseparable aspect. But if we never experience anything but what is *not* an inseparable aspect of *that* experience, how can we infer that anything whatever, let alone *everything*, is an inseparable aspect of *any* experience? How utterly unfounded is the assumption that '*esse* is *percipi*' appears in the clearest light.

But further I think it may be seen that if the object of an Idealist's sensation were, as he supposes, *not* the object but merely the content of that sensation, if, that is to say, it really were an inseparable aspect of his experience, each Idealist could never be aware either of himself or of any other real thing. For the relation of a sensation to its object is certainly the same as that of any other instance of experience to its object; and this, I think, is generally admitted even by Idealists: they state as readily that *what* is judged or thought or perceived is the *content* of that judgment or thought or perception, as that blue is the content of the sensation of blue. But, if so, then when any Idealist thinks he is *aware* of himself or of any one else, this cannot really be the case. The fact is, on his own theory, that himself and that other person are in reality mere *contents* of an awareness, which is aware *of* nothing whatever. All that can be said is that there is an awareness in him, *with* a certain content: it can never be true that there is in him a consciousness *of* any-thing. And similarly he is never aware either of the fact that he exists or that reality is spiritual. The real fact, which he describes in those terms, is that his existence and the spirituality of reality are *contents* of an awareness, which is aware of nothing – certainly not, then, of its own content.

And further if everything, of which he thinks he is aware, is in reality merely a content of his own experience he has certainly no *reason* for holding that anything does exist except himself: it will, of course, be possible that other persons do exist; solipsism will not be necessarily true; but he cannot possibly infer from anything he holds that it is not true. That he himself exists will of course follow from his premiss that many things are contents of *his* experience. But since everything, of which he thinks himself aware, is in reality merely an inseparable aspect of that awareness; this premiss allows no inference that any of these contents, far less any other consciousness, exists at all except as an inseparable aspect of his awareness, that is, as part of himself.

Such, and not those which he takes to follow from it, are the consequences which *do* follow from the Idealist's supposition that the object of an experience is in reality merely a content or inseparable aspect of that experience. If, on the other hand, we clearly recognise the nature of that peculiar relation which I have called 'awareness of anything'; if we see that *this* is in-volved equally in the analysis of *every* experience – from the merest sensation to the most developed perception or reflexion, and that *this* is in fact the only essential element in an experience

– the only thing that is both common and peculiar to all experiences – the only thing which gives us reason to call any fact mental; if, further, we recognise that this awareness is and must be in all cases of such a nature that its object, when we are aware of it, is precisely what it would be, if we were not aware: then it becomes plain that the existence of a table in space is related to my experience of *it* in precisely the same way as the existence of my own experience is related to my experience of *that*. Of both we are merely aware: if we are aware that the one exists, we are aware in precisely the same sense that the other exists; and if it is true that my experience can exist, even when I do not happen to be aware of its existence, we have exactly the same reason for supposing that the table can do so also. When, therefore, Berkeley, supposed that the only thing of which I am directly aware is my own sensations and ideas, he supposed what was false; and when Kant supposed that the objectivity of things in space *consisted* in the fact that they were '*Vorstellungen*' having to one another different relations from those which the same '*Vorstellungen*' have to one another in subjective experience, he supposed what was equally false. I am as directly aware of the existence of material things in space as of my own sensations; and *what* I am aware of with regard to each is exactly the same – namely that in one case the material thing, and in the other case my sensation does really exist. The question requiring to be asked about material things is thus not: What reason have we for supposing that anything exists *corresponding* to our sensations? but: What reason have we for supposing that material things do *not* exist, since *their* existence has precisely the same evidence as that of our sensations? That either exist *may* be false; but if it is a reason for doubting the existence of matter, that it is an inseparable aspect of our experience, the same reasoning will prove conclusively that our experience does not exist either, since that must also be an inseparable aspect of our experience of *it*. The only *reasonable* alternative to the admission that matter exists *as well* as spirit, is absolute Scepticism – that, as likely as not *nothing* exists at all. All other suppositions – the Agnostic's, that something, at all events, does exist, as much as the Idealist's, that spirit does – are, if we have no reason for believing in matter, as baseless as the grossest superstitions.

4

SENSE-DATA

I have said that I shall now begin discussing the various ways in which we know of the existence of material objects – *supposing* that we do know of their existence. I do not want to assume, to begin with, that we *certainly do* know that they exist. I only want to consider what sort of a thing our knowledge of them is, *supposing* that it is really knowledge. I shall afterwards consider whether it *is* really knowledge.

And I said I should begin with the most primitive sort of way in which we commonly suppose that we have knowledge of them – namely, that kind of knowledge, which we should call knowledge *by means of the senses* – the knowledge which we have, for instance, by seeing and feeling, as when we feel an object over with our hands. This way of knowing material objects, by means of the senses, is, of course, by no means the only way in which we commonly suppose we know of their existence. For instance, each of us knows of the past existence of many material objects by means of memory; we remember the existence of objects which we are no longer perceiving by any of our senses. We know of others again, which we ourselves have never perceived by our senses and cannot therefore remember, by the testimony of other persons who *have* perceived them by their senses. And we know also, we suppose, by means of inference, of others which nobody has ever perceived by his senses: we know, for instance, in this way that there is another surface of the moon, different from that which is constantly

First published in *Some Main Problems of Philosophy* (George Allen & Unwin, London: 1953) pp.28–40. This lecture was originally written for delivery in 1910. While preparing it for publication during 1952 Moore added some footnotes which are reproduced here: they all end with the sign '(1952)'.

turned to the earth. All these other ways of knowing material objects, I shall have presently to consider, and to contrast them with sense-perception. But all these other ways do seem, in a sense, to be *based* upon sense-perception, so that *it* is, in a sense, the most primitive way of knowing material objects: it seems, in fact, to be true, that if I had not known of *some* material objects by means of sense-perception, I could never possibly have known of any others in any of these other ways; and this seems to be true universally: no man could ever know of the existence of any material objects at all, unless he first knew of *some* by means of his senses. The evidence of the senses is, therefore, the evidence upon which all our other ways of knowing material objects seems to be based.

And what I want first to consider is what sort of a thing this evidence of the senses is; or in other words what it is that happens when (as we should say) we see, or feel, a material object, or perceive one by any other sense. And I propose to take as an instance, for the sake of simplicity, a single sense *only* – namely, the sense of sight: I shall use what happens when we *see*, as an illustration of what happens in sense-perception generally. All the general principles which I point out with regard to the sense of seeing, will, I think, be easily transferable, *mutatis mutandis*, to all the other senses by which we can be said to perceive material objects.

My first question is, then: What exactly is it that happens, when (as we should say) we *see* a material object? And I should explain, perhaps, to avoid misunderstanding, that the occurrence which I mean here to analyse is merely the *mental* occurrence – the act of consciousness – which we call *seeing*. I do not mean to say anything at all about the bodily processes which occur in the eye and the optic nerves and the brain. I have no doubt, myself, that these bodily processes *do* occur, when we see; and that physiologists really do *know* a great deal about them. But all that I shall mean by *'seeing'*, and all that I wish to talk about, is the mental occurrence – the act of consciousness – which occurs (as is supposed) as a consequence of or accompaniment of these bodily processes. This mental occurrence, which I call 'seeing', is known to us in a much more simple and direct way, than are the complicated physiological processes which go on in our eyes and nerves and brains. A man cannot directly observe the minute processes which go on in his own eyes and nerves and brain when he sees; but all of us who are not blind can directly observe this mental occurrence, which we mean by seeing. And it is solely with *seeing*, in this sense – seeing, as an act of consciousness which we can all of us directly observe as happening in our own minds – that I am now concerned.

And I wish to illustrate what I have to say about seeing by a direct practical example; because, though I dare say many of you are perfectly familiar with the sort of points I wish to raise, it is, I think, very important for every one, in these subjects, to consider carefully single concrete instances, so that there may be no mistake as to exactly what it is that is being talked about. Such mistakes are, I think, very apt to happen, if one talks merely in generalities; and moreover one is apt to overlook important points. I propose, therefore, to hold up an envelope in my hand, and to ask you all to look at it for a moment; and then to consider with me exactly what it is that happens, when you see it: *what* this occurrence, which we call the *seeing* of it, *is*.

I hold up this envelope, then: I look at it, and I hope you all will look at it. And now I put it down again. Now what has happened? We should certainly say (if you have looked at it) that we all *saw* that envelope, that we all saw *it*, *the same* envelope: *I* saw it, and you all saw it. We all saw *the same* object. And by the *it*, which we all saw, we mean an object, which, at any one of the moments when we were looking at it, occupied just *one* of the many places that constitute the whole of space. Even during the short time in which we were looking at it, it may have moved – occupied successively several different places; for the earth, we believe, is constantly going round on its axis, and carrying with it all the objects on its surface, so that, even while we looked at the envelope, it probably moved and changed its position in space, though we did not see it move. But at any *one* moment, we should say, this *it*, the envelope, which we say we all saw, was at some *one* definite place in space.

But now, what happened to each of us, when we saw that envelope? I will begin by describing *part* of what happened to me. I saw a patch* of a particular whitish colour, having a certain size, and a certain shape, a shape with rather sharp

* I am so extending the use of the word 'patch' that, e.g., the very small black dot which I directly apprehend when I see a full-stop, or the small black line which I directly apprehend when I see a hyphen, are, each of them, in the sense in which I am using the word, a 'patch of colour' (1952).

angles or corners and bounded by fairly straight lines. These things: this patch of a whitish colour, and its size and shape I did actually see. And I propose to call these things, the colour and size and shape, *sense-data*,[†] things *given* or presented by the senses – given, in this case, by my sense of sight. Many philosophers have called these things which I call sense-data, *sensations*. They would say, for instance, that that particular patch of colour was a sensation. But it seems to me that this term 'sensation' is liable to be misleading. We should certainly say that I *had* a sensation, when I saw that colour. But when we say that I *had* a sensation, what we mean is, I think, that I had the experience which consisted in my *seeing* the colour. That is to say, what we mean by a sensation in this phrase, is my *seeing* of the colour, not the colour which I saw: this colour does not seem to be what I mean to say that I *had*, when I say I *had* a sensation of colour. It is very unnatural to say that I *had* the colour, that I *had* that particular whitish grey or that I *had* the patch which was of that colour. What I certainly did *have* is the experience which consisted in my seeing the colour and the patch. And when, therefore, we talk of *having* sensations, I think what we mean by 'sensations' is the experiences which consist in apprehending certain sense-data, *not* these sense-data themselves. I think, then, that the term 'sensation' is liable to be misleading, because it may be used in two different senses, which it is very important to distinguish from one another. It may be used *either* for the colour which I saw *or* for the experience which consisted in my seeing it. And it is, I think very important, for several reasons, to distinguish these two things. I will mention only two of these reasons. In the first place, it is, I think, quite conceivable (I do not say it is actually true) but *conceivable* that the patch of colour which I saw may have continued to exist after I saw it: whereas, of course, when I ceased to see it, *my seeing* of it ceased to exist. I will illustrate what I mean, by holding up the envelope again, and looking at it. I look at it, and I again see a *sense-datum*, a patch of a whitish colour. But now I immediately turn away my eyes, and I no longer see that sense-datum: my seeing of it has ceased to exist. But I am by no means sure that the sense-datum

---

† I should now make, and have for many years made, a sharp distinction between what I have called the 'patch', on the one hand, and the colour, size and shape, *of* which it is, on the other; and should call, and have called, *only* the patch, *not* its colour, size or shape, a 'sense-datum' (1952).

– that very same patch of whitish colour which I saw – is not still *existing* and still there. I do not say, for certain, that it is: I think very likely it is not. But I have a strong inclination to believe that it is. And it seems to me at least *conceivable* that it should be still existing, whereas my *seeing* of it certainly has ceased to exist. This is one reason for distinguishing between the sense-data which I see, and my seeing of them. And here is another. It seems to me *conceivable* – here again I do not say it is true but *conceivable* – that some sense-data   this whitish colour for instance – are in the place in which the material object – the envelope, is. It seems to me *conceivable* that this whitish colour is really on the surface of the material envelope. Whereas it does not seem to me that my *seeing* of it is in that place. My seeing of it is in another place – somewhere within my body. Here, then, are two reasons for distinguishing between the *sense-data* which I see, and my *seeing* of them. And it seems to me that both of these two very different things are often meant when people talk about 'sensations'. In fact, when you are reading any philosopher who is talking about sensations (or about sense-*impressions* or *ideas* either), you need to look very carefully to see which of the two he is talking about in any particular passage – whether of the sense-data themselves or of our apprehension of them: you will, I think, almost invariably find that he is talking now of the one and now of the other, and very often that he is assuming that what is true of the one must also be true of the other – an assumption which does not seem to be at all justified. I think, therefore, that the term 'sensation' is liable to be very misleading. And I shall, therefore, never use it. I shall always talk of *sense-data*, when what I mean is such things as this colour and size and shape or the patch which is *of* this colour and size and shape, which I actually see. And when I want to talk of my seeing of them, I shall expressly call this the seeing of sense-data; or, if I want a term which will apply equally to all the senses, I shall speak of the *direct apprehension of* sense-data. Thus when I see this whitish colour, I am *directly apprehending* this whitish colour: my seeing of it, as a mental act, an act of consciousness, just consists in my direct apprehension of it; – so too when I hear a sound, I directly apprehend the sound; when I feel a tooth-ache I directly apprehend the ache: and all these things – the whitish colour, the sound and the ache are *sense-data*.

To return, then, to what happened to us, when we all saw the same envelope. Part, at least, of what happened to me, I can now express by saying that I saw certain sense-data: I saw a whitish patch of colour, of a particular size and shape. And I have no doubt whatever that this is part, at least, of what happened to all of you. You also saw certain sense-data; and I expect also that the sense-data which you saw were more or less similar to those which I saw. You also saw a patch of colour which might be described as whitish, of a size not very different from the size of the patch which I saw, and of a shape similar at least in this that it had rather sharp corners and was bounded by fairly straight lines. But now, what I want to emphasize is this. Though we all did (as we should say) see *the same* envelope, no two of us, in all probability, saw exactly the *same sense-data*. Each of us, in all probability, saw, to begin with, a slightly different shade of colour. All these colours may have been whitish; but each was probably at least slightly different from all the rest, according to the way in which the light fell upon the paper, relatively to the different positions you are sitting in; and again according to differences in the strength of your eye-sight, or your distance from the paper. And so too, with regard to the size of the patch of colour which you saw: differences in the strength of your eyes and in your distance from the envelope probably made slight differences in the size of the patch of colour, which you saw. And so again with regard to the shape. Those of you on that side of the room will have seen a rhomboidal figure, while those in front of me will have seen a figure more nearly rectangular. Those on my left will have seen a figure more like this which you in front now see, and which you see is different from *this* which you then saw. And those in front of me will have seen a figure like that which you on the left now see, and which, you see, is different from *this*, which you saw before. Those directly in front of me, may, indeed, have all seen very nearly the same figure – perhaps, even, exactly the same. But we should not say we *knew* that any two did; whereas we should say we did *know* that we all saw the *same* envelope. That you did all see the same envelope, would, indeed, be accepted in ordinary life as a certainty of the strongest kind. Had you all seen me commit a murder, as clearly as you all saw this envelope, your evidence would be accepted by any jury as sufficient to hang me. Such evidence would be accepted in any court of law as quite conclusive; we should take such a responsibility as that of hanging a man, upon it. It would be accepted, that is, that you had all seen me, *the same man*, commit a murder; and not merely that you had all seen some man or other, possibly each of you a different man in each case, commit one. And yet, in this case, as in the case of the envelope, the sense-data which you had all seen, would have been different sense-data: you could not swear in a court of law that you had all seen exactly the *same sense-data*.

Now all this seems to me to shew very clearly, that, *if* we *did* all see the same envelope, the envelope which we saw was not *identical with* the sense-data which we saw: the envelope cannot be exactly the same thing as each of the sets of sense-data, which we each of us saw; for these were in all probability each of them slightly different from all the rest, and they cannot, therefore, *all* be exactly the same thing as the envelope.

But it might be said: Of course, when we say that we all saw the envelope, we do not mean that we all saw the *whole* of it. I, for instance, only saw *this* side of it, whereas all of you only saw *that* side. And generally, when we talk of seeing an object we only mean seeing some *part* of it. There is always more in any object which we see, than the *part* of it which we see.

And this, I think, is quite true. Whenever we talk roughly of seeing any object, it is true that, in another and stricter sense of the word *see*, we only see *a part of* it. And it might, therefore, be suggested that why we say we all saw this envelope, when we each, in fact, saw a different set of sense-data, is because each of these *sets of sense-data* is, in fact, a *part* of the envelope.

But it seems to me there is a great difficulty even in maintaining that the different sense-data we all saw are parts of the envelope. What do we mean by a *part* of a material object? We mean, I think, at least this. What we call a part of a material object must be something which occupies a part of the volume in space occupied by the whole object. For instance, this envelope occupies a certain volume in space: that is to say, it occupies a space which has breadth and thickness as well as length. And anything which is a *part* of the envelope at any moment, must be *in* some part of the volume of space occupied by the whole envelope at that moment: it must be somewhere within that volume, or at some point in the surfaces bounding that volume.

Are, then, any of the sense-data we saw *parts* of the envelope in this sense?

The sense-data I mentioned were these three – the colour – the whitish colour; the *size* of this colour; its *shape*.* And of these three it is only the colour, which could, in the sense defined, possibly be supposed to be a *part* of the envelope. The colour might be supposed to occupy a *part* of the volume occupied by the envelope – one of its bounding surfaces,† for instance. But the size and shape could hardly be said to *occupy* any part of this volume. What might be true of them is that the size I saw *is* the size of one surface of the envelope; and that the shape *is* the shape of this surface of the envelope. The side of the envelope which I say I saw certainly *has* some size and some shape; and the sense-data – the size and shape, which I saw as the size and shape of a patch of colour – might possibly *be* the size and shape of this side of the envelope.

Let us consider whether these things are so.

And, first, as to the colours. Can these possibly be parts of the envelope? What we supposed is that each of you probably saw a slightly different colour. And if we are to suppose that *all* those colours are parts of the envelope, then we must suppose that *all* of them are in the same place. We must suppose that ever so many different colours all of them occupy the same surface – this surface of the envelope which you now see. And I think it is certainly difficult to suppose this, though not absolutely impossible. It is not absolutely impossible, I think, that all the different colours which you see are really all of them in the same place. But I myself find it difficult to believe that this is so; and you can understand, I think, why most philosophers should have declared it to be impossible. They have declared, chiefly, I think, on grounds like this, that none of the colours which any of us ever see are ever parts of material objects: they have declared that none of them are ever in any part of the places where material objects (if there are any material objects) are. This conclusion does, indeed, go beyond what the premises justify, even if we accept the premise that several different colours cannot all be in

* I had here forgotten that one of the sense-data mentioned was the *patch* which *has* that colour and shape and size – the *patch* which, I should now say, is the *only* sense-datum, having to do with the envelope, which I then saw (1952).
† I should now say that any part of the *surface* of a volume is *not* a part of the volume, because it is not itself a volume (1952).

exactly the same place. For it remains possible that the colour, which some *one* of you sees, is really on the surface of the envelope; whereas the colours which all the rest of you see are *not* there. But if so, then we must say that though all of you are seeing the same side of the envelope, yet only one of you is seeing a sense-datum which is a part of that side: the sense-data seen by all the rest are *not* parts of the envelope. And this also, I think, is difficult to believe. It might be, indeed, that those of you who are seeing a colour, which is *not* a part of the envelope, might yet be seeing a size and a shape which really *is* the size and shape of one side of the envelope; and we will go on to consider whether *this* is so.

And, first, as to the size. I assumed that the sense-given sizes, which you see, are all of them probably slightly different from one another. And, if this be so, then certainly it seems to be absolutely impossible that they should *all* of them be the size of this side of the envelope. This side of the envelope can only really have *one* size; it cannot have several different sizes. But it may not seem quite clear, that you all do see different sizes; the differences between the different distances at which you are from the envelope are not so great, but what the patches of colour you all see might be, at least, of *much the same* size. So I will give a hypothetical instance to make my point clearer. Suppose this room were so large that I could carry the envelope two or three hundred yards away from you. The sense-given size which you would then see, when I was three hundred yards off, would certainly be appreciably smaller than what you see now. And yet you would still be seeing this same envelope. It seems quite impossible that these two very different sizes should both of them be *the* size of the envelope. So that here the *only* possibility is that the size which you see at some *one* definite distance or set of distances, should be the envelope's real size, *if* you ever see its real size at all. This may be so: it may be that some one of the sense-given sizes which we see is the envelope's real size. But it seems also possible that none of them are; and in any case we all see the envelope, just the same, *whether* we see its real size or not.

And now for the shape. Here again it seems quite impossible that *all* the shapes we see can be the envelope's real shape. This side of the envelope can have but *one* shape: it cannot be both rhomboidal, as is the shape which you on the left see, and also rectangular, as is the shape seen by those in front; the angles at its corners cannot be both right angles and also very far from right angles. Certainly, therefore, the sense-given shape which some of you see is *not* the shape of this side of the envelope. But here it may be said, it is plain enough that one of the sense-given shapes seen *is* its real shape. You may say: The shape seen by those in front *is* its real shape; the envelope *is* rectangular. And I quite admit that this is so: I think we do know, in fact, that the envelope really is *roughly* rectangular. But here I want to introduce a distinction. There are two different senses in which we may talk of *the* shape of anything. A rectangle of the size of this envelope, and a rectangle of the size of this blackboard, may both, in a sense, have exactly *the same* shape. They may have the same shape in the sense, that all the angles of both are right angles, and that the proportions between the sides of the one, and those between the sides of the other, are the same. They may, in fact, have the same shape, in the sense in which a big square always has the same shape as a small square, however big the one may be and however small the other. But there is another sense in which *the* shape of a big square is obviously not *the same* as that of a small square. We may mean by *the* shape of a big square the actual lines bounding it; and if we mean this, *the* shape of a big square cannot possibly be the *same* as *the* shape of a smaller one. The lines bounding the two cannot possibly be the *same* lines. And the same thing may be true, even when there is no difference in size between two shapes. Imagine *two* squares, of the same size, side by side. The lines bounding the one are *not* the same lines as those bounding the other: though each is both *of* the same shape and *of* the same size as the other. The difference between these two senses in which we may talk of *the* shape of anything, may be expressed by saying that the shape of the big square is the same *in quality* – qualitatively identical – with that of the small square, but is not *numerically* the same – not numerically identical: the shape of the big square is *numerically* different from that of the small, in the sense that they are *two* shapes, and not one only, of which we are talking, though both are the same in quality: both are *squares*, but the one is *one* square and the other is *another* square. There is, then, a difference between two different kinds of identity: qualitative identity and numerical identity; and we are all perfectly familiar with the difference between the two, though the names may sound strange. I shall in future use these names: qualitative identity and numerical identity. And now to return to the case of the envelope. Even supposing that the sense-given shape which you in front see is rectangular, and that the real shape of the envelope is also rectangular, and that both are rectangles of exactly the same shape; it still does not follow that the sense-given shape which you see is *the* shape of the envelope. The sense-given shape and the shape of the envelope, even if they are qualitatively the same, *must* still be *two* different shapes, *numerically* different, unless they are *of the same size*; just as *the* shape of a large square must be numerically different from *the* shape of a smaller one. And we saw before how difficult it was to be sure that any of the sizes which you saw were the *real* size of the envelope. And even if the sense-given size which some one of you sees *is* the real size of the envelope, it still does not follow that the sense-given *shape* which you see is numerically the same as the shape of the envelope. The two may be numerically different, just as in the case of two different squares, side by side, of the same shape and size, *the* shape of the one *is* not *the* shape of the other; they are two numerically different shapes. We may say, then, that if those of you who see rectangular shapes, do see rectangular shapes of different sizes, only one of these can possibly be *the* shape of the envelope: all the others may be *of* the same shape – the same in quality – but they cannot be *the* shape of the envelope. And even if some *one* of you does see a shape, which is of the same size as *the* shape of the envelope, as well as being of the same shape (and it is very doubtful whether any of you does) it would yet be by no means certain that this sense-given shape which you saw was *the* shape of the envelope. It might be a shape *numerically* different from *the* shape of the envelope, although exactly similar both in shape and size. And finally there is some reason to suppose that none of the sense-given shapes which any of you see are *exactly* the same, even in quality, as *the* shape of the envelope. The envelope itself probably has a more or less irregular edge; there are probably ups and downs in the line bounding its side, which you at that distance cannot see.

Of the three kinds of sense-data,* then, which you all of you

---

* The *patch* itself, which *has* that colour and shape and size, again forgotten! (1952).

saw, when I held up the envelope, namely, the whitish colour, its size, and its shape, the following things seem to be true. First, as regards the colour, no one of you can be sure that the exact colour which you saw was really a part of the envelope – was really in any part of the space, which the real envelope (if there was a real envelope) occupied. Then as regards the size, no one of you can be sure that the size which you saw was the real size of the envelope. And finally as regards the shape, no one of you can be sure that the shape which you saw was really of exactly the same shape as that of the envelope; still less can you be sure that it was *the* shape of the envelope, that the bounding lines which composed it were numerically the same bounding lines as those which enclosed the envelope. And not only can none of you be sure of these things. As regards the sizes and shapes which you saw, it seems quite certain that some of you saw sizes and shapes which were *not* the real size and shape of the envelope; because it seems quite certain that some of you saw sizes and shapes different from those seen by others, and that these different sizes and shapes cannot possibly *all* be *the* size and shape of the envelope. And as regards the colours it seems fairly certain, that the colours which you saw cannot all have been *in* the envelope; since it seems fairly certain that you all saw slightly different colours, and it is difficult to believe, though not absolutely impossible, that all these different colours were really in the same place at the same time.

This seems to be the state of things with regard to these sense-data – the colour, the size and the shape. They seem, in a sense, to have had very little to do with the real envelope, if there *was* a real envelope. It seems very probable that *none* of the colours seen was really a part of the envelope; and that *none* of the sizes and shapes seen were the size or the shape of the real envelope.

But now I wish to mention one other sense-datum, of a kind that we all saw, which might be thought to have more to do with the real envelope. Besides the patch of colour and its shape and size, we did, in a sense, all see the *space* which this patch of colour occupied. The patch of colour seemed to occupy a certain area; and we can by abstraction distinguish this area from the patch of colour occupying it. This area was also a sense-datum. And in this area we can distinguish parts – this part, and this part, and this. And it might be thought with regard to parts, at least, of this area, that two things are true. Firstly, that part at least of the sense-given area which each of you saw, is really numerically identical with some part of that seen by all the rest. And secondly, that *this* part, which you all saw, is also a part of the area occupied by the real envelope. In other words, you might comfort yourselves by supposing, that even if the colour presented by your senses is *not* a part of the real envelope, and even if the shape and size presented by your senses are not the shape and size of the real envelope, yet at least there is presented by your senses a *part* of the *space occupied by* the real envelope. And against this supposition I confess I cannot find any argument, which seems to me very strong. We are all, I think, very strongly tempted to suppose that this is so. That, for instance, this space which I touch is really seen by all of you – this very same place – and that it also is part of the space which the real envelope occupies. The best argument I can think of against this supposition is the following; and I think it is enough to render the supposition doubtful. If we are to say that part of this sense-given area which I see is really numerically the same with part of those which you see, and that it is also numerically the same as part of the area occupied by the real envelope, then we must either again accept the hypothesis that all the different colours which we see as occupying the area are really in the same place and in the same place as the real envelope, or else we must say that the colours only *seem* to be in this sense-given area and are not really there. But there is the former objection to supposing that several different colours are all really in the same place. And as to the only remaining possibility, namely, that they only *seem* to be in this sense-given area; it may be objected that so far as the sense-given area is concerned, the colours we see *really do* occupy it – that they not only seem to be but *really are* there – that there can be no doubt about this. If we are talking of the area really presented by the senses as occupied by the colours, *this* area, it may be said, undoubtedly *is* occupied by the colours: it *is* nothing but the space over which the colour is spread. So that, if the area, which I see, really is numerically the same as those which you see, then it will follow that all the different colours we see really are in the same place. This argument, I say, does not seem to me to be absolutely conclusive. It does seem to me possible that the colour I see only *seems* to be in the sense-given area, which I see. But it is, I think, sufficient to suggest a doubt whether any part of this sense-given

area seen by me really is numerically the same as any part of any
of those seen by you.[1]

NOTE

1 This is not the end of Moore's lecture on 'Sense-Data'. He proceeds to
discuss the view that sense-data exist only in the minds of those who
apprehend them, without either accepting or rejecting this view, and
then to discuss the implications of this view for an account of the
perception of material objects.

5

HUME'S THEORY EXAMINED

I have just been occupied mainly in stating one particular answer, which I called Hume's answer, to the following question: Under what circumstances (if any) does a man ever *know* of the existence, past, present, or future, of anything whatever, which he himself is not directly apprehending at the moment, and has not directly apprehended in the past?

And the answer to this question which I represented as given by Hume, was in two parts.

The first part was this. Let us say that the existence of one thing, A, is a *sure sign* of the existence of another thing, B, whenever you can truly say: *Since* A exists, it is *certain* that B did exist before it, does exist at the same time, or will exist after it. And let us say that the existence of one thing, A, is a *probable sign* of the existence of another thing, B, whenever you can truly say: *Since* A exists, it is *probable* that B did exist before it, does exist at the same time, or will exist after it. Well then, the first part of Hume's answer consists in saying two things. Firstly: Nobody ever knows that anything, B, which he himself has not directly apprehended, *certainly* did exist, or does exist, or will exist, unless he knows that the existence of some thing or set of things, A, which he *has* directly apprehended, is a *sure sign* of the existence of B. And secondly: Nobody ever knows that anything, B, which he himself has not directly apprehended, *probably* did exist, or does exist, or will exist, unless he knows that the existence of some thing or set of things, A, which he *has* directly apprehended, is a *probable* sign of the existence of B.

First published in *Some Main Problems of Philosophy* (George Allen & Unwin, London: 1953), pp.108–26. This lecture was originally written for delivery in 1910.

This was the first part of Hume's answer to our question; and the second part was this.

Let us say that a man has experienced a *general conjunction* between *things like* A and *things like* B, if, when he has directly apprehended a thing like A in the past, he has *generally* directly apprehended a thing like B, either before or after, or at the same time. *'Conjunction'*, a word which Hume himself uses, is a convenient word, because we can say that things like A are *generally conjoined* with things like B, *both* when we mean that they generally precede them, *and* when we mean that they generally follow them, *and* when we mean that they generally accompany them. Let us say, then, that a man has experienced a *general conjunction* between things like A and things like B, if, when he has directly apprehended a thing like A in the past, he has *generally* directly apprehended a thing like B also, either before or after or at the same time. Well then, if we understand the phrase 'experienced a general conjunction' in this sense, the second part of Hume's answer consists in saying this. No man, he says, ever knows that the existence of any one thing, A, is either a *sure sign* or even a *probable sign* of the existence of another thing, B, unless *somebody* has in the past experienced a general conjunction between *things like* A and *things like* B. But obviously something more can be added to this answer. For even if somebody else has experienced a general conjunction between *things like* A and *things like* B, yet if I myself have not, and also I do not *know* that anybody else has, I shall be as far as ever from knowing that the existence of A is a sign of the existence of B. But the fact that anybody else has ever experienced anything whatever is always a fact which I myself have never directly apprehended. If, therefore, I am to know that anybody else has experienced any general conjunction, I must know that some thing, A, which I *have* directly apprehended, is a *sign* that they have. And I can only know this if I *myself* have experienced a conjunction between things like A and things like the fact that somebody else has experienced the conjunction in question.

This was the second part of Hume's answer to our question. And these two rules or principles were what I tried to explain at length last time. They are, I think, very difficult to express quite accurately: I have not even tried to express them *quite* accurately even now: and yet, I think, it is very easy to see almost exactly what is meant by them, although they are so difficult to express. I will call the first the rule: That nobody can ever know of the existence of anything which he has not directly apprehended, unless he knows that something which he has directly apprehended is *a sign* of its existence. And I will call the second the rule: That nobody can ever know that the existence of any one thing, A is a *sign* of the *existence* of another thing, B, unless he himself (or, under certain conditions, somebody else) has experienced a *general conjunction* between *things like* A and *things like* B. And the important thing to remember about this second rule is that nobody can be said to have *experienced a conjunction* between any two things, unless he has *directly apprehended* both the things. I will call these two rules, then, Hume's first rule, and Hume's second rule. But, when I call them Hume's, I ought, perhaps, to warn you of two things. If you were to look for them in Hume, you would not find either of them expressed exactly in the form in which I have expressed them; and also you *would* find, mingled with statements which seem to be statements of these rules, other statements which mean something very different indeed, and which Hume himself does not seem to distinguish very clearly from these two rules. I do not pretend, then, that these two rules are at all a complete statement of what Hume has to say about our knowledge of the existence of things which we do not directly apprehend. All that I do mean to claim is that they certainly do express a part, and a very important part, of what he did think about this subject; and so far as I know, he was the first philosopher who did definitely think of these two rules.

But now I said that many philosophers seem to me to have been led to conclude that we cannot ever know of the existence of any material object, by the assumption, conscious or unconscious, that these rules of Hume's are true. They have, I think, argued first, with some plausibility, that, *if* these rules are true, then none of us ever knows of the existence of any material object; and *then* they have concluded that, *since* these rules *are* true, none of us does ever know that any material object exists – not even that there is the slightest probability of its existence. Both steps in this argument, I said, do seem to me plausible enough to need an answer; and I said that in this lecture I should do my best to meet it. Obviously it must be met, if at all, in one or other of two ways: you must either try to shew that,

even if Hume's rules are true, we might yet know of the existence of material objects; or you must try to shew that Hume's
rules are not true. I shall presently consider both of these two
ways of meeting it. But first of all, I want to try to state more
clearly exactly what the point at issue is.

There are, I think, two views, both very plausible and both
very commonly held, which owe their plausibility, in the way I
have suggested, to the assumption that Hume's rules are true.

Both of them start by admitting, as Hume does, that every
man can know of the existence of things which he himself is
directly apprehending at the moment, or has directly apprehended in the past and now remembers. But they hold that the only
existing things which any man ever does directly apprehend are
(1) his own acts of consciousness and (2) his own private sense-
data and images. And, except for the possibility that some of the
sense-data which we directly apprehend may not be *private* to us
– the possibility, that is, that two or more of us may sometimes
directly apprehend the very same sense-datum – I think they are
plainly quite right so far. Nobody, I think, does ever learn by
direct apprehension of the existence of anything whatever except his own acts of consciousness, on the one hand, and sense-
data and images on the other: and these sense-data and images
may, I think, as these views hold, be *all* of them always *private* to
the person who directly apprehends them: I think this is very
possibly so, only I do not feel quite sure. At all events, nobody
ever does know, by direct apprehension, of the existence of
anything whatever except his own acts of consciousness and the
sense-data and images which he directly apprehends. As to this
we are agreed. The only question is as to what things *beside* his
own acts of consciousness and the sense-data and images which
he directly apprehends a man can ever know to exist: and it is
here that Hume's rules come in.

One of the two views I am speaking of, holds this, namely:
That every man's knowledge as to what exists, or even *probably*
exists, *beyond* what he himself has directly apprehended, is
entirely confined to two classes of things. A man may know, it
says, to a certain extent, what acts of consciousness he himself is
likely to perform in the future, and what sense-data and images
he is likely to directly apprehend; and so too he may be able to
know that he himself has in the past, or probably has, performed certain acts of consciousness and directly apprehended

certain sense-data, even though he has quite forgotten them. This is one class of things which he may know to exist, probably or certainly, by inference, according to Hume's rules. Let us say that this class consists entirely of *contents*, past and future, of his own mind – assuming, that is, that the sense-data and images which he directly apprehends are in his own mind – are *contained* in it. And the other class of things which, according to this view, a man may know to exist (probably or certainly) consists, in the same sense, entirely of the *contents of other people's minds*. A man may know, that is, that other people, beside himself, have performed, are performing, and probably will perform certain acts of consciousness; and that they also have directly apprehended, are directly apprehending and probably will directly apprehend certain sense-data. These two classes of things – certain contents past and future of his own mind – and certain contents, past, present, and future, of other people's minds, a man may know to exist, at least *probably*, even though he has not directly apprehended them, or, if he has, has quite forgotten them. *But* (this view says) nobody can ever know, even probably, that anything else whatever, not belonging to these two classes, does exist or will exist in the Universe at all. Nobody can know that there even probably has existed, does exist, or will exist in the Universe anything else whatever except certain things which are in his own mind or else in somebody else's mind. This is one view, which has, I think, been very commonly held, and which is, I think, plainly due to the assumption that Hume's rules are true. Hume's second rule states that nobody can ever know of the existence of anything which he himself has not directly apprehended, unless he has previously apprehended something *like* it. But the only existing things which any man ever has directly apprehended are things in his own mind – either his own acts of consciousness, or the sense-data and images which he has directly apprehended. It is then argued, with some plausibility, that anything else which is sufficiently *like* these to be inferred according to Hume's rule, must also be something in somebody's mind. And hence it is concluded that nobody ever does know of the existence of anything whatever except what is in somebody's mind, either his own mind or somebody else's.

This, then, is one of the two views, which seems to me to be due to the assumption that Hume's rules are true. And the second is exactly like it except in one respect. This view also holds that the only definite kinds of things which Hume's rules allow me to infer are certain contents, past and future, of my own mind and certain contents past, present, and future, of other people's minds. But it holds also that none of the events in my own mind or in other people's, which I can thus know of, are sufficient to *account for* the existence of the sense-data, which I or other people directly apprehend. This view holds, therefore, that I *can* know that *something else* exists in the Universe – because something else must have existed, in order to *cause* the existence of my own and other people's sense-data. But, it says, I cannot possibly know whether this something else, which is the cause of sense-data, is or is not in any respect *like* anything which anybody has ever directly apprehended. I cannot possibly know, for instance, whether it has shape or is situated in space or not. I cannot possibly know whether it is or is not in anybody's mind. The only means by which I can know what *sort* of a thing is likely to have caused any particular kind of thing is by means of Hume's rules. But Hume's rules only allow me to infer the existence of certain things in my own mind and in other people's minds. I *know* that these things, which I can infer, are *not* sufficient to cause my own sense-data and other people's sense-data. I know, therefore, that *something else* must exist in the Universe. But with regard to this something else I know nothing whatever except simply that it does exist and that it causes my own and other people's sensations. I cannot possibly know that it is in the least respect similar to anything whatever which I or anybody else has ever directly apprehended.

These two views, then, I say, both deny that we can ever know of the existence of any material object – they both deny that we can ever know that any material object even *probably* exists. But curiously enough many of those who hold them have thought that they were not denying our knowledge of material objects. They have thought that, to allow that we do know of the things, which they say that we do know of, is *the same thing* as to allow that we do know of the existence of material objects. They have thought that they were not denying our power to know anything which Common Sense supposes itself to know. And what I wish now, first of all, to make plain is that both of these views *do* deny our power to know of the existence of material objects; and that in doing so they do flatly contradict Common

Sense. I want to make plain how utterly and extremely different these views are from those which we take, when we do believe in the existence of material objects. And thus, at the same time, to make plain exactly what the question at issue is, when it is asked whether we can, if Hume's rules are true, ever know of the existence of any material object.

Let us take a particular instance. Look at this pencil. It is just an ordinary wooden pencil. And, when you see it, you directly apprehend a patch of brownish colour, bounded on two sides by fairly long parallel straight lines, and at the ends by much shorter lines, which, in the case of some of you, are probably curved. You directly apprehend these sense-data, and both the two views we are considering allow that, when you directly apprehend these sense-data, you may know them – these visual sense-data – to exist. But you have all often seen a pencil before; that is to say, you have directly apprehended sense-data similar to these that you are now seeing. And when you did so, you may often have directly apprehended *other sense-data* in *conjunction* with visual sense-data similar to those you are now directly apprehending. For instance, you may often have felt a pencil in your hands; and you all know the sort of sense-data you directly apprehend, when you do this – the feeling of smoothness and hardness and of a cylindrical shape. Again you have probably sometimes split a pencil in halves longwise along this line of division, and you know what sort of sense-data you would see and feel, if you looked at the pencil or felt it after doing this. Again you have probably cut one through its breadth, so, and you know what sort of sense-data, you would see and feel, if you looked at and felt the two new ends, after cutting it. These past experiences, which you may have had, of the *conjunction* of other sense-data, visual and tactual, with visual sense-data similar to those which you are now directly apprehending, are what are often called by those who hold the views I am now discussing 'routines of sensations'. And both views allow that on the ground of these past 'routines', you may, according to Hume's rules, know *now* that you *would*, if you did certain things – that is to say, if you directly apprehended the sense-data which you would directly apprehend, if you took this pencil in your hand and split it or cut it – that you *would*, that is under certain conditions, directly apprehend other sense-data, visual and tactual, of the sort to which I have referred. They allow, that is, that these sense-data, which you now directly apprehend, really are *signs* of *something* else: are *signs*, not indeed that anything else *will*, even probably, exist, but only that certain other sense-data *would* exist, *if* in addition to the sense-data which you now directly apprehend, you were also to apprehend directly certain others. But neither view pretends that these other sense-data, of which those which you now see are in this remote way *signs*, do exist *now*. Neither view pretends that that cylindrical shape, which you would feel, if you handled the pencil, exists *now*; or that the sense-data, which you might feel or see, if you split the pencil or cut it open, exist *now*. And as regards the first view, it holds that the sense-data which you now see cannot be known by you to be a sign of the *present* existence of *anything whatever*. The pencil, so far as you mean by the pencil something which you know, even probably, to exist *now*, consists *solely* of those visual sense-data which you are now directly apprehending; *either* of these alone or, perhaps it would be said, also of any images, which you may now be directly apprehending – images of sense-data which you *would* see or feel under other circumstances. But it is not pretended that these images, even if some of them are images of what you would see or feel, if you cut the pencil open, are *inside* the pencil now. The pencil simply has no inside, so far as you know. You cannot possibly know that it has any. All that the sense-data, which you now see, are a *sign* of, is not anything which exists now, but only of certain other sense-data, which you would see or feel, *if* certain other conditions also were realised, which may never be realised.

This is what the first view holds. And the second merely adds to it this. It adds that the visual sense-data you now see really can be known to be a sign of the present existence of *something* else: not, indeed, quite strictly, of the *present* existence of anything else; since this something else can only be known as the *cause* of what you now see, and the *cause* must exist *before* the effect. But it does allow that you may know that these sense-data are a sign that *something* existed a moment ago – something different from anything which you or anybody else, so far as you know, directly apprehended at that moment. But with regard to this something else, it says, you cannot possibly know that it has any shape, or is situated anywhere in space, or that it is in any respect similar to anything which you have ever directly apprehended. You cannot know, for instance, that what causes the sense-data you see is part of a cylindrical surface, or that there is anything whatever *inside* that cylindrical surface. You could not know this, even if you had the advantages which I enjoy, and could examine the pencil both by touch and sight as closely as I can. So far as the sense-data which I directly apprehend can be known to be signs of anything having shape and occupying space at all, they can only, as the first view said, be signs of certain other sense-data, which *would* be seen or felt, under other conditions, which may perhaps never be realised: they are *not* signs of the *present* or *past* existence of anything that has shape or occupies space at all.

Now it seems to me quite plain that these views are utterly different from what we all commonly believe, when we believe in the existence of material objects. What we believe is that these sense-data which we now directly apprehend are signs of the existence of something which exists *now*, or at least did exist a moment ago – not merely of something, which *would* exist, under conditions similar to what we have experienced in the past. And we believe – we all cannot help believing, even though we may hold philosophical views to the contrary – that this something which exists now or existed a moment ago, is not merely a something which may or may not have shape or be situated in space – something with regard to which we cannot possibly tell whether it has a shape or not. We believe quite definitely that the sense-data which we now see are *signs* of the present or immediately past existence of something, which certainly has a cylindrical shape – roughly cylindrical – and which certainly has an inside. I, for instance, claim to *know* that there does exist now, or did a moment ago, not only these sense-data which I am directly apprehending – seeing and feeling – but *also* something else which I am not directly apprehending. And I claim to know not merely that this something else is the *cause* of the sense-data which I am seeing or feeling: I claim to know that this cause is situated *here*; and though by *here* I do not necessarily mean *in* the space which I directly apprehend, yet I do mean *in space* – somewhere in *some* space. And moreover I claim to know, not merely that the cause of my sensations is situated here in space, and has therefore some shape, but also roughly *what* its shape is. I claim to know that the cause of the sense-data I am now directly apprehending is part of the surface of something which is really roughly cylindrical; and that what is enclosed within this cylindrical surface is something different from what is here just outside it. It is, I think, plainly things like these that we all of us believe, when we believe in the existence of material objects. We do not always believe we know exactly what the shape of the objects is, but we do believe that they have some shape. We do take the sense-data which we directly apprehend to be *signs* of the *present*, or *immediately past* existence, of something having shape and in space: *not* merely to be signs of the *possible* future existence of something having shape and in space; *nor* merely signs of the present or immediately past existence of a bare something – something with regard to which we cannot tell whether it has shape or not.

The question is, then, whether we can, consistently with Hume's second rule, ever know that the sense-data which we directly apprehend are *signs* of the existence of a material object in this sense. And in considering this question we may as well again take this pencil as an example. If I do not know *now* that these sense-data, which I now directly apprehend, are really signs of the present or immediately past existence of a body, which I do not directly apprehend, but which is really roughly cylindrical; then, I think, I must admit that I do not ever *know* of the existence of *any* material object. If I do not know of the existence of this pencil now and here, I can hardly ever know of the existence of any material object at all. I do not suppose I have ever had better evidence for the existence of any than I have for this. Can I, then, if Hume's second rule is true, really know now that this cylindrical body, in whose existence I believe but which I *do not* directly apprehend, does, even probably, now exist, or did, even probably, exist a moment ago?

What makes it, at first sight, seem possible that I might know this, even if Hume's second rule were true, is, I think, the following circumstance. Namely, I certainly have directly apprehended in the past, *in conjunction* with sense-data similar to those which I now directly apprehend, other sense-data which were really similar, in some respects, to *parts* of the material object, in whose existence I believe. I believe, for instance, that this material object – this pencil – really is composed of a number of surfaces, similar to that which I now directly apprehend when I look at this end or feel it with my hand, in respect of the fact that they are *circular* or very nearly circular. And I have in the past, when I cut a pencil through, directly apprehended circular surfaces of this sort standing in a certain relation to sense-data similar to those which I now directly apprehend when I look at the length of the pencil. I might, therefore, it would seem, in accordance with Hume's rule, possibly know that there really exist at this moment circular surfaces standing to every point in this length which I directly apprehend in a similar relation to that in which I have found similar surfaces conjoined to points in a similar length before. I might, that is, possibly know that there really exist *at this moment*, all along this pencil a series of circular patches of colour, similar to those which I should see, if I cut it through at any point; and also a series of circular patches of smoothness and hardness, or whatever the qualities may be which I should feel, if I felt the ends, after cutting it through. Also, I or somebody else, may have sometimes examined a circular patch, similar to this, under the microscope, and have then directly apprehended colours and forms different from those which I now apprehend by the naked eye but still all enclosed in a circle. And I might, therefore, know that there really exist at this moment all along the length of this pencil, not only circular patches of colour similar to those which I should see, if I cut through the pencil, and then looked at the ends with the naked eye, but also, and *in the same place*, patches similar to those which I should see, if I looked at the ends through a microscope. It seems to me that I might, according to Hume's second rule, possibly know that these sense-data which I now directly apprehend really are signs of the present or immediately past existence of sense-data of all these kinds; are *signs* that all these sense-data really do exist *now*, though I do not directly apprehend them, and not merely that they *would* exist in the future, *if* certain other conditions were also fulfilled. I might, that is, possibly know that there really do exist now not only those sense-data which I *do* directly apprehend, but also, in certain relations to them, immense numbers of others, which I do not directly apprehend, but similar to those which I have directly apprehended in the past in conjunction with sense-data similar to these. And these other sense-data would really be similar to parts of the material object – the pencil – in whose existence I do believe. For I do believe that there are, all along this pencil, circular surfaces, and that there are, within the circle which bounds each of these surfaces things having shapes similar to those which I should see with the naked eye, if I cut

69

the pencil and looked at the ends: for instance, the smaller circle, of a different colour, within the larger circle, which represents the place where the lead is: I believe that there really is within this pencil, all along it, *something* similar in shape to this round surface of lead which I now see within the larger circle. And also that there really are within it, all along it, differences of structure similar in shape to those which I should see, if I cut it and examined it with a microscope. The material object, in whose present existence I believe, is, therefore, really in many respects similar to sense-data, which I *should* see in conjunction with these, which I now see, under certain circumstances; and similar also therefore, to sense-data which I have directly apprehended in conjunction with sense-data like these in the past. And Hume's second rule would, so far as I can see, allow us to infer that these sense-data, which I should see under certain circumstances, do all really exist *now*.

I might, therefore, even if Hume's second rule were true, *know of* the present existence of something very *like* in many respects to the material object, in which I believe; something consisting of parts very similar in shape, to the parts of the object which I believe to exist. I might know, that there really do exist *now* sense-data of a sort, which, according to the two views I am attacking, I can only know *would* exist under certain conditions, that are *not* now fulfilled. Hume's rule would, therefore, allow of my knowing something much more *like* what I believe, than these two views did.

But nevertheless it seems to me it would *not* allow me to know of the existence of exactly that, in which I believe – the material object, the pencil. For all these things similar in shape to parts of the pencil, which it would allow me to know of, are, it must be remembered, patches of *colour* of a certain shape, patches of *hardness*, and *smoothness* or *roughness* of a certain shape. And even if it might be true that there do really exist inside the pencil now colours similar to those which I should see, if I cut it open; and even if it might be true that different colours, of different sizes, might all exist in the same place: yet these patches of colour and of hardness and smoothness certainly do not constitute the *whole* of the material object in which I believe. Even if there are *here* now all sorts of colours, which I do not see, and all sorts of tactual qualities, which I do not feel, yet the pencil, in which I believe, certainly does not consist *solely* of colours and of tactual qualities: what I believe when I believe that the pencil exists is that there exists something which really is cylindrical in shape, but which does not consist *merely* of any number of patches of colour or of smoothness or hardness, or any other sort of sense-data which I have ever directly apprehended. Even if sense-data of all these kinds really are now in the same place where the pencil is – and I think there are good reasons for doubting whether they are – I certainly believe that there is in that place *something else besides*. This something else, even if it be not the *whole* material object, is certainly a *part* of it. And it seems to me that, if Hume's second rule were true, I could not possibly know of the existence of this something else. For I have never directly apprehended in the past anything whatever that was like *it*: I have only directly apprehended sense-data which had a similar *shape* to that which it has.

I think, therefore, those philosophers who argue, on the ground of Hume's principles, that nobody can ever know of the existence of any material object, are right so far as the first step in their argument is concerned. They are right in saying: *If* Hume's principles are true, nobody can ever *know* of the existence of any material object – nobody can ever know that any such object even probably exists: meaning by a material object, an object which has shape and is situated in space, but which *is not* similar, except in these respects, to any of the sense-data which we have ever directly apprehended. But are they also right in the second step of their argument? Are they also right, in concluding: *Since* Hume's principles are true, nobody ever *does* know, even probably, of the existence of any material object? In other words: Are Hume's principles true?

You see, the position we have got to is this. If Hume's principles are true, then, I have admitted, I do *not* know *now* that this pencil – the material object – exists. If, therefore, I am to prove that I *do* know that this pencil exists, I must prove, somehow, that Hume's principles, one or both of them, are *not* true. In what sort of way, by what sort of argument, can I prove this?

It seems to me that, in fact, there really is no stronger and better argument than the following. I *do* know that this pencil exists; but I could not know this, if Hume's principles were true; *therefore*, Hume's principles, one or both of them, are false. I think this argument really is as strong and good a one as any that could be used: and I think it really is conclusive. In other words, I think that the fact that, if Hume's principles were true, I could not know of the existence of this pencil, is a *reductio ad absurdum* of those principles. But, of course, this is an argument which will not seem convincing to those who believe that the principles are true, nor yet to those who believe that I really do not know that this pencil exists. It seems like begging the question. And therefore I will try to show that it really is a good and conclusive argument.

Let us consider what is necessary in order that an argument may be a good and conclusive one. A really conclusive argument is one which enables us to *know* that its conclusion is true. And one condition, which must be satisfied, if an argument is to enable us to know this, is that the conclusion must really follow from the premisses. Let us see, first, how my argument compares with that of my opponent in this respect.

My argument is this: I do know that this pencil exists; therefore Hume's principles are false. My opponent's argument on the contrary is: Hume's principles are true; therefore you do not know that this pencil exists. And obviously in respect of the certainty with which the conclusion follows from the premiss, these two arguments are equally good. *If* my opponent's conclusion follows from his premiss, my conclusion must certainly also follow from mine. For my opponent's conclusion does not follow from his premiss, except on one condition, namely, unless the following hypothetical proposition is true: *If* Hume's principles are true, then I do not know that this pencil exists. But if this proposition is true, then *my* conclusion also follows from my premiss. In fact, both arguments depend in this respect on exactly the same hypothetical proposition – the proposition which both I and my opponent have admitted to be true: namely that: If Hume's principles are true, then I do not know that this pencil exists. Neither conclusion follows from its premiss, unless this proposition is true; and each does follow from its premiss, if this proposition is true. And this state of things is an excellent illustration of a principle, which many philosophers are, I think, apt to forget: namely, that the mere fact that one proposition coheres with or follows from another does not by itself give us the slightest presumption in favour of its truth. My conclusion coheres with my premiss, exactly as strongly as my opponent's coheres with *his*. And yet obviously this mere fact does not give the slightest presumption in favour of either.

Both arguments, therefore, equally satisfy the first condition that is necessary to make an argument conclusive. Both equally satisfy the condition that the conclusion must follow from the premiss. What other condition, then, is necessary if an argument is to enable us to *know* that its conclusion is true?

The second condition, that is necessary, is this: namely that we should *know* the premiss to be true. Obviously, I think, this condition must be satisfied, if the argument is to enable us to *know* that its conclusion is true. It is not sufficient merely that the premiss should *be* true, if we do not *know* that it is so. For suppose that the premiss is true, and the conclusion does follow from it, and *yet* I do not *know* that the premiss is true. How can this state of things possibly enable me to know that the conclusion is true? Obviously so long as this is the whole state of the case, I shall be just as far from *knowing* that the conclusion is true, as if I had never thought of the premiss at all. The argument may be, and is, a good argument in the sense that the conclusion does follow from the premiss, that the premiss is, in fact, true, and that, therefore the conclusion also is in fact true. But it is not a good argument in the sense that it can possibly enable either me or any one else to *know* that the conclusion is true. The mere fact that the premiss *is* true will not, by itself, enable anyone whatever to know that the conclusion is so. If anybody whatever is to be enabled by the argument absolutely to *know* the conclusion, that person must himself first absolutely *know* that the premiss is true. And the same holds not only for absolute certainty but also for every degree of probability short of it. If any argument whatever is to enable me to know that its conclusion is in any degree probable, I must first know that its premiss is probable in at least the same degree. In other words, no argument is a good one, even in the sense that it enables us to know its conclusion to have any probability whatever, unless its premiss is at least as certain as its conclusion: meaning by 'certain', not merely true or probably true, but *known* to be so.

The only way, then, of deciding between my opponent's argument and mine, as to which is the better, is by deciding which premiss is known to be true. My opponent's premiss is that Hume's principles are true; and unless this premiss not merely *is* true, but is absolutely known to be so, his argument to prove that I do not know of the existence of this pencil cannot be conclusive. Mine is that I do know of the existence of this pencil; unless this premiss not only *is* true, but is absolutely known to be so, my argument to prove that Hume's principles are false cannot be conclusive. And moreover the degree of certainty of the conclusion, in either case, supposing neither is quite certain, will be in proportion to the degree of certainty of the premiss. How is it to be decided which premiss, if either, is known? Or which is the more certain?

One condition under which a premiss may be known to be true, is a condition which we have already stated. Namely, any proposition is known to be true, if we have a conclusive argument in its favour; if, that is to say, it does really follow from some premiss or set of premisses already *known* to be true. I say some premiss or *set of premisses*; and this new qualification should be noticed, because it introduces a complication. If any argument from a *single* premiss is to be conclusive, the *single* premiss must, as we have seen, be at least as certain as the conclusion: the conclusion cannot, by the help of any such argument, be known with more certainty than the premiss. But obviously in the case of a set of premisses, the conclusion may be *more* certain than any *single* one of the premisses. Here, too, however, each of the premisses must be known to be at least probable in some degree: no amount of premisses, which were not known to be probable at all, could enable us to know that the conclusion which followed from them all was even in the least degree probable. One way, therefore, in which a proposition can be known to be true, is if it follows from some premiss or set of premisses, each of which is already known to be so with some degree of certainty. And some philosophers seem to have thought that this is the only way in which any proposition can ever be known to be true. They seem to have thought, that is, that no proposition can ever be known to be true, unless it follows from some other proposition or set of propositions already known to be so.

But it is, I think, easy to see that, if this view were true, no man ever has known any proposition whatever to be in the slightest degree probable. For if I cannot know any proposition whatever to be either true or probably true, unless I have first known some other proposition, from which it follows, to be so; then, of course, I cannot have known this other proposition, unless I have first known some third proposition, before *it*; nor this third proposition, unless I have first known a fourth before it; and so on *ad infinitum*. In other words, it would follow that no man has ever known any proposition whatever to be even probably true, unless he has previously known an absolutely infinite series of other propositions. And it is quite certain that no man ever has thus known a really infinite series of propositions. If this view were true, then, neither my argument nor my opponent's argument could possibly be a good argument: neither of them could enable us to know that the conclusion was even in the least degree probable. And the same would be true of every other argument whatsoever. So that if this view – the view that we can never know any proposition whatever, unless we have a good argument for it – were true, then it would follow that we cannot ever know any proposition whatever to be true, since we never can have any good argument for it.

If, therefore, either my argument or my opponent's, or any other argument whatever, is to be a good one, it must be the case that we are capable of knowing at least *one* proposition to be true, *without* knowing any other proposition whatever from which it follows. And I propose to call this way of knowing a proposition to be true, *immediate* knowledge. And I wish to insist for a moment upon what *immediate* knowledge is. It is something utterly different from what I have called *direct apprehension*; and that is why I have chosen a different name for it, though, in fact, both of them are very often called by both names – they are both often called direct knowledge and both often called immediate knowledge. One difference between them is that *direct apprehension*, as I explained, is a relation which you may have to a proposition, equally when you believe it and when you do not, and equally when it is true and when it is false; whereas immediate knowledge is one form of the relation which I called knowledge *proper*: and knowledge *proper*, you may remember, is a relation which you never have to a proposition, unless, besides directly apprehending it, you also believe it; and unless, besides this, the proposition itself is true, *and also* some fourth condition is satisfied as well. And another difference between direct apprehension and immediate knowledge is that direct apprehension is a relation which you may have to things which are *not* propositions, whereas immediate knowledge, being a form of knowledge proper, is a relation which you can only have to propositions. For instance, at this moment, I directly apprehend the whitish colour of this paper; but I do not *immediately know* this whitish colour. When I directly apprehend it, I may *also*, if I happen to think of them, immediately know the proposition that I directly apprehend it and also the proposition that it exists. But both these propositions are something quite different from the whitish colour itself; and I may at a given moment directly apprehend a colour, without at the same time immediately knowing either proposition; although, whenever I do directly apprehend a colour or any other sense-datum, I *can, if I happen to think of them*, also *know both* the proposition that I directly apprehend it *and* also the proposition that it exists. Immediate knowledge is, therefore, something quite different from direct apprehension. And there is one other point about it which should be mentioned. I have said it is the kind of way in which you know a proposition to be true – really *know* it, not merely directly apprehend it – when you *do not* know any other proposition from which it follows. And of course, if you do not know any proposition from which it follows, then, if you know it at all, you can only know it immediately. But it is important to insist that even when you do know a proposition immediately, you *may* also at the same time know some proposition from which it follows: you may know it *both* immediately and *also* because you know some other proposition from which it follows. If, therefore, we give the name *mediate* knowledge to all cases in which you know a proposition, because you know some other from which it follows; the result is that you may at one and the same time know the same proposition *both* mediately *and* also immediately. The relation, therefore, between mediate and immediate knowledge is very different from that between direct and indirect apprehension. When you are apprehending a thing directly you are never at the same time also apprehending it indirectly; and when you are apprehending a thing indirectly, you are never at the same time also apprehending it directly. But you may, at one and the same time, *know* a proposition both mediately and immediately. Of course, cases do occur where you *only* know a proposition mediately – *only* because you know some other proposition from which it follows; but it is important to distinguish such cases from cases where, though you do know the proposition, *because* you know some other from which it follows, and therefore do know it mediately, you do not know it *only* because of this, but *also* immediately.

It is certain, then, that if any proposition whatever is ever known by us mediately, or because some other proposition is known from which it follows, some one proposition at least, must also be known by us *immediately*, or *not merely* because some other proposition is known from which it follows. And hence it follows that the conditions necessary to make an argument good and conclusive may just as well be satisfied, when the premiss is only known *immediately*, as when there are other arguments in its favour. It follows, therefore, that my argument: 'I know this pencil to exist; therefore Hume's principles are false'; may be just as good an argument as any other, even though its premiss – the premiss that I do know that this pencil exists – is only known immediately.

But is this premiss in fact known by me immediately? I am inclined to think that it is, though this might be disputed, for the following reasons. It must be noticed, that the premiss is: I know that this pencil exists. What, therefore, I am claiming to know immediately is *not*, that this pencil exists, but that I know it to exist. And it may be said: Can I possibly know immediately such a thing as this? Obviously, I cannot know *that* I know that the pencil exists, unless I do know that the pencil exists; and it might, therefore, be thought that the first proposition can only be mediately known – known *merely* because the second is known. But it is, I think, necessary to make a distinction. From the mere fact that I should not know the first, *unless* I knew the second, it does not follow that I know the first *merely* because I know the second. And, in fact, I think I do know *both* of them immediately. This might be disputed in the case of the second also. It might be said: I certainly do not know immediately that the pencil exists; for I should not know it at all, unless I were directly apprehending certain sense-data, and knew that they were signs of its existence. And of course I admit, that I should not know it, unless I were directly apprehending certain sense-data. But this is again a different thing from admitting that I do not know it immediately. For the mere fact that I should not know it, unless certain other things were happening, is quite a different thing from knowing it *only* because I know *some other proposition*. The mere direct apprehension of certain sense-data is quite a different thing from the knowledge of any proposition;

and yet I am not sure that it is not by itself quite sufficient to enable me to know that the pencil exists.

But whether the exact proposition which formed my premiss, namely: I do know that this pencil exists; or only the proposition: This pencil exists; or only the proposition: The sense-data which I directly apprehend are a sign that it exists; is known by me immediately, one or other of them, I think, certainly is so. And all three of them are much more certain than any premiss which could be used to prove that they are false; and also much more certain than any other premiss which could be used to prove that they are true. That is why I say that the strongest argument to prove that Hume's principles are false is the argument from a particular case, like this in which we do know of the existence of some material object. And similarly, if the object is to prove *in general* that we do know of the existence of material objects, no argument which is really stronger can, I think, be brought forward to prove this than particular instances in which we do in fact know of the existence of such an object. I admit, however, that other arguments may be more convincing; and perhaps some of you may be able to supply me with one that is. But, however much more *convincing* it may be, it is, I think, sure to depend upon some premiss which is, in fact, less certain than the premiss that I do know of the existence of this pencil; and so, too, in the case of any arguments which can be brought forward to prove that we do not know of the existence of any material object.

6

EXTERNAL AND INTERNAL RELATIONS[1]

In the index to *Appearance and Reality* (first edition)[2] Mr Bradley declares that *all* relations are 'intrinsical'; and the following are some of the phrases by means of which he tries to explain what he means by this assertion. 'A relation must at both ends *affect*, and pass into, the being of its terms' (p.364).[3] 'Every relation essentially penetrates the being of its terms, and is, in this sense, intrinsical' (p.392).[4] 'To stand in a relation and not to be relative, to support it and yet not to be infected and undermined by it, seems out of the question' (p.142).[5] And a good many other philosophers seem inclined to take the same view about relations which Mr Bradley is here trying to express. Other phrases which seem to be sometimes used to express it, or a part of it, are these: 'No relations are purely external'; 'All relations qualify or modify or make a difference to the terms between which they hold'; 'No terms are independent of any of the relations in which they stand to other terms'. (See e.g., Joachim, *The Nature of Truth*, pp.11, 12, 46.[6])

It is, I think, by no means easy to make out exactly what these philosophers mean by these assertions. And the main object of this paper is to try to define clearly one proposition, which, even if it does not give the whole of what they mean, seems to me to be always implied by what they mean, and to be certainly false. I shall try to make clear the exact meaning of this proposition, to point out some of its most important consequences, and to distinguish it clearly from certain other propositions which are, I think, more or less liable to be confused with it. And I shall

Originally published in G.E. Moore, *Philosophical Studies* (Kegan Paul Trench Trubner & Co, London: 1922), pp.276–309.

maintain that, if we give to the assertion that a relation is 'internal' the meaning which this proposition would give to it, then, though, in that sense, *some* relations are 'internal', others, no less certainly, are not, but are 'purely external'.

To begin with, we may, I think, clear the ground, by putting on one side two propositions about relations, which, though they seem sometimes to be confused with the view we are discussing, do, I think, quite certainly not give the whole meaning of that view.

The first is a proposition which is quite certainly and obviously true of all relations, without exception, and which, though it raises points of great difficulty, can, I think, be clearly enough stated for its truth to be obvious. It is the proposition that, in the case of any relation whatever, the kind of fact which we express by saying that a given term A has that relation to another term, B, or to a pair of terms B and C, or to three terms B, C, and D, and so on, in no case simply consists in the terms in question *together with* the relation. Thus the fact which we express by saying that Edward VII was father of George V, obviously does not simply consist in Edward, George, *and* the relation of fatherhood. In order that the fact may be, it is obviously not sufficient that there should merely be George and Edward and the relation of fatherhood; it is further necessary that the relation should *relate* Edward to George, and not only so, but also that it should relate them in the particular way which we express by saying that Edward was father of George, and not merely in the way which we should express by saying that George was father of Edward. This proposition is, I think, obviously true of all relations without exception: and the only reason why I have mentioned it is because, in an article in which Mr Bradley criticises Mr Russell (*Mind*, 1910, p.179),[7] he seems to suggest that it is inconsistent with the proposition that any relations are merely external, and because, so far as I can make out, some other people who maintain that all relations are internal seem sometimes to think that their contention follows from this proposition. The way in which Mr Bradley puts it is that such facts are unities which are not *completely analysable*; and this is, of course, true, if it means merely that in the case of no such fact is there any set of constituents of which we can truly say: This fact is *identical with* these constituents. But whether from this it follows that all relations are internal must of course depend upon what is meant by the latter statement. If it be merely used to express this proposition itself, or anything which follows from it, then, of course, there can be no doubt that all relations are internal. But I think there is no doubt that those who say this do not mean by their words *merely* this obvious proposition itself; and I am going to point out something which I think they always imply, and which certainly does *not* follow from it.

The second proposition which, I think, may be put aside at once as certainly not giving the whole of what is meant, is the proposition which is, I think, the natural meaning of the phrases 'All relations modify or affect their terms' or 'All relations make a difference to their terms'. There is one perfectly natural and intelligible sense in which a given relation may be said to modify a term which stands in that relation, namely, the sense in which we should say that, if, by putting a stick of sealing-wax into a flame, we make the sealing-wax melt, its relationship to the flame has modified the sealing-wax. This is a sense of the word 'modify' in which part of what is meant by saying of any term that it is modified, is that it has actually undergone a change: and I think it is clear that a sense in which this is part of its meaning is the only one in which the word 'modify' can properly be used. If, however, those who say that all relations modify their terms were using the word in this, its proper, sense, part of what would be meant by this assertion would be that all terms which have relations at all actually undergo changes. Such an assertion would be obviously false, for the simple reason that there are terms which have relations and which yet never change at all. And I think it is quite clear that those who assert that all relations are internal, in the sense we are concerned with, mean by this something which could be consistently asserted to be true of all relations without exception, even if it were admitted that some terms which have relations do not change. When, therefore, they use the phrase that all relations 'modify' their terms as equivalent to 'all relations are internal', they must be using 'modify' in some metaphorical sense other than its natural one. I think, indeed, that most of them would be inclined to assert that in every case in which a term A comes to have to another term B a relation, which it did not have to B in some immediately preceding interval, its having of that relation to that term causes it to undergo some change, which it would not have undergone if it

81

had not stood in precisely that relation to B and I think perhaps they would think that this proposition follows from some proposition which is true of all relations, without exception, and which is what they mean by saying that all relations are internal. The question whether the coming into a new relation does thus always cause some modification in the term which comes into it is one which is often discussed, as if it had something to do with the question whether all relations are internal; as when, for instance, it is discussed whether knowledge of a thing alters the thing known. And for my part I should maintain that this proposition is certainly not true. But what I am concerned with now is not the question whether it is true, but simply to point out that, so far as I can see, it can have nothing to do with the question whether all relations are internal, for the simple reason that it cannot possibly follow from any proposition with regard to *all* relations without exception. It asserts with regard to all relational properties of a certain kind, that they have a certain kind of *effect*; and no proposition of this sort can, I think follow from any universal proposition with regard to *all* relations.

We have, therefore, rejected as certainly not giving the whole meaning of the dogma that all relations are internal: (1) the obviously true proposition that no relational facts are *completely* analysable, in the precise sense which I gave to that assertion; and (2) the obviously false proposition that all relations modify their terms, in the natural sense of the term 'modify', in which it always has as part of its meaning 'cause to undergo a change'. And we have also seen that this false proposition that any relation which a term comes to have always causes it to undergo a change is wholly irrelevant to the question whether *all* relations are internal or not. We have seen finally that if the assertion that all relations modify their terms is to be understood as equivalent to the assertion that all are internal, 'modify' must be understood in some metaphorical sense. The question is: What is this metaphorical sense?

And one point is, I think, pretty clear to begin with. It is obvious that, in the case of some relations, a given term A may have the relation in question, not only to one other term, but to several different terms. If, for instance, we consider the relation of fatherhood, it is obvious that a man may be father, not only of one, but of several different children. And those who say that all relations modify their terms always mean, I think, not merely that every different relation which a term has modifies it; but also that, where the relation is one which the term has to several different other terms, then, in the case of *each* of these terms, it is modified by the fact that it has the relation in question to that particular term. If, for instance, A is father of three children, B, C, and D, they mean to assert that he is modified, not merely by being a father, but by being the father of B, also by being the father of C, and also by being the father of D. The mere assertion that all *relations* modify their terms does not, of course, make it quite clear that this is what is meant; but I think there is no doubt that it is always meant; and I think we can express it more clearly by using a term, which I have already introduced, and saying the doctrine is that all *relational properties* modify their terms, in a sense which remains to be defined. I think there is no difficulty in understanding what I mean by a *relational property*. If A is father of B, then what you assert of A when you say that he is so is a *relational property* – namely the property of being father of B; and it is quite clear that this property is not itself a *relation*, in the same fundamental sense in which the relation of fatherhood is so; and also that, if C is a different child from B, then the property of being father of C is a different relational property from that of being father of B, although there is only *one* relation, that of fatherhood, from which both are derived. So far as I can make out, those philosophers who talk of all *relations* being internal, often actually mean by 'relations' 'relational properties'; when they talk of all the 'relations' of a given term, they mean all its relational properties, and not merely all the different relations, of each of which it is true that the term has that relation to something. It will, I think, conduce to clearness to use a different word for these two entirely different uses of the term 'relation' to call 'fatherhood' a relation, and 'fatherhood of B' a 'relational property'. And the fundamental proposition, which is meant by the assertion that all relations are internal, is, I think, a proposition with regard to relational properties, and not with regard to relations properly so-called. There is no doubt that those who maintain this dogma mean to maintain that all relational properties are related in a peculiar way to the terms which possess them – that they modify or are internal to them, in some metaphorical sense. And once we have defined what this sense is in which a *relational property* can be said to be internal to a term which possesses it, we can easily derive from it a corresponding sense in which the *relations*, strictly so called, from which relational properties are derived, can be said to be internal.

Our question is then: What is the metaphorical sense of 'modify' in which the proposition that all relations are internal is equivalent to the proposition that all relational properties 'modify' the terms which possess them? I think it is clear that the term 'modify' would never have been used at all to express the relation meant, unless there had been some analogy between this relation and that which we have seen is the proper sense of 'modify', namely, *causes* to change. And I think we can see where the analogy comes in by considering the statement, with regard to any particular term A and any relational property Φ which belongs to it, that A *would have been different from what it is if it had not had* Φ: the statement, for instance, that Edward VII would have been different if he had not been father of George V. This is a thing which we can obviously truly say of A and Φ, in some sense, whenever it is true of Φ that it *modified* A in the proper sense of the word: if the being held in the flame causes the sealing-wax to melt, we can truly say (in some sense) that the sealing-wax would not have been in a melted state if it had not been in the flame. But it seems as if it were a thing which might also be true of A and Φ where it is *not* true that the possession of Φ *caused* A to change; since the mere assertion that A would have been different, if it had not had Φ, does not necessarily imply that the possession of Φ *caused* A to have any property which it would not have had otherwise. And those who say that all relations are internal do sometimes tend to speak as if what they meant could be put in the form: In the case of every relational property which a thing has, it is always true that the thing which has it would have been different if it had not had that property; they sometimes say even: If Φ be a relational property and A a term which has it, then it is always true that A *would not have been* A if it had not had Φ. This is, I think, obviously a clumsy way of expressing anything which could possibly be true, since, taken strictly, it implies the self-contradictory proposition that if A had not had Φ, it would not have been true that A did not have Φ. But it is nevertheless a more or less natural way of expressing a proposition which might quite well be true, namely, that, supposing A has Φ, then anything which had not had Φ would necessarily have been different from A. This is the proposition which I wish to suggest as giving the metaphorical meaning of 'Φ *modifies* A', of which we are in search. It is a proposition to which I think a perfectly precise meaning can be given, and one which does not at all imply that the possession of Φ *caused* any change in A, but which might conceivably be true of all terms and all the relational properties they have, without exception. And it seems to me that it is not unnatural that the proposition that this is true of Φ and A, should have been expressed in the form, 'Φ modifies A', since it can be more or less naturally expressed in the perverted form, 'If A had not had Φ it would have been different' – a form of words, which, as we saw, can also be used whenever Φ does, in the proper sense, modify A.

I want to suggest, then, that one thing which is always implied by the dogma that, 'All relations are internal', is that, in the case of every relational property, it can always be truly asserted of any term A which has that property, that any term which had not had it would necessarily have been different from A.

This is the proposition to which I want to direct attention. And there are two phrases in it, which require some further explanation.

The first is the phrase 'would necessarily have been'. And the meaning of this can be explained in a preliminary way, as follows: To say of a pair of properties Φ and Ψ that any term which had had Φ would necessarily have had Ψ, is equivalent to saying that, in every case, from the proposition with regard to any given term that it has Φ, it *follows* that that term has Ψ: *follows* being understood in the sense in which from the proposition with regard to any term, that it is a right angle, it *follows* that it is an angle, and in which from the proposition with regard to any term that it is red it *follows* that it is coloured. There is obviously some very important sense in which from the proposition that a thing is a right angle, it does follow that it is an angle, and from the proposition that a thing is red it does follow that it is coloured. And what I am maintaining is that the metaphorical sense of 'modify', in which it is maintained that all relational properties modify the subjects which possess them, can be defined by reference to this sense of 'follows'. The definition is: To say of a given relational property Φ that it modifies or is internal to a given term A which possesses it, is to

85

say that from the proposition that a thing has not got Φ it follows that that thing is different from A. In other words, it is to say that the property of *not* possessing Φ, and the property of being different from A are related to one another in the peculiar way in which the property of being a right-angled triangle is related to that of being a triangle, or that of being red to that of being coloured.

To complete the definition it is necessary, however, to define the sense in which 'different from A' is to be understood. There are two different senses which the statement that A is different from B may bear. It may be meant merely that A is *numerically* different from B, *other* than B, not identical with B. Or it may be meant that not only is this the case, but also that A is related to B in a way which can be roughly expressed by saying that A is *qualitatively* different from B. And of these two meanings, those who say 'All relations make a *difference* to their terms', always, I think, mean difference in the latter sense and not merely in the former. That is to say, they mean, that if Φ be a relational property which belongs to A, then the absence of Φ entails not only numerical difference from A, but qualitative difference. But, in fact, from the proposition that a thing is qualitatively different from A, it does follow that it is also numerically different. And hence they are maintaining that every relational property is 'internal to' its terms in both of two different senses at the same time. They are maintaining that, if Φ be a relational property which belongs to A, then Φ is internal to A both in the sense (1) that the absence of Φ entails qualitative difference from A; and (2) that the absence of Φ entails numerical difference from A. It seems to me that neither of these propositions is true; and I will say something about each in turn.

As for the first, I said before that I think some relational properties really are 'internal to' their terms, though by no means all are. But, if we understand 'internal to' in this first sense, I am not really sure that any are. In order to get an example of one which was, we should have, I think, to say that any two different qualities are always *qualitatively* different from one another: that, for instance, it is not only the case that anything which is pure red is qualitatively different from anything which is pure blue, but that the quality pure red itself is qualitatively different from the quality 'pure blue'. I am not quite sure that we can say this, but I think we can; and if so, it is easy to get an example of a relational property which is internal in our first sense. The quality 'orange' is intermediate in shade between the qualities yellow and red. This is a relational property, and it is quite clear that, on our assumption, it is an internal one. Since it is quite clear that any quality which were *not* intermediate between yellow and red, would necessarily be *other* than orange; and if any quality *other* than orange must be *qualitatively* different from orange, then it follows that 'intermediate between yellow and red' is internal to 'orange'. That is to say, the absence of the relational property 'intermediate between yellow and red', *entails* the property 'different in quality from orange'.

There is then, I think, a difficulty in being sure that *any* relational properties are internal in this first sense. But, if what we want to do is to show that some are *not* and that therefore the dogma that all relations are internal is false, I think the most conclusive reason for saying this is that if *all* were internal in this first sense, all would necessarily be internal in the second, and that this is plainly false. I think, in fact, the most important consequence of the dogma that all relations are internal, is that it follows from it that all relational properties are internal in this second sense. I propose, therefore, at once to consider this proposition, with a view to bringing out quite clearly what it means and involves, and what are the main reasons for saying that it is false.

The proposition in question is that, if Φ be a relational property and A a term to which it does in fact belong, then, no matter what Φ and A may be, it may always be truly asserted of them, that any term which had *not* possessed Φ would necessarily have been other than – numerically different from – A: or in other words, that A would necessarily, in all conceivable circumstances, have possessed Φ. And with this sense of 'internal', as distinguished from that which says *qualitatively different*, it is quite easy to point out some relational properties which certainly are internal in this sense. Let us take as an example the relational property which we assert to belong to a visual sense-datum when we say of it that it has another visual sense-datum as a spatial part: the assertion, for instance, with regard to a coloured patch half of which is red and half yellow: 'This whole patch contains this patch' (where 'this patch' is a proper name for the red half). It is here, I think, quite plain that, in a perfectly clear and intelligible sense, we can say that any whole, which had not contained that red patch, could not have been identical with the whole in question: that from the proposition with regard to any term whatever that it does not contain *that* particular patch it *follows* that that term is *other* than the whole in question – though *not* necessarily that it is qualitatively different from it. *That* particular whole could not have existed without having that particular patch for a part. But it seems no less clear, at first sight, that there are many other relational properties of which this is not true. In order to get an example, we have only to consider the relation which the red patch has to the whole patch, instead of considering as before that which the whole has to it. It seems quite clear that, though the whole could not have existed without having the red patch for a part, the red patch might perfectly well have existed without being part of that particular whole. In other words, though every relational property of the form 'having *this* for a spatial part' is 'internal' in our sense, it seems equally clear that every property of the form 'is a spatial part of this whole' is *not* internal, but purely external. Yet this last, according to me, is one of the things which the dogma of internal relations denies. It implies that it is just as necessary that anything, which is in fact a part of a particular whole, should be a part of that whole, as that any whole, which has a particular thing for a part, should have that thing for a part. It implies, in fact, quite generally, that any term which does in fact have a particular relational property, could not have existed without having that property. And in saying this it obviously flies in the face of common sense. It seems quite obvious that in the case of many relational properties which things have, the fact that they have them is *a mere matter of fact*: that the things in question *might* have existed without having them. That this, which seems obvious, is true, seems to me to be the most important thing that can be meant by saying that some relations are purely external. And the difficulty is to see how any philosopher could have supposed that it was not true: that, for instance, the relation of part to whole is no more external than that of whole to part. I will give at once one main reason which seems to me to have led to the view, that *all* relational properties are internal in this sense.

What I am maintaining is the common sense view, which seems obviously true, that it may be true that A has in fact got Φ and yet also true that A might have existed without having Φ. And I say that this is equivalent to saying that it may be true that A has Φ, and yet *not* true that from the proposition that a thing has *not* got Φ it *follows* that that thing is *other* than A – numerically different from it. And one reason why this is disputed is, I think, simply because it is in fact true that if A has Φ, and *x* has *not*, it *does* follow that *x* is other than A. These two propositions, the one which I admit to be true (1) that if A has Φ, and *x* has not, it does follow that *x* is other than A, and the one which I maintain to be false (2) that if A has Φ, then from the proposition with regard to any term *x* that it has not got Φ, it *follows* that *x* is other than A, are, I think, easily confused with one another. And it is in fact the case that if they are not different, or if (2) follows from (1), then no relational properties are external. For (1) is certainly true, and (2) is certainly equivalent to asserting that none are. It is therefore absolutely essential, if we are to maintain external relations, to maintain that (2) does *not* follow from (1). These two propositions (1) and (2), with regard to which I maintain that (1) is true, and (2) is false, can be put in another way, as follows: (1) asserts that if A has Φ, then any term which has not, *must* be other than A. (2) asserts that if A has Φ then any term which had not, *would necessarily be* other than A. And when they are put in this form, it is, I think, easy to see why they should be confused: you have only to confuse 'must' or 'is necessarily' with 'would necessarily be'. And their connexion with the question of external relations can be brought out as follows: To maintain external relations you have to maintain such things as that, though Edward VII was in fact father of George V, he *might* have existed without being father of George V. But to maintain this, you have to maintain that it is *not* true that a person who was *not* father of George would necessarily have been other than Edward. Yet it is, in fact, the case, that any person who was not the father of George, *must* have been other than Edward. Unless, therefore, you can maintain that from this true proposition it does not follow that any person who was *not* father of George *would necessarily* have been other than Edward, you will have to give up the view that Edward might have existed without being father of George.

By far the most important point in connexion with the dogma of internal relations seems to me to be simply to see clearly the difference between these two propositions (1) and (2), and that

(2) does *not* follow from (1). If this is not understood, nothing in connexion with the dogma, can, I think, be understood. And perhaps the difference may seem so clear, that no more need be said about it. But I cannot help thinking it is not clear to everybody, and that it does involve the rejection of certain views, which are sometimes held as to the meaning of 'follows'. So I will try to put the point again in a perfectly strict form.

Let Φ be a relational property, and A a term to which it does in fact belong. I propose to define what is meant by saying that Φ is internal to A (in the sense we are now concerned with) as meaning that from the proposition that a thing has not got Φ, it 'follows' that it is *other* than A.

That is to say, this proposition asserts that between the two properties 'not having Φ' and 'other than A', there holds that relation which holds between the property 'being a right angle' and the property 'being an angle', or between the property 'red' and the property 'coloured', and which we express by saying that, in the case of any thing whatever, from the proposition that that thing is a right angle it follows, or is deducible, that it is an angle.

Let us now adopt certain conventions for expressing this proposition.

We require, first of all, some term to express the *converse* of that relation which we assert to hold between a particular proposition *q* and a particular proposition *p*, when we assert that *q* *follows from* or *is deducible from p*. Let us use the term 'entails' to express the converse of this relation. We shall then be able to say truly that '*p* entails *q*', when and only when we are able to say truly that '*q* follows from *p*' or 'is deducible from *p*', in the sense in which the conclusion of a syllogism in Barbara follows from the two premisses, taken as one conjunctive proposition; or in which the proposition 'This is coloured' follows from 'This is red'. '*p* entails *q*' will be related to '*q* follows from *p*' in the same way in which 'A is greater than B' is related to 'B is less than A'.

We require, next, some short and clear method of expressing the proposition, with regard to two properties Φ and Ψ, that *any* proposition which asserts of a given thing that it has the property Φ *entails* the proposition that the thing in question also has the property Ψ. Let us express this proposition in the form

$$\Phi x \text{ entails } \Psi x.[8]$$

That is to say 'Φx entails Ψx' is to mean the same as 'Each one of all the various propositions, which are alike in respect of the fact that each asserts with regard to some given thing that that thing has Φ, entails *that one* among the various propositions, alike in respect of the fact that each asserts with regard to some given thing that that thing has Ψ, which makes this assertion with regard to the *same thing*, with regard to which the proposition of the first class asserts that it has Φ'. In other words 'Φx entails Ψx' is to be true, if and only if the proposition 'ΦA entails ΨA' is true, and if also all propositions which resemble this, in the way in which 'ΦB entails ΨB' resembles it, are true also; where 'ΦA' means the same as 'A has Φ', 'ΨA' the same as 'A has Ψ' etc., etc.

We require, next, some way of expressing the proposition, with regard to two properties Φ and Ψ, that any proposition which *denies* of a given thing that it has Φ *entails* the proposition, with regard to the thing in question, that it has Ψ.

Let us, in the case of any proposition, p, express the contradictory of that proposition by $\sim (p)$. The proposition 'It is not the case that A has Φ' will then be expressed by $\sim(\Phi A)$; and it will then be natural, in accordance with the last convention to express the proposition that any proposition which *denies* of a given thing that it has Φ *entails* the proposition, with regard to the thing in question, that it has Ψ, by

$$\sim\Phi x \text{ entails } \Psi x.$$

And we require, finally, some short way of expressing the proposition, with regard to two things B and A, that B is *other* than (or not identical with) A. Let us express 'B is identical with A' by 'B $=$ A'; and it will then be natural, according to the last convention, to express 'B is not identical with A' by

$$\sim(B = A).$$

We have now got everything which is required for expressing, in a short symbolic form, the proposition, with regard to a given thing A and a given relational property Φ, which A in fact possesses, that Φ is *internal* to A. The required expression is

$$\sim(\Phi x) \text{ entails } \sim(x = A)$$

which is to mean the same as 'Every proposition which asserts of any given thing that it has not got Φ *entails* the proposition, with regard to the thing in question, that it is other than A'. And this proposition is, of course, logically equivalent to

$$(x = A) \text{ entails } \Phi x$$

where we are using 'logically equivalent' in such a sense that to say of any proposition p that it is logically equivalent to another proposition q is to say that both p entails q and q entails p. This last proposition again, is, so far as I can see, either identical with or logically equivalent to the propositions expressed by 'anything which were identical with A would, in any conceivable universe, necessarily have Φ' or by 'A could not have existed in any possible world without having Φ'; just as the proposition expressed by 'In any possible world a right angle must be an angle' is, I take it, either identical with or logically equivalent to the proposition '(x is a right angle) entails (x is an angle)'.

We have now, therefore, got a short means of symbolising, with regard to any particular thing A and any particular property Φ, the proposition that Φ is *internal* to A in the second of the two senses distinguished on p.86. But we still require a means of symbolising the general proposition that *every* relational property is internal to any term which possesses it – the proposition, namely, which was referred to on p.87 as the most important consequence of the dogma of internal relations, and which was called (2) on p.89.

In order to get this, let us first get a means of expressing with regard to some one particular relational property Φ, the proposition that Φ is internal to *any* term which possesses it. This is a proposition which takes the form of asserting with regard to one particular property, namely Φ, that any term which possesses that property also possesses another – namely the one expressed by saying that Φ is internal to it. It is, that is to say, an ordinary universal proposition, like 'All men are mortal'. But such a form of words is, as has often been pointed out, ambiguous. It may stand for either of two different propositions. It may stand merely for the proposition 'There is nothing, which both is a man, and is not mortal' – a proposition which may also be expressed by 'If anything is a man, that thing is mortal', and which is distinguished by the fact that it makes no assertion as to whether there are any men or not; or it may stand for the conjunctive proposition 'If anything is a man, that thing is mortal, *and there are men*'. It will be sufficient for our purposes to deal with propositions of the first kind – those namely, which assert with regard to some two properties, say Ψ and X, that there is nothing which both does possess Ψ and does not possess X, without asserting that anything does possess Ψ. Such a proposition is obviously equivalent to the assertion that *any* pair of propositions which resembles the pair 'ΨA' and 'XA', in respect of the fact that one of them asserts of some particular thing that it has Ψ and the other, of the same thing, that it has X, stand to one another in a certain relation: the relation, namely, which, in the case of 'ΨA' and 'XA', can be expressed by saying that 'It is not the case both that A has Ψ and that A has not got X'. When we say 'There is nothing which does possess Ψ and does not possess X' we are obviously saying something which is either identical with or logically equivalent to the proposition 'In the case of every such pair of propositions it is not the case both that the one which asserts a particular thing to have Ψ is true, and that the one which asserts it to have X is false'. We require, therefore, a short way of expressing the relation between two propositions p and q, which can be expressed by 'It is not the case that p is true and q false'. And I am going, quite arbitrarily to express this relation by writing

$$p \supset q$$

for 'It is not the case that p is true and q false'.

The relation in question is one which logicians have sometimes expressed by 'p implies q'. It is, for instance, the one which Mr Russell in the *Principles of Mathematics*[9] calls 'material implication', and which he and Dr Whitehead in *Principia Mathematica* call simply 'implication'.[10] And if we do use 'implication' to stand for this relation, we, of course, get the apparently paradoxical results that every false proposition implies every other proposition, both true and false, and that every true proposition implies every other true proposition: since it is quite clear that if p is false then, whatever q may be, 'it is not the case that p is true and q false', and quite clear also, that if p and q are both true, then also 'it is not the case that p is true and q false'. And these results, it seems to me, appear to be paradoxical, solely because, if we use 'implies' in any ordinary sense, they are quite certainly false. Why logicians should have thus chosen to use the word 'implies' as a name for a relation, for which it never is used by any one else, I do not know. It is partly, no doubt, because the relation for which they do use it – that expressed by saying 'It is not the case that p is true and q false' – is one for which it is very important that they should have a short name, because it is a relation which is very fundamental and about which they need constantly to talk, while (so far as I can discover) it simply has no short name in ordinary life. And it is partly, perhaps, for a reason which leads us back to our present reason for giving some name to this relation. It is, in fact, natural to use 'p implies q' to mean the same as 'If p then q'. And though 'If p then q' is hardly ever, if ever, used to mean the same as 'It is not the case that p is true and q false'; yet the expression 'If *anything* has Ψ, *it* has X' may, I think, be naturally used to express the proposition that, in the case of *every* pair of propositions which resembles the pair ΨA and XA in respect of the fact that the first of the pair asserts of some particular thing that it has Ψ and the second, of the same thing, that it has X, it is not the case that the first is true and the second false. That is to say, if (as I propose to do) we express 'It is not the case both that ΨA is true and XA false' by

$$\Psi A \supset XA,$$

and if, further (on the analogy of the similar case with regard to 'entails'), we express the proposition that of *every* pair of propositions which resemble ΨA and XA in the respect just mentioned, it is true that the first has the relation '$\supset$' to the second by

$$\Phi x \supset X x$$

then, it *is* natural to express $\Phi x \supset X x$ by 'If *anything* has Ψ, then *that thing* has X'. And logicians may, I think, have falsely inferred that *since* it is natural to express '$\Psi x \supset X x$' by 'If *anything* has Ψ, then *that thing* has X', it *must* be natural to express '$\Psi A \supset XA$' by 'If ΨA, then XA', and therefore also by 'ΨA implies XA'. If this has been their reason for expressing '$p \supset q$' by 'p implies q' then obviously their reason is a fallacy. And, whatever the reason may have been, it seems to me quite certain that '$\Psi A \supset XA$' cannot be properly expressed either by 'ΨA implies XA' or by 'If ΨA then XA', although '$\Psi x \supset X x$' can be properly expressed by 'If anything has Ψ, then that thing has X'.

I am going, then, to express the universal proposition, with regard to two particular properties Ψ and X, which asserts that

'Whatever has Ψ, has X' or 'If anything has Ψ, it has X', without asserting that anything has Ψ, by

$$\Psi x \supset Xx$$

– a means of expressing it, which since we have adopted the convention that '$p \supset q$' is to mean the same as 'It is not the case that p is true and q false', brings out the important fact that this proposition is either identical with or logically equivalent to the proposition that of *every* such pair of propositions as ΨA and XA, it is true that it is not the case that the first is true and the second false. And having adopted this convention, we can now see how, in accordance with it, the proposition, with regard to a particular property Φ, that Φ is *internal* to *everything* which possesses it, is to be expressed. We saw that Φ is *internal* to A is to be expressed by

$$\sim (\Phi x) \text{ entails } \sim (x = A)$$

or by the logically equivalent proposition

$$(x = A) \text{ entails } \Phi x.$$

And we have now only to express the proposition that *anything* that has Φ, has also the property that Φ is *internal* to it. The required expression is obviously as follows. Just as 'Anything that has Ψ, has X' is to be expressed by

$$\Psi x \supset Xx$$

so 'Anything that has Φ, has also the property that Φ is internal to it' will be expressed by

$$\Phi x \supset \{ \sim (\Phi y) \text{ entails } \sim (y = x) \}$$

or by

$$\Phi x \supset \{(y = x) \text{ entails } \Phi y\}.$$

We have thus got, in the case of any particular property Φ, a means of expressing the proposition that it is *internal* to *every* term that possesses it, which is both short and brings out clearly the notions that are involved in it. And we do not need, I think, any further special convention for symbolising the proposition that *every* relational property is internal to any term which possesses it – the proposition, namely, which I called (2) above (p.89), and which on p.87 I called the most important consequence of the dogma of internal relations. We can express it simply enough as follows:

(2) = 'What we assert of Φ when we say

$$\Phi x \supset \{\sim (\Phi y) \text{ entails } \sim (y = x)\}$$

can be truly asserted of every relational property'.

And now, for the purpose of comparing (2) with (1), and seeing exactly what is involved in my assertion that (2) does not follow from (1), let us try to express (1) by means of the same conventions.

Let us first take the assertion with regard to a particular thing A and a particular relational property Φ that, from the proposition that A has Φ it *follows* that nothing which has not got Φ is identical with A. This is an assertion which is quite certainly true; since, if anything which had not got Φ were identical with A, it would follow that $\sim(\Phi A)$; and from the proposition ΦA, it certainly *follows* that $\sim(\Phi A)$ is false, and therefore also that 'Something which has not got Φ is identical with A' is false, or that 'Nothing which has not got Φ is identical with A' is true. And this assertion, in accordance with the conventions we have adopted, will be expressed by

$$\Phi A \text{ entails } \{\sim(\Phi x) \supset \sim (x = A)\}.$$

We want, next, in order to express (1), a means of expressing with regard to a particular relational property Φ, the assertion that, from the proposition, with regard to *anything* whatever, that that thing has got Φ, it *follows* that nothing which has not got Φ is identical with the thing in question. This also is an assertion which is quite certainly true; since it merely asserts (what is obviously true) that what

$$\Phi A \text{ entails } \{\sim(\Phi x) \supset \sim (x = A)\}$$

asserts of A, can be truly asserted of anything whatever. And this assertion, in accordance with the conventions we have adopted, will be expressed by

$$\Phi x \text{ entails } \{\sim(\Phi y) \supset \sim (y = x)\}.$$

The proposition, which I meant to call (1), but which I expressed before rather clumsily, can now be expressed by

(1) = 'What we assert of Φ, when we say,

$$\Phi x \text{ entails } \{\sim(\Phi y) \supset \sim (y = x)\}$$

can be truly asserted of every relational property'.

This is a proposition which is again quite certainly true; and, in order to compare it with (2), there is, I think, no need to adopt any further convention for expressing it, since the questions whether it is or is not different from (2), and whether (2) does or does not follow from it, will obviously depend on the same questions with regard to the two propositions, with regard to the particular relational property, Φ,

$$\Phi x \text{ entails } \{\sim(\Phi y) \supset \sim (y = x)\}$$

and

$$\Phi x \supset \{\sim(\Phi y) \text{ entails } \sim (y = x)\}.$$

Now what I maintain with regard to (1) and (2) is that, whereas (1) is true, (2) is false. I maintain, that is to say, that the proposition 'What we assert of Φ, when we say

$$\Phi x \supset \{\sim(\Phi y) \text{ entails } \sim (y = x)\}$$

is true of *every* relational property' is false, though I admit that what we here assert of Φ is true of *some* relational properties. Those of which it is true, I propose to call *internal* relational properties, those of which it is false *external* relational properties. The dogma of internal relations, on the other hand, implies that (2) is true; that is to say, that *every* relational property is *internal*, and that there are no *external* relational properties. And what I suggest is that the dogma of internal relations has been held only because (2) has been falsely thought to follow from (1)

And that (2) does not follow from (1), can, I think, be easily seen as follows. It can follow from (1) only if from any proposition of the form

$$p \text{ entails } (q \supset r)$$

there follows the corresponding proposition of the form

$$p \supset (q \text{ entails } r),$$

and that this is not the case can, I think, be easily seen by considering the following three propositions. Let $p =$ 'All the books on this shelf are blue', let $q =$ 'My copy of the *Principles of Mathematics* is a book on this shelf', and let $r =$ 'My copy of the

97

Principles of Mathematics is blue'. Now p here does absolutely *entail* $(q \supset r)$. That is to say, it absolutely follows from p that 'My copy of the *Principles* is on this shelf', and 'My copy of the *Principles* is *not* blue', are not, as a matter of fact, both true. But it by no means follows from this that $p \supset (q$ entails $r)$. For what this latter proposition means is 'It is not the case both that p is true and that $(q$ entails $r)$ is false'. And, as a matter of fact $(q$ entails $r)$ is quite certainly false; for from the proposition 'My copy of the *Principles* is on this shelf' the proposition 'My copy of the *Principles* is blue' does *not* follow. It is simply not the case that the second of these two propositions can be deduced from the first *by itself*: it is simply not the case that it stands to it in the relation in which it does stand to the conjunctive proposition 'All the books on this shelf are blue *and* my copy of the *Principles* is on this shelf'. This conjunctive proposition really does *entail* 'My copy of the *Principles* is blue'. But 'My copy of the *Principles* is on this shelf', *by itself*, quite certainly does not entail 'My copy of the *Principles* is blue'. It is simply not the case that my copy of the *Principles couldn't* have been on this shelf without being blue. $(q$ entails $r)$ is, therefore, false. And hence '$p \supset (q$ entails $r)$', can only follow from 'p entails $(q \supset r)$', if from this latter proposition $\sim p$ follows. But $\sim p$ quite certainly does not follow from this proposition: from the fact that $(q \supset r)$ is deducible from p, it does not in the least follow that $\sim p$ is true. It is, therefore, clearly not the case that every proposition of the form

$$p \text{ entails } (q \supset r)$$

entails the corresponding proposition of the form

$$p \supset (q \text{ entails } r),$$

since we have found one particular proposition of the first form which does *not* entail the corresponding proposition of the second.

To maintain, therefore, that (2) follows from (1) is mere confusion. And one source of the confusion is, I think, pretty plain. (1) does allow you to assert that, if ΦA is true, then the proposition '$\Phi y \supset \{\sim (y = A)\}$' *must* be true. What the 'must' here expresses is merely that this proposition follows from ΦA, not that it is in itself a necessary proposition. But it is supposed, through confusion, that what is asserted is that it is not the case both that ΦA is true and that '$\sim(\Phi y) \supset \{\sim(y = A)\}$' is not, *in itself*, a necessary proposition; that is to say, it is supposed that what is asserted is '$\Phi A \supset \{\sim (\Phi y)$ entails $\sim (y = A)\}$'; since to say that '$\sim (\Phi y) \supset \sim (y = A)$' is, *in itself*, a necessary proposition is the same thing as to say that '$\sim (\Phi y)$ entails $\sim (y = A)$' is also true. In fact it seems to me pretty plain that what is meant by saying of propositions of the form '$\Phi x \supset \Psi x$' that they are *necessary* (or 'apodeictic') propositions, is merely that the corresponding proposition of the form 'Φx entails Ψx' is also true. 'Φx *entails* Ψx' is not *itself* a necessary proposition; but, if 'Φx entails Ψx' is *true*, then '$\Phi x \supset \Psi x$' is a necessary proposition – and a necessary truth, since no false propositions are necessary in themselves. Thus what is meant by saying that 'Whatever is a right angle, is also an angle' is a necessary truth, is, so far as I can see, simply that the proposition '(x is a right angle) entails (x is an angle)' is also true. This seems to me to give what has, in fact, been generally meant in philosophy by 'necessary truths', e.g., by Leibniz; and to point out the distinction between them and those true universal propositions which are 'mere matters of fact'. And if we want to extend the meaning of the name 'necessary truth' in such a way that some singular propositions may also be said to be 'necessary truths', we can, I think, easily do it as follows. We can say that ΦA is itself a necessary truth, if and only if the universal proposition '($x = A$) $\supset \Phi x$' (which, as we have seen, follows from ΦA) is a necessary truth: that is to say, if and only if ($x = A$) entails Φx. With this definition, what the dogma of internal relations asserts is that in every case in which a given thing actually has a given relational property, the fact that it has that property is a necessary truth; whereas what I am asserting is that, if the property in question is an 'internal' property, then the fact in question will be a necessary truth, whereas if the property in question is 'external', then the fact in question will be a mere 'matter of fact'.

So much for the distinction between (1) which is true, and (2), or the dogma of internal relations, which I hold to be false. But I said above, in passing, that my contention that (2) does not follow from (1), involves the rejection of certain views that have sometimes been held as to the meaning of 'follows'; and I think it is worth while to say something about this.

It is obvious that the possibility of maintaining that (2) does not follow from (1), depends upon its being true that from '$\Phi x \supset \Psi x$' the proposition 'Φx entails Ψx' does not follow. And this has sometimes been disputed, and is, I think, often not clearly seen.

To begin with, Mr Russell, in the *Principles of Mathematics* (p.34), treats the phrase '*q* can be deduced from *p*' as if it meant exactly the same thing as '*p* ⊃ *q*' or '*p* materially implies *q*'; and has repeated the same error elsewhere, e.g., in *Philosophical Essays* (p.166),[11] where he is discussing what *he* calls the axiom of internal relations. And I am afraid a good many people have been led to suppose that, since Mr Russell has said this, it must be true. If it were true, then, of course, it would be impossible to distinguish between (1) and (2), and it would follow that, since (1) certainly is true, what I am calling the dogma of internal relations is true too. But I imagine that Mr Russell himself would now be willing to admit that, so far from being true, the statement that '*q* can be deduced from *p*' means the same as '*p* ⊃ *q*' is simply an enormous 'howler'; and I do not think I need spend any time in trying to show that it is so.

But it may be held that, though '*p* entails *q*' does not mean the same as '*p* ⊃ *q*', yet nevertheless from 'Φ*x*⊃Ψ*x*' the proposition 'Φ*x* entails Ψ*x*' does follow, for a somewhat more subtle reason; and, if this were so, it would again follow that what I am calling the dogma of internal relations must be true. It may be held, namely, that though 'ΦA entails ΨA' does not mean simply 'ΦA⊃ΨA' yet what it does mean is simply the conjunction 'ΦA⊃ΨA *and* this proposition is an instance of a true formal implication' (the phrase 'formal implication' being understood in Mr Russell's sense, in which 'Φ*x*⊃Ψ*x*' asserts a formal implication). This view as to what 'ΦA entails ΨA' means, has, for instance, if I understand him rightly, been asserted by Mr O. Strachey in *Mind*, n.s., 93.[12] And the same view has been frequently suggested (though I do not know that he has actually asserted it) by Mr Russell himself (e.g., *Principia Mathematica*, p.21). If this view were true, then, though 'Φ*x* entails Ψ*x*' would not be identical in meaning with 'Φ*x*⊃Ψ*x*', yet it would follow from it; since, if

$$\Phi x \supset \Psi x$$

were true, then every particular assertion of the form ΦA⊃ΨA, would not only be true, but would be an instance of a true formal implication (namely 'Φ*x*⊃Ψ*x*') and this, according to the proposed definition, is all that 'Φ*x* entails Ψ*x*' asserts. If, there-

fore, it were true, it would again follow that all relational properties must be internal. But that this view also is untrue appears to
me perfectly obvious. The proposition that I am in this room
does 'materially imply' that I am more than five years old, since
both are true; and the assertion that it does is also an instance of
a true formal implication, since it is in fact true that all the
persons in this room are more than five years old; but nothing
appears to me more obvious than that the second of these two
propositions can *not* be deduced from the first – that the kind of
relation which holds between the premisses and conclusion of a
syllogism in *Barbara* does *not* hold between them. To put it in
another way: it seems to me quite obvious that the properties
'being a person in this room' and 'being more than five years
old' are not related in the kind of way in which 'being a right
angle' *is* related to 'being an angle', and which we express by
saying that, in the case of every term, the proposition that that
term is an angle can be deduced from the proposition that it is a
right angle.

These are the only two suggestions as to the meaning of '*p*
entails *q*' known to me, which, if true, would yield the result
that (2) does follow from (1), and that therefore all relational
properties are internal; and both of these, it seems to me, are
obviously false. All other suggested meanings, so far as I know,
would leave it true that (2) does not follow from (1), and therefore that I may possibly be right in maintaining that some
relational properties are external. It might, for instance, be
suggested that the last proposed definition should be amended
as follows – that we should say: '*p* entails *q*' means '*p* ⊃ *q* and* this
proposition is an instance of a formal implication, which is not
merely true but *self-evident*, like the laws of Formal Logic'. This
proposed definition would avoid the paradoxes involved in Mr
Strachey's definition, since such true formal implications as 'all
the persons in this room are more than five years old' are
certainly not self-evident; and, so far as I can see, it may state
something which is in fact true of *p* and *q*, whenever and only
when *p* entails *q*. I do not myself think that it gives the *meaning*
of '*p* entails *q*', since the kind of relation which I see to hold
between the premisses and conclusion of a syllogism seems to
me to be one which is purely 'objective' in the sense that no
psychological term, such as is involved in the meaning of 'self-
evident', is involved in its definition (if it has one). I am not,

however, concerned to dispute that some such definition of 'p entails q' as this may be true. Since it is evident that, even if it were, my proposition that 'Φx entails Ψx' does *not* follow from '$\Phi x \supset \Psi x$', would still be true; and hence also my contention that (2) does not follow from (1).

So much by way of arguing that we are not bound to hold that all relational properties are internal in the particular sense, with which we are now concerned, in which to say that they are means that in every case in which a thing A has a relational property, it follows from the proposition that a term has *not* got that property that the term in question is *other* than A. But I have gone further and asserted that some relational properties certainly are *not* internal. And in defence of this proposition I do not know that I have anything to say but that it seems to me evident in many cases that a term which *has* a certain relational property *might* quite well not have had it: that, for instance, from the mere proposition that this is this, it by no means follows that this has to other things all the relations which it in fact has. Everybody, of course, must admit that if all the propositions which assert of it that it has these properties, do in fact follow from the proposition that this is this, we cannot see that they do. And so far as I can see, there is no reason of any kind for asserting that they do, except the confusion which I have exposed. But it seems to me further that we can see in many cases that the proposition that this has that relation does *not* follow from the fact that it is this: that, for instance, the proposition that Edward VII was father of George V *is* a *mere* matter of fact.

I want now to return for a moment to that other meaning of 'internal' (p.86), in which to say that Φ is internal to A means not merely that anything which had not Φ would necessarily be *other* than A, but that it would necessarily be *qualitatively* different. I said that this was the meaning of 'internal' in which the dogma of internal relations holds that all relational properties are 'internal'; and that one of the most important consequences which followed from it, was that all relational properties are 'internal' in the less extreme sense that we have just been considering. But, if I am not mistaken, there is another important consequence which also follows from it, namely, the Identity of Indiscernibles. For if it be true, in the case of every relational property, that any term which had not that property

102

would necessarily be qualitatively different from any which had, it follows of course that, in the case of two terms one of which has a relational property, which the other has not the two are qualitatively different. But, from the proposition that x is other than y, it *does* follow that x has some relational property which y has not; and hence, if the dogma of internal relations be true, it will follow that if x is other than y, x is always also qualitatively different from y, which is the principle of Identity of Indiscernibles. This is, of course, a further objection to the dogma of internal relations, since I think it is obvious that the principle of Identity of Indiscernibles is not true. Indeed, so far as I can see, the dogma of internal relations essentially consists in the joint assertion of two indefensible propositions: (1) the proposition that in the case of no relational property is it true of any term which has got that property, that it *might* not have had it and (2) the Identity of Indiscernibles.

I want, finally, to say something about the phrase which Mr Russell uses in the *Philosophical Essays* to express the dogma of internal relations. He says it may be expressed in the form 'Every relation is grounded in the natures of the related terms' (p.160).[13] And it can be easily seen, if the account which I have given be true, in what precise sense it does hold this. Mr Russell is uncertain as to whether by 'the nature' of a term is to be understood the term itself or something else. For my part it seems to me that by a term's nature is meant, not the term itself, but what may roughly be called all its qualities as distinguished from its relational properties. But whichever meaning we take, it will follow from what I have said, that the dogma of internal relations does imply that every relational property which a term has is, in a perfectly precise sense, *grounded* in its nature. It will follow that every such property is *grounded* in *the term*, in the sense that, in the case of every such property, it *follows* from the mere proposition that that term is that term that it has the property in question. And it will also follow that any such property is grounded in the qualities which the term has, in the sense, that if you take *all* the qualities which the term has, it will again follow in the case of each relational property, from the proposition that the term has *all* those qualities that it has the relational property in question; since this is implied by the proposition that in the case of any such property, any term which had not had it would necessarily have been different in

103

quality from the term in question. In both of these two senses, then, the dogma of internal relations does, I think, imply that every relational property is grounded in the nature of every term which possesses it; and in this sense that proposition is false. Yet it is worth noting, I think, that there is another sense of 'grounded' in which it may quite well be true that every relational property *is* grounded in the nature of any term which possesses it. Namely that, in the case of every such property, the term in question has some quality *without* which it could not have had the property. In other words that the relational property *entails* some quality in the term, though no quality in the term *entails* the relational property.

NOTES

1 This paper is a revised version of the paper of the same title published in *The Proceedings of the Aristotelian Society* XX (1919–20) pp.40–62. As Moore explains in the Preface to *Philosophical Studies*, the printers of that book could not cope with the symbolism of *Principia Mathematica* which he had previously employed, so he had to use different symbols, and most of the revisions to the text concern these symbols whose use Moore felt he should explain in detail. Despite Moore's explanations, his unfamiliar symbols make the revised paper hard to read. So I have taken the opportunity to revert to a simplified version of the original symbolism.
2 F.H. Bradley, *Appearance and Reality* (Swan Sonneschein, London: 1893). The second edition published by George Allen & Unwin (London: 1897) preserves the original pagination; but the ninth impression of this edition published by Clarendon (Oxford: 1930) has a different pagination.
3 Clarendon edition, p.322.
4 Clarendon edition, p.347.
5 Moore's reference here is a mistake; there is no such passage on p.142 (first edition). I have not been able to locate the passage Moore here cites.
6 H. Joachim, *The Nature of Truth* (Clarendon, Oxford: 1906).
7 Moore refers here to F.H. Bradley, 'On Appearance, Error, and Contradiction', *Mind* n.s.19 (1910). This paper is reprinted in F.H. Bradley, *Essays on Truth and Reality* (Clarendon, Oxford: 1914); the passage Moore refers to occurs here on p.281.
8 In the first version of this paper Moore employs a universal quantifier to state general claims of this kind – so he would have here '(x) (Φx entails Ψx)'. In the revised version reproduced here he systematically omits the quantifier, and I have not reversed this change.
9 B. Russell, *The Principles of Mathematics* (George Allen & Unwin, London: 1903), p.14.

10 B. Russell and A. Whitehead, *Principia Mathematica* (Cambridge University Press, Cambridge: 1910), vol. I, p.7.
11 B. Russell, *Philosophical Essays* (George Allen & Unwin, London: 1910). In the revised edition of this book (1966) the reference is to p.144. Moore is alluding to Russell's remark that 'from a false hypothesis anything can be deduced'.
12 This reference is meaningless. But Moore clearly intends to refer to O. Strachey's 'Mr Russell and criticism of his views', *Mind* n.s.24 (1915), pp.26–8.
13 *Op. cit.* p.139 in the revised edition.

7

A DEFENCE OF COMMON SENSE

In what follows I have merely tried to state, one by one, some of the most important points in which my philosophical position differs from positions which have been taken up by *some* other philosophers. It may be that the points which I have had room to mention are not really the most important, and possibly some of them may be points as to which no philosopher has ever really differed from me. But, to the best of my belief, each is a point as to which many have really differed; although (in most cases, at all events) each is also a point as to which many have agreed with me.

I. The first point is a point which embraces a great many other points. And it is one which I cannot state as clearly as I wish to state it, except at some length. The method I am going to use for stating it is this. I am going to begin by enunciating, under the heading (1), a whole long list of propositions, which may seem, at first sight, such obvious truisms as not to be worth stating: they are, in fact, a set of propositions, every one of which (in my own opinion) I *know*, with certainty, to be true. I shall, next, under the heading (2), state a single proposition which makes an assertion about a whole set of *classes* of propositions – each class being defined, as the class consisting of all propositions which resemble *one* of the propositions in (1) in a certain respect. (2), therefore, is a proposition which could not be stated, until the list of propositions in (1), or some similar list, had already been given. (2) is itself a proposition which may seem such an

Originally published in *Contemporary British Philosophy* (second series), ed. J.H. Muirhead (George Allen & Unwin, London: 1925), pp.192–233.

obvious truism as not to be worth stating: and it is also a proposition which (in my own opinion) I *know*, with certainty, to be true. But, nevertheless, it is, to the best of my belief, a proposition with regard to which many philosophers have, for different reasons, differed from me; even if they have not directly denied (2) itself, they have held views incompatible with it. My first point, then, may be said to be that (2), together with all its implications, some of which I shall expressly mention, is true.

(1) I begin, then, with my list of truisms, every one of which (in my own opinion) I *know*, with certainty, to be true. The propositions to be included in this list are the following:

There exists at present a living human body, which is *my* body. This body was born at a certain time in the past, and has existed continuously ever since, though not without undergoing changes; it was, for instance, much smaller when it was born, and for some time afterwards, than it is now. Ever since it was born, it has been either in contact with or not far from the surface of the earth; and, at every moment since it was born, there have also existed many other things, having shape and size in three dimensions (in the same familiar sense in which it has), from which it has been *at various distances* (in the familiar sense in which it is now at a distance both from that mantelpiece and from that bookcase, and at a greater distance from the bookcase than it is from the mantelpiece); also there have (very often, at all events) existed some other things of this kind with which it was *in contact* (in the familiar sense in which it is now in contact with the pen I am holding in my right hand and with some of the clothes I am wearing). Among the things which have, in this sense, formed part of its environment (i.e., have been either in contact with it, or at *some* distance from it, however *great*) there have, at every moment since its birth, been large numbers of other living human bodies, each of which has, like it, (*a*) at some time been born, (*b*) continued to exist from some time after birth, (*c*) been, at every moment of its life after birth, either in contact with or not far from the surface of the earth; and many of these bodies have already died and ceased to exist. But the earth had existed also for many years before my body was born; and for many of these years, also, large numbers of human bodies had, at every moment, been alive upon it; and many of these bodies had died and ceased to exist before it was born. Finally (to come to a different class of propositions), I am a human being, and I have, at different times since my body was born, had many different experiences, of each of many different kinds: e.g., I have often perceived both my own body and other things which formed part of its environment, including other human bodies; I have not only perceived things of this kind, but have also observed facts about them, such as, for instance, the fact which I am now observing, that that mantelpiece is at present nearer to my body than that bookcase; I have been aware of other facts, which I was not at the time observing, such as, for instance, the fact, of which I am now aware, that my body existed yesterday and was then also for some time nearer to that mantelpiece than to that bookcase; I have had expectations with regard to the future, and many beliefs of other kinds, both true and false; I have thought of imaginary things and persons and incidents, in the reality of which I did not believe; I have had dreams; and I have had feelings of many different kinds. And, just as my body has been the body of a human being, namely myself, who has, during his lifetime, had many experiences of each of these (and other) different kinds; so, in the case of very many of the other human bodies which have lived upon the earth, each has been the body of a different human being, who has, during the lifetime of that body, had many different experiences of each of these (and other) different kinds.

(2) I now come to the single truism which, as will be seen, could not be stated except by reference to the whole list of truisms, just given in (1). This truism also (in my own opinion) I *know*, with certainty, to be true; and it is as follows:

In the case of *very many* (I do not say *all*) of the human beings belonging to the class (which includes myself) defined in the following way, i.e., as human beings who have had human bodies, that were born and lived for some time upon the earth, and who have, during the lifetime of those bodies, had many different experiences of each of the kinds mentioned in (1), it is true that each has frequently, during the life of his body, known, with regard to *him*self or *his* body, and with regard to some time earlier than any of the times at which I wrote down the propositions in (1), a proposition *corresponding* to each of the propositions in (1), in the sense that it asserts with regard to *him*self or *his* body and the earlier time in question (namely, in each case, the time at which he knew it), just what the corresponding proposition in (1) asserts with regard to *me* or *my* body and the time at which I wrote that proposition down.

In other words what (2) asserts is only (what seems an obvious enough truism) that each of *us* (meaning by 'us', very many human beings of the class defined) has frequently *known*, with regard to *him*self or *his* body and the time at which he knew it, everything which, in writing down my list of propositions in (1), I was claiming to know about *my*self or *my* body and the time at which I wrote that proposition down, i.e., just as *I* knew (when I wrote it down) 'There exists at present a living human body which is my body', so each of us has frequently known with regard to himself and some other time the different but corresponding proposition, which *he* could *then* have properly expressed by, 'There exists *at present* a human body which is *my* body'; just as *I* know 'Many human bodies other than mine have before now lived on the earth', so each of us has frequently known the different but corresponding proposition 'Many human bodies other than *mine* have before *now* lived on the earth'; just as *I* know 'Many human beings other than myself have before now perceived, and dreamed, and felt', so each of *us* has frequently known the different but corresponding proposition 'Many human beings other than *myself* have before *now* perceived, and dreamed, and felt'; and so on, in the case of *each* of the propositions enumerated in (1).

I hope there is no difficulty in understanding, so far, what this proposition (2) asserts. I have tried to make clear by examples what I mean by 'propositions *corresponding* to each of the propositions in (1)'. And what (2) asserts is merely that each of us has frequently known to be true a proposition *corresponding* (in that sense) to each of the propositions in (1) – a *different* corresponding proposition, of course, at each of the times at which he knew such a proposition to be true.

But there remain two points, which, in view of the way in which some philosophers have used the English language, ought, I think, to be expressly mentioned, if I am to make quite clear exactly how much I am asserting in asserting (2).

The first point is this. Some philosophers seem to have thought it legitimate to use the word 'true' in such a sense that a proposition which is partially false may nevertheless also be true; and some of these, therefore, would perhaps *say* that propositions like those enumerated in (1) are, in their view, true, when all the time they believe that every such proposition is partially false. I wish, therefore, to make it quite plain that I am not using 'true' in any such sense. I am using it in such a sense (and I think this is the ordinary usage) that if a proposition is partially false, it follows that it is *not* true, though, of course, it may be *partially* true. I am maintaining, in short, that all the propositions in (1), and also many propositions corresponding to each of these, are *wholly* true; I am asserting this in asserting (2). And hence any philosopher, who does in fact believe, with regard to any or all of these classes of propositions, that every proposition of the class in question is partially false, is, in fact, disagreeing with me and holding a view incompatible with (2), even though he may think himself justified in *saying* that he believes some propositions belonging to all of these classes to be 'true'.

And the second point is this. Some philosophers seem to have thought it legitimate to use such expressions as, e.g. 'The earth has existed for many years past', as if they expressed something which they really believed, when in fact they believe that every proposition, which such an expression would *ordinarily* be understood to express, is, at least partially, false; and all they really believe is that there is some *other* set of propositions, related in a certain way to those which such expressions do actually express, which, unlike these, really are true. That is to say, they use the expression 'The earth has existed for many years past' to express, not what it would ordinarily be understood to express, but the proposition that some proposition, related to this in a certain way, is true; when all the time they believe that the proposition, which this expression would ordinarily be understood to express, is, at least partially, false. I wish, therefore, to make it quite plain that I was not using the expressions I used in (1) in any such subtle sense. I meant by each of them precisely what every reader, in reading them, will have understood me to mean. And any philosopher, therefore, who holds that any of these expressions, if understood in this popular manner, expresses a proposition which embodies some popular error, is disagreeing with me and holding a view incompatible with (2), even though he may hold that there is some *other*, true, proposition which the expression in question might be legitimately used to express.

In what I have just said, I have assumed that there is some meaning which is *the* ordinary or popular meaning of such expressions as 'The earth has existed for many years past'. And this, I am afraid, is an assumption which some philosophers are capable of disputing. They seem to think that the question 'Do you believe that the earth has existed for many years past?' is not a plain question, such as should be met either by a plain 'Yes' or 'No', or by a plain 'I can't make up my mind', but is the sort of question which can be properly met by: 'It all depends on what you mean by "the earth" and "exists" and "years": if you mean so and so, and so and so, and so and so, then I do; but if you mean so and so, and so and so, and so and so, or so and so, and so and so, and so and so, or so and so, and so and so, and so and so, then I don't, or at least I think it is extremely doubtful'. It seems to me that such a view is as profoundly mistaken as any view can be. Such an expression as 'The earth has existed for many years past' is the very type of an unambiguous expression, the meaning of which we all understand. Anyone who takes a contrary view must, I suppose, be confusing the question whether we understand its meaning (which we all certainly do) with the entirely different question whether we *know what it means*, in the sense that we are able to *give a correct analysis* of its meaning. The question what is the correct analysis of *the* proposition meant *on any occasion* (for, of course, as I insisted in defining (2), a different proposition is meant at every different time at which the expression is used) by 'The earth has existed for many years past' is, it seems to me, a profoundly difficult question, and one to which, as I shall presently urge, no one knows the answer. But to hold that we do not know what, in certain respects, is the analysis of what we understand by such an expression, is an entirely different thing from holding that we do not understand the expression. It is obvious that we cannot even raise the question how what we do understand by it is to be analysed, unless we do understand it. So soon, therefore, as we know that a person who uses such an expression is using it in its ordinary sense, we understand his meaning. So that in explaining that I was using the expressions used in (1) in their ordinary sense (those of them which have an ordinary sense, which is not the case with quite all of them), I have done all that is required to make my meaning clear.

But now, assuming that the expressions which I have used to

express (2) are understood, I think, as I have said, that many philosophers have really held views incompatible with (2). And the philosophers who have done so may, I think, be divided into two main groups. A. What (2) asserts is, with regard to a whole set of *classes* of propositions, that we have, each of us, frequently *known* to be true propositions belonging to *each* of these classes. And one way of holding a view incompatible with this proposition is, of course, to hold, with regard to one or more of the classes in question, that *no* propositions of that class *are* true – that all of them are, at least partially, false; since if, in the case of any one of these classes, *no* propositions of that class *are* true, it is obvious that nobody can have *known* any propositions of that class to be true, and therefore that *we* cannot have known to be true propositions belonging to *each* of these classes. And my first group of philosophers consists of philosophers who have held views incompatible with (2) for this reason. They have held, with regard to one or more of the classes in question, simply that no propositions of that class *are* true. Some of them have held this with regard to *all* the classes in question; some only with regard to *some* of them. But, of course, whichever of these two views they have held, they have been holding a view inconsistent with (2). B. Some philosophers, on the other hand, have not ventured to assert, with regard to *any* of the classes in (2), that no propositions of that class *are* true, but what they have asserted is that, in the case of some of these classes, no human being has ever *known*, with certainty, that any propositions of the class in question are true. That is to say, they differ profoundly from philosophers of group A, in that they hold that propositions of *all* these classes *may* be true; but nevertheless they hold a view incompatible with (2) since they hold, with regard to some of these classes, that none of us has ever *known* a proposition of the class in question to be true.

A. I said that some philosophers, belonging to this group, have held that no propositions belonging to *any* of the classes in (2) are wholly true, while others have only held this with regard to *some* of the classes in (2). And I think the chief division of this kind has been the following. Some of the propositions in (1) (and, therefore, of course, all propositions belonging to the corresponding classes in (2)) are propositions which cannot be true, unless some *material things* have existed and have stood *in*

spatial relations to one another: that is to say, they are propositions which, *in a certain sense*, imply *the reality of material
things*, and *the reality of Space*. E.g., the proposition that my body
has existed for many years past, and has, at every moment
during that time been either in contact with or not far from the
earth, is a proposition which implies both the *reality of material
things* (provided you use 'material things' in such a sense that to
deny the reality of material things implies that no proposition
which asserts that human bodies have existed, or that the earth
has existed, is wholly true) and also the *reality of Space* (provided, again, that you use 'Space' in such a sense that to deny
the reality of Space implies that no proposition which asserts
that anything has ever been in contact with or at a distance from
another, in the familiar senses pointed out in (1), is wholly true).
But others among the propositions in (1) (and, therefore, propositions belonging to the corresponding classes in (2)), do not (at
least obviously) imply either the reality of material things or the
reality of Space: e.g., the propositions that I have often had
dreams, and have had many different feelings at different times.
It is true that propositions of this second class do imply one
thing which is also implied by all propositions of the first,
namely that (*in a certain sense*) *Time is real*, and imply also one
thing not implied by propositions of the first class, namely that
(*in a certain sense*) *at least one Self is real*. But I think there are some
philosophers, who, while denying that (in the senses in question) either material things or Space are real, have been willing
to admit that Selves and Time are real, in the sense required.
Other philosophers, on the other hand, have used the expression 'Time is not real', to express some view that they held;
and some, at least, of these have, I think, meant by this expression something which is incompatible with the truth of *any*
of the propositions in (1) – they have meant, namely, that *every*
proposition of the sort that is expressed by the use of 'now' or 'at
present', e.g., 'I am now both seeing and hearing' or 'There
exists at present a living human body', or by the use of a *past*
tense, e.g., 'I *have* had many experiences in the past', or 'The
earth *has* existed for many years', are, at least partially, false.

All the four expressions I have just introduced, namely 'Material things are not real', 'Space is not real', 'Time is not real',
'The Self is not real', are, I think, unlike the expressions I used in
(1), really ambiguous. And it may be that, in the case of each of

113

them, some philosopher has used the expression in question to express some view he held which was not incompatible with (2). With such philosophers, if there are any, I am not, of course, at present concerned. But it seems to me that the most natural and proper usage of each of these expressions is a usage in which it *does* express a view incompatible with (2); and, in the case of each of them, some philosophers have, I think, really used the expression in question to express such a view. All such philosophers have, therefore, been holding a view incompatible with (2).

All such views, whether incompatible with *all* of the propositions in (1), or only with *some* of them, seem to me to be quite certainly false; and I think the following points are specially deserving of notice with regard to them.

(a) If *any* of the classes of propositions in (2) is such that no proposition of that class is true, then no philosopher has ever existed, and therefore none can ever have held with regard to any such class, that no proposition belonging to it is true. In other words, the proposition that some propositions belonging to each of these classes are true is a proposition which has the peculiarity, that, if any philosopher has ever denied it, it follows from the fact that he has denied it, that he must have been wrong in denying it. For when I speak of 'philosophers' I mean, of course (as we all do), exclusively philosophers who have been human beings, with human bodies that have lived upon the earth, and who have at different times had many different experiences. If, therefore, there have been any philosophers, there have been human beings of this class; and if there have been human beings of this class, all the rest of what is asserted in (1) is certainly true too. Any view, therefore, incompatible with the proposition that many propositions corresponding to each of the propositions in (1) are true, can only be true, on the hypothesis that no philosopher has ever held any such view. It follows, therefore, that, in considering whether this proposition is true, I cannot consistently regard the fact that many philosophers, whom I respect, have, to the best of my belief, held views incompatible with it, as having any weight at all against it. Since, if I know that they have held such views, I am, *ipso facto*, knowing that they were mistaken; and, if I have no reason to believe that the proposition in question is true, I have still less reason to believe that they have held views incompatible with it;

since I am more certain that they have existed and held *some* views, i.e., that the proposition in question is true, than that they have held any views incompatible with it.

(*b*) It is, of course, the case that all philosophers who have held such views have repeatedly, even in their philosophical works, expressed other views inconsistent with them: i.e., no philosopher has ever been able to hold such views consistently. One way in which they have betrayed this inconsistency, is by alluding to the existence of other philosophers. Another way is by alluding to the existence of the human race, and in particular by using 'we' in the sense in which I have already constantly used it, in which any philosopher who asserts that 'we' do so and so, e.g., that *'we* sometimes believe propositions that are not true', is asserting not only that he himself has done the thing in question, but that *very many other human beings, who have had bodies and lived upon the earth*, have done the same. The fact is, of course, that all philosophers have belonged to the class of human beings which exists only if (2) be true: that is to say, to the class of human beings who have frequently *known* propositions corresponding to each of the propositions in (1). In holding views incompatible with the proposition that propositions of all these classes are true, they have, therefore, been holding views inconsistent with propositions which they themselves *knew* to be true; and it was, therefore, only to be expected that they should sometimes betray their knowledge of such propositions. The strange thing is that philosophers should have been able to hold sincerely, as part of their philosophical creed, propositions inconsistent with what they themselves *knew* to be true; and yet, so far as I can make out, this has really frequently happened. My position, therefore, on this first point, differs from that of philosophers belonging to this group A, not in that I hold anything which they don't hold, but only in that I don't hold, as part of my philosophical creed, things which they do hold as part of theirs – that is to say, propositions inconsistent with some which they and I both hold in common. But this difference seems to me to be an important one.

(*c*) Some of these philosophers have brought forward, in favour of their position, arguments designed to show, in the case of some or all of the propositions in (1), that no propositions of that type can possibly be wholly true, because every such proposition entails both of two incompatible propositions.

And I admit, of course, that if any of the propositions in (1) did entail both of two incompatible propositions it could not be true. But it seems to me I have an absolutely conclusive argument to show that none of them does entail both of two incompatible propositions. Namely this: All of the propositions in (1) are true; no true proposition entails both of two incompatible propositions; therefore, none of the propositions in (1) entails both of two incompatible propositions.

(d) Although, as I have urged, no philosopher who has held with regard to any of these types of proposition that no propositions of that type are true, has failed to hold also other views inconsistent with his view in this respect, yet I do not think that the view, with regard to any or all of these types, that no proposition belonging to them is true, is *in itself* a self-contradictory view, i.e., entails both of two incompatible propositions. On the contrary, it seems to me quite clear that it *might* have been the case that Time was not real, material things not real, space not real, selves not real. And in favour of my view that none of these things, whcih might have been the case, *is* in fact the case, I have, I think, no better argument than simply this – namely, that all the propositions in (1) are, in fact, true.

B. This view, which is usually considered a much more modest view than A, has, I think, the defect that, unlike A, it really is self-contradictory, i.e., entails both of two mutually incompatible propositions.

Most philosophers who have held this view, have held, I think, that though each of us knows propositions corresponding to *some* of the propositions in (1), namely to those which merely assert that *I* myself have had in the past experiences of certain kinds at many different times, yet none of us knows *for certain* any propositions either of the type (a) which assert the existence of *material things* or of the type (b) which assert the existence of *other* selves, beside myself, and that *they* also have had experiences. They admit that we do in fact *believe* propositions of both these types, and that they *may* be true: some would even say that we know them to be highly probable; but they deny that we ever know them, *for certain*, to be true. Some of them have spoken of such beliefs as 'beliefs of Common Sense', expressing thereby their conviction that beliefs of this kind are very commonly entertained by mankind: but they are convinced that these things are, in all cases, only *believed*, not known for certain;

and some have expressed this by saying that they are matters of Faith, not of Knowledge.

Now the remarkable thing which those who take this view have not, I think, in general duly appreciated, is that, in each case, the philosopher who takes it is making an assertion about 'us' – that is to say, not merely about himself, but about *many other human beings as well*. When he says 'No human being has ever *known* of the existence of other human beings', he is saying: 'There have been many other human beings beside myself, and none of them (including myself) has ever known the existence of other human beings'. If he says: 'These beliefs are beliefs of Common Sense, but they are not matters of *knowledge*', he is saying: 'There have been many other human beings, beside myself, who have shared these beliefs, but neither I nor any of the rest have ever known them to be true'. In other words, he asserts with confidence that these beliefs *are* beliefs of Common Sense, and seems often to fail to notice that, *if* they are, they must be true; since the proposition that they are beliefs of Common Sense is one which logically entails the proposition both of type (*a*) and of type (*b*); it logically entails the proposition that many human beings, beside the philosopher himself, have had human bodies, which lived upon the earth, and have had various experiences, including beliefs of this kind. This is why this position, as contrasted with positions of group A, seems to me to be self-contradictory. Its difference from A consists in the fact that it is making a proposition about *human knowledge* in general, and therefore is actually asserting the existence of many human beings, whereas philosophers of group A in stating their position are not doing this: they are only contradicting *other* things which they hold. It is true that a philosopher who says 'There have existed many human beings beside myself, and none of us has ever known the existence of any human beings beside himself', is only contradicting himself if what he holds is 'There have *certainly* existed many human beings beside myself' or, in other words, '*I* know that there have existed other human beings beside myself'. But this, it seems to me, is what such philosophers have in fact been generally doing. They seem to me constantly to betray the fact that they regard the proposition that those beliefs *are* beliefs of Common Sense, or the proposition that they themselves are not the only members of the human race, as not merely true, but *certainly* true; and *certainly* true it cannot be, unless one member, at least, of the human race, namely themselves, has *known* the very things which that member is declaring that no human being has ever known.

Nevertheless, my position that I *know*, with certainty, to be true all of the propositions in (1), is certainly not a position, the denial of which entails both of two incompatible propositions. If I do *know* all these propositions to be true, then, I think, it is quite certain that other human beings also have known corresponding propositions: that is to say (2) also *is* true, and *I* know it to be true. But do I really *know* all the propositions in (1) to be true? Isn't it possible that I merely believe them? Or know them to be highly probable? In answer to this question, I think I have nothing better to say than that it seems to me that I *do* know them, with certainty. It is, indeed, obvious that, in the case of most of them, I do not know them *directly*: that is to say, I only know them because, in the past, I have known to be true *other* propositions which were evidence for them. If, for instance, I do know that the earth had existed for many years before I was born, I certainly only know this because I have known other things in the past which were evidence for it. And I certainly do not know exactly what the evidence was. Yet all this seems to me to be no good reason for doubting that I do know it. We are all, I think, in this strange position that we do *know* many things, with regard to which we *know* further that we must have had evidence for them, and yet we do not know *how* we know them, i.e., we do not know what the evidence was. If there is any 'we', and if we know that there is, this must be so: for that there is a 'we', is one of the things in question. And that I do know that there is a 'we', that is to say, that many other human beings, with human bodies, have lived upon the earth, it seems to me that I do know, for certain.

If this first point in my philosophical position, namely my belief in (2), is to be given any name, which has actually been used by philosophers in classifying the positions of other philosophers, it would have, I think, to be expressed by saying that I am one of those philosophers who have held that the 'Common Sense view of the world' is, in certain fundamental features, *wholly* true. But it must be remembered that, according to me, *all* philosophers, without exception, have agreed with me in holding this: and that the real difference, which is commonly expressed in this way, is only a difference between those philosophers, who have *also* held views inconsistent with these features in 'the Common Sense view of the world', and those who have not.

The features in question (namely, propositions of any of the classes defined in defining (2)) are all of them features, which have this peculiar property – namely, that *if we know that they are features in the 'Common Sense view of the world', it follows that they are true*: it is self-contradictory to maintain that *we* know them to be features in the Common Sense view, and that yet they are not true; since to say that *we* know this, is to say that they are true. And many of them also have the further peculiar property that, *if they are features in the Common Sense view of the world (whether 'we' know this or not), it follows that they are true*, since to say that there is a 'Common Sense view of the world', is to say that they are true. The phrases 'Common Sense view of the world' or 'Common Sense beliefs' (as used by philosophers) are, of course, extraordinarily vague; and, for all I know, there may be many propositions which may be properly called features in 'the Common Sense view of the world' or 'Common Sense beliefs', which are not true, and which deserve to be mentioned with the contempt with which some philosophers speak of 'Common Sense beliefs'. But to speak with contempt of those 'Common Sense beliefs' which I have mentioned is quite certainly the height of absurdity. And there are, of course, enormous numbers of other features in 'the Common Sense view of the world' which, if these are true, are quite certainly true too: e.g., that there have lived upon the surface of the earth not only human beings, but also many different species of plants and animals, etc., etc.

II. What seems to me the next in importance of the points in which my philosophical position differs from positions held by *some* other philosophers, is one which I will express in the following way. I hold, namely, that there is no good reason to suppose either (A) that *every* physical fact is *logically* dependent upon some mental fact or (B) that *every* physical fact is *causally* dependent upon some mental fact. In saying this, I am not, of course, saying that there *are* any physical facts which are wholly independent (i.e., both logically and causally) of mental facts: I do, in fact, believe that there are; but that is not what I am asserting. I am only asserting that there is *no good reason* to suppose the contrary; by which I mean, of course, that none of the human beings, who have had human bodies that lived upon the earth, have, during the lifetime of their bodies, had any good reason to suppose the contrary. Many philosophers have, I think, not only believed either that *every* physical fact is *logically* dependent upon some mental fact ('physical fact' and 'mental fact' being understood in the sense in which I am using these terms) or that *every* physical fact is *causally* dependent upon some mental fact, or both, but also that they themselves had good reason for these beliefs. In this respect, therefore, I differ from them.

In the case of the term 'physical fact', I can only explain how I am using it by giving examples. I mean by 'physical facts', facts *like* the following: 'That mantelpiece is at present nearer to this body than that bookcase is', 'The earth has existed for many years past', 'The moon has at every moment for many years past been nearer to the earth than to the sun', 'That mantelpiece is of a light colour'. But, when I say 'facts *like* these', I mean, of course, facts like them *in a certain respect*; and what this respect is I cannot define. The term 'physical fact' is, however, in common use; and I think that I am using it in its ordinary sense. Moreover, there is no need for a definition to make my point clear; since among the examples I have given there are some with regard to which I hold that there is no reason to suppose *them* (i.e., these particular physical facts) either logically or causally dependent upon any mental fact.

'Mental fact', on the other hand, is a much more unusual expression, and I am using it in a specially limited sense, which, though I think it is a natural one, does need to be explained. There may be many other senses in which the term can be properly used, but I am only concerned with this one; and hence it is essential that I should explain what it is.

There may, possibly, I hold, be 'mental facts' of three different kinds. It is only with regard to the first kind that I am sure that there are facts of that kind; but if there were any facts of either of the other two kinds, they would be 'mental facts' in my limited sense, and therefore I must explain what is meant by the hypothesis that there are facts of those two kinds.

(*a*) My first kind is this. I am conscious now; and also I am seeing something now. These two facts are both of them mental facts of my first kind; and my first kind consists exclusively of facts which resemble one or other of the two *in a certain respect*.

(α) The fact that I am conscious now is obviously, in a certain sense, a fact, with regard to a particular individual and a particular time, to the effect that that individual is conscious at that time. And every fact which resembles this one in that respect is to be included in my first kind of mental fact. Thus the fact that I was also conscious at many different times yesterday is not itself a fact of this kind: but it entails that there *are* (or, as we should commonly say, because the times in question are past times, 'were') many other facts of this kind, namely each of the facts, which, at each of the times in question, I could have properly expressed by 'I am conscious *now*'. *Any* fact which is, in this sense, a fact with regard to an individual and a time (whether the individual be myself or another, and whether the time be past or present), to the effect that that individual *is* conscious at that time, is to be included in my first kind of mental fact: and I call such facts, facts of class (α).

(β) The second example I gave, namely the fact that I am seeing something now, is obviously related to the fact that I am conscious now in a peculiar manner. It not only *entails* the fact that I am conscious now (for from the fact that I am seeing something it *follows* that I am conscious: I *could* not have been seeing anything, unless I had been conscious, though I might quite well have been conscious without seeing anything) but it also is a fact, with regard to a *specific way* (or mode) of being conscious, to the effect that I am conscious in that way: in the same sense in which the proposition (with regard to any particular thing) 'This is red' both entails the proposition (with regard to the same thing) 'This is coloured', and is also a proposition, with regard to a *specific way* of being coloured, to the effect that that thing is coloured in that way. And any fact which is related in this peculiar manner to any fact of class (α), is also to be included in my first kind of mental fact, and is to be called a fact of class (β). Thus the fact that I am hearing now is, like the fact that I am seeing now, a fact of class (β); and so is any fact, with regard to myself and a past time, which could at that time have been properly expressed by 'I am dreaming now', 'I am imagining now', 'I am at present aware of the fact that . . .', etc., etc. In short, any fact, which is a fact with regard to a particular individual (myself or another), a particular time (past or present),

121

and *any particular kind of experience*, to the effect that that individual is having at that time an experience of that particular kind, is a fact of class (β): and only such facts are facts of class (β).

My first kind of mental facts consists exclusively of facts of classes (α) and (β), and consists of *all* facts of either of these kinds.

(*b*) That there are many facts of classes (α) and (β) seems to me perfectly certain. But many philosophers seem to me to have held a certain view with regard to the *analysis* of facts of class (α), which is such that, if it were true, there would be facts of another kind, which I should wish also to call 'mental facts'. I don't feel at all sure that this analysis is true; but it seems to me that it *may* be true; and since we can understand what is meant by the supposition that it is true, we can also understand what is meant by the supposition that there are 'mental facts' of this second kind.

Many philosophers have, I think, held the following view as to the analysis of what each of us knows, when he knows (at any time) 'I am conscious now'. They have held, namely, that there is a certain intrinsic property (with which we are all of us familiar and which might be called that of 'being an experience') which is such that, at any time at which any man knows 'I am conscious now', he is knowing, with regard to that property and himself and the time in question, 'There is occurring now an event which has this property (i.e., "is an experience") and which is an experience of *mine*', and such that this fact is what he expresses by 'I am conscious now'. And if this view is true, there must be many facts of each of three kinds, each of which I should wish to call 'mental facts'; *viz.* (1) facts with regard to some event, which has this supposed intrinsic property, and to some time, to the effect that that event is occurring at that time, (2) facts with regard to this supposed intrinsic property and some time, to the effect that *some* event which has that property is occurring at that time, and (3) facts with regard to some property, which is a *specific way* of having the supposed intrinsic property (in the sense above explained in which 'being red' is a specific way of 'being coloured') and some time, to the effect that some event which has that specific property is occurring at that time. Of course, there not only are not, but *cannot* be, facts of any of these kinds, unless there is an intrinsic property related to what each of us (on any occasion) expresses by 'I am conscious now', in the manner defined above; and I feel very doubtful whether there is any such property; in other words, although I know for certain both that I have had many experiences, and that I have had experiences of many different kinds, I feel very doubtful whether to say the first is the same thing as to say that there have been many events, each of which was an experience and an experience of mine, and whether to say the second is the same thing as to say that there have been many events, each of which was an experience of mine, and each of which also had a different property, which was a specific way of being an experience. The proposition that I have had experiences does not necessarily entail the proposition that there have been any events which were experiences; and I cannot satisfy myself that I am acquainted with any events of the supposed kind. But yet it seems to me possible that the proposed analysis of 'I am conscious now' is correct: that I am really acquainted with events of the supposed kind, though I cannot see that I am. And *if* I am, then I should wish to call the three kinds of facts defined above 'mental facts'. Of course, if there are 'experiences' in the sense defined, it would be possible (as many have held) that there *can* be no experiences which are not *some individual's* experiences; and in that case any fact of any of these three kinds would be logically dependent on, though not necessarily identical with, some fact of class (α) or class (β). But it seems to me also a possibility that, if there are 'experiences', there might be experiences which did not belong to any individual; and, in that case, there would be 'mental facts' which were neither identical with nor logically dependent on any fact of class (α) or class (β).

(c) Finally some philosophers have, so far as I can make out, held that there are or may be facts which are facts with regard to some individual, to the effect that he is conscious, or is conscious in some specific way, but which differ from facts of classes (α) and (β), in the important respect that they are not facts *with regard to any time*: they have conceived the possibility that there may be one or more individuals, who are *timelessly* conscious, and timelessly conscious in specific modes. And others, again, have, I think, conceived the hypothesis that the intrinsic property defined in (b) may be one which does not belong only to *events*, but may also belong to one or more wholes, which do *not* occur at any time: in other words, that there may be one or more *timeless* experiences, which might or might not be the experiences of some individual. It seems to me very doubtful whether any of these hypotheses are even possibly true; but I cannot see for certain that they are not possible: and, if they are possible, then I should wish to give the name 'mental fact' to any fact (if there were any) of any of the five following kinds, *viz.* (1) to any fact which is the fact, with regard to any individual, that he is *timelessly* conscious, (2) to any fact which is the fact, with regard to any individual, that he is *timelessly* conscious in any specific way, (3) to any fact which is the fact with regard to a *timeless* experience that it exists, (4) to any fact which is the fact with regard to the supposed intrinsic property 'being an experience', that something timelessly exists which has that property, and (5) to any fact which is the fact, with regard to any property, which is a specific mode of this supposed intrinsic property, that something timelessly exists which has that property.

I have, then, defined three different kinds of facts, each of which is such that, if there *were* any facts of that kind (as there certainly *are*, in the case of the first kind), the facts in question *would be* 'mental facts' in my sense; and to complete the definition of the limited sense in which I am using 'mental facts', I have only to add that I wish also to apply the name to one *fourth* class of facts: namely to any fact, which is the fact, with regard to any of these three kinds of facts, or any kinds included in them, *that there are facts of the kind in question*; i.e., not only will each individual fact of class (α) be, in my sense, a 'mental fact', but also the general fact 'that there are facts of class (α)', will itself be a 'mental fact'; and similarly in all other cases: e.g., not only will the fact that I am now perceiving (which is a fact of class (β)) be a 'mental fact', but also the general fact that *there are* facts, with regard to individuals and times, to the effect that the individual in question is perceiving at the time in question, will be a 'mental fact'.

A. Understanding 'physical fact' and 'mental fact' in the senses just explained, I hold, then, that there is no good reason to suppose that *every* physical fact is *logically* dependent upon some mental fact. And I use the phrase, with regard to two facts, F_1 and F_2, 'F_1 is *logically dependent* on F_2', wherever and only where F_1 *entails* F_2, either in the sense in which the proposition 'I am seeing now' *entails* the proposition 'I am conscious

124

now', or the proposition (with regard to any particular thing) 'This is red' entails the proposition (with regard to the same thing) 'This is coloured', or else in the more strictly logical sense in which (for instance) the conjunctive proposition 'All men are mortal, and Mr Baldwin is a man' entails the proposition 'Mr Baldwin is mortal'. To say, then, of two facts, F_1 and F_2, that F_1 is *not* logically dependent upon F_2, is only to say that F_1 *might* have been a fact, even if there had been no such fact as F_2; or that the conjunctive proposition 'F_1 is a fact, but there is no such fact as F_2' is a proposition which is not self-contradictory, i.e., does not entail both of two mutually incompatible propositions.

I hold, then, that, in the case of *some* physical facts, there is no good reason to suppose that there is some mental fact, such that the physical fact in question could not have been a fact unless the mental fact in question had also been one. And my position is perfectly definite, since I hold that this is the case with all the four physical facts, which I have given as examples of physical facts. For example, there is no good reason to suppose that there is any mental fact whatever, such that the fact that that mantelpiece is at present nearer to my body than that bookcase could not have been a fact, unless the mental fact in question had also been a fact; and, similarly, in all the other three cases.

In holding this I am certainly differing from some philosophers. I am, for instance, differing from Berkeley, who held that that mantelpiece, that bookcase, and my body are, all of them, either 'ideas' or 'constituted by ideas', and that no 'idea' can possibly exist without being perceived. He held, that is, that this physical fact is logically dependent upon a mental fact of my fourth class: namely a fact which is the fact that there is at least one fact, which is a fact with regard to an individual and the present time, to the effect that that individual is now perceiving something. He does not say that this physical fact is logically dependent upon any fact which is a fact of any of my first three classes, e.g., on any fact which is the fact, with regard to a particular individual and the present time, that *that* individual is now perceiving something: what he does say is that the physical fact couldn't have been a fact, unless it had been a fact that there was *some* mental fact of this sort. And it seems to me that many philosophers, who would perhaps disagree either with Berkeley's assumption that my body is an 'idea' or 'constituted by ideas', or with his assumption that 'ideas' cannot exist without being perceived, or with both, nevertheless would agree with him in thinking that this physical fact is logically dependent upon *some* 'mental fact': e.g., they might say that it could not have been a fact, unless there had been, at some time or other, or, were timelessly, *some* 'experience'. Many, indeed, so far as I can make out, have held that *every* fact is logically dependent on every other fact. And, of course, they have held in the case of their opinions, as Berkeley did in the case of his, that they had good reasons for them.

B. I also hold that there is no good reason to suppose that *every* physical fact is *causally* dependent upon some mental fact. By saying that F_1 is *causally* dependent on F_2, I mean only that F_1 *wouldn't* have been a fact unless F_2 had been; *not* (which is what 'logically dependent' asserts) that F_1 *couldn't conceivably* have been a fact, unless F_2 had been. And I can illustrate my meaning by reference to the example which I have just given. The fact that that mantelpiece is at present nearer to my body than that bookcase, is (as I have just explained) so far as I can see, not *logically* dependent upon any mental fact; it *might* have been a fact, even if there had been no mental facts. But it certainly is *causally* dependent on many mental facts: my body *would* not have been here unless I had been conscious in various ways in the past; and the mantelpiece and the bookcase certainly *would* not have existed, unless other men had been conscious too.

But with regard to two of the facts, which I gave as instances of physical facts, namely the fact that the earth has existed for many years past, and the fact that the moon has for many years past been nearer to the earth than to the sun, I hold that there is no good reason to suppose that these are *causally* dependent upon any mental fact. So far as I can see, there is no reason to suppose that there is any mental fact of which it could be truly said: unless this fact had been a fact, the earth would not have existed for many years past. And in holding this, again, I think I differ from some philosophers. I differ, for instance, from those who have held that all material things were created by God, and that they had good reasons for supposing this.

III. I have just explained that I differ from those philosophers who have held that there is good reason to suppose that all material things were created by God. And it is, I think, an important point in my position, which should be mentioned, that I differ also from all philosophers who have held that there is good reason to suppose that there is a God at all, whether or not they have held it likely that he created all material things.

And similarly, whereas some philosophers have held that there is good reason to suppose that we, human beings, shall continue to exist and to be conscious after the death of our bodies, I hold that there is no good reason to suppose this.

IV. I now come to a point of a very different order.

As I have explained under I, I am not at all sceptical as to the *truth* of such propositions as 'The earth has existed for many years past', 'Many human bodies have each lived for many years upon it', i.e., propositions which assert the existence of material things: on the contrary, I hold that we all know, with certainty, many such propositions to be true. But I am very sceptical as to what, in certain respects, the correct *analysis* of such propositions is. And this is a matter as to which I think I differ from many philosophers. Many seem to hold that there is no doubt at all as to their *analysis*, nor, therefore, as to the analysis of the proposition 'Material things have existed', in certain respects in which I hold that the analysis of the propositions in question is extremely doubtful; and some of them, as we have seen, while holding that there is no doubt as to their *analysis*, seem to have doubted whether any such propositions are *true*. I, on the other hand, while holding that there is no doubt whatever that many such propositions are wholly true, hold also that no philosopher, hitherto, has succeeded in suggesting an analysis of them, as regards certain important points, which comes anywhere near to being certainly true.

It seems to me quite evident that the question how propositions of the type I have just given are to be analysed, depends on the question how propositions of another and simpler type are to be analysed. I know, at present, that I am perceiving a human hand, a pen, a sheet of paper, etc.; and it seems to me that I cannot know how the proposition 'Material things exist' is to be analysed, until I know how, in certain respects, these simpler propositions are to be analysed. But even these are not simple enough. It seems to me quite evident that my knowledge that I am now perceiving a human hand is a deduction from a pair of propositions simpler still – propositions which I can only express in the form 'I am perceiving *this*' and '*This* is a human hand'. It is the analysis of propositions of the latter kind which seems to me to present such great difficulties, while nevertheless the whole question as to the *nature* of material things obviously depends upon their analysis. It seems to me a surprising thing that so few philosophers, while saying a great deal as to what material things *are* and as to what it is to perceive them, have attempted to give a clear account as to what precisely they suppose themselves to *know* (or to *judge*, in case they have held that we don't *know* any such propositions to be true, or even that no such propositions *are* true) when they know or judge such things as 'This is a hand', 'That is the sun', 'This is a dog', etc., etc., etc.

Two things only seem to me to be quite certain about the analysis of such propositions (and even with regard to these I am afraid some philosophers would differ from me) namely that whenever I know, or judge, such a proposition to be true, (1) there is always some *sense-datum* about which the proposition in question is a proposition – some sense-datum which is *a* subject (and, in a certain sense, the principal or ultimate subject) of the proposition in question, and (2) that, nevertheless, *what* I am knowing or judging to be true about this sense-datum is not (in general) that it is *itself* a hand, or a dog, or the sun, etc., etc., as the case may be.

Some philosophers have I think doubted whether there are any such things as other philosophers have meant by 'sense-data' or 'sensa'. And I think it is quite possible that some philosophers (including myself, in the past) have used these terms in senses such that it is really doubtful whether there are any such things. But there is no doubt at all that there are sense-data, in the sense in which I am now using that term. I am at present seeing a great number of them, and feeling others. And in order to point out to the reader what sort of things I mean by sense-data, I need only ask him to look at his own right hand. If he does this he will be able to pick out something (and, unless he is seeing double, *only* one thing) with regard to which he will see that it is, at first sight, a natural view to take that that thing is identical, not, indeed, with his whole right hand, but with that part of its surface which he is actually seeing, but will also (on a little reflection) be able to see that it is doubtful whether it can be identical with the part of the surface of his hand in question. Things *of the sort* (in a certain respect) of which this thing is, which he sees in looking at his hand, and with regard to which he can understand how some philosophers should have supposed it to *be* the part of the surface of his hand which he is seeing, while others have supposed that it can't be, are what I mean by 'sense-data'. I therefore define the term in such a way that it is an open question whether the sense-datum which I now see in looking at my hand and which is a sense-datum of my hand is or is not identical with that part of its surface which I am now actually seeing.

That what I know, with regard to this sense-datum, when I know 'This is a human hand', is not that it is *itself* a human hand, seems to me certain because I know that my hand has many parts (e.g., its other side, and the bones inside it), which are quite certainly *not* parts of this sense-datum.

I think it certain, therefore, that the analysis of the proposition 'This is a human hand' is, roughly at least, of the form 'There is a thing, and only one thing, of which it is true both that it is a human hand and that *this surface* is a part of its surface'. In other words, to put my view in terms of the phrase 'theory of representative perception', I hold it to be quite certain that I do not *directly* perceive *my hand*; and that when I am said (as I may be correctly said) to 'perceive' it, that I 'perceive' it means that I perceive (in a different and more fundamental sense) something which is (in a suitable sense) *representative* of it, namely, a certain part of its surface.

This is all that I hold to be *certain* about the analysis of the proposition 'This is a human hand'. We have seen that it includes in its analysis a proposition of the form 'This is part of the surface of a human hand' (where 'This', of course, has a different meaning from that which it has in the original proposition which has now been analysed). But this proposition also is undoubtedly a proposition about the sense-datum, which I am seeing, which is a sense-datum *of* my hand. And hence the further question arises: *What*, when I know *'This is part of the surface of* a human hand', am I knowing about the sense-datum in question? Am I, in this case, really knowing about the sense-datum in question that it *itself* is part of the surface of a human hand? Or, just as we found in the case of 'This is a human hand', that what I was knowing about the sense-datum was certainly not that it *itself* was a human hand, so, is it perhaps the case, with this new proposition, that even here I am not knowing, with regard to the sense-datum, that it is *itself* part of the surface of a hand? And, if so, what is it that I am knowing about the sense-datum itself?

This is the question to which, as it seems to me, no philosopher has hitherto suggested an answer which comes anywhere near to being *certainly* true.

There seem to me to be three, and only three, alternative types of answer possible; and to any answer yet suggested, of any of these types, there seem to me to be very grave objections.

(1) Of the first type, there is but one answer: namely, that in this case what I am knowing really is that the sense-datum *itself* is part of the surface of a human hand. In other words that, though I don't perceive *my hand* directly, I do *directly* perceive part of its surface; that the sense-datum itself *is* this part of its surface and not merely something which (in a sense yet to be determined) 'represents' this part of its surface; and that hence the sense in which I 'perceive' this part of the surface of my hand, is not in its turn a sense which needs to be defined by reference to yet a third more ultimate sense of 'perceive', which is the only one in which perception is direct, namely that in which I perceive the sense-datum.

If this view is true (as I think it may just possibly be), it seems to me certain that we must abandon a view which has been held to be certainly true by most philosophers, namely the view that our sense-data always really have the qualities which they sensibly appear to us to have. For I know that if another man were looking through a microscope at the same surface which I am seeing with the naked eye, the sense-datum which he saw would sensibly appear to him to have qualities very different from and incompatible with those which my sense-datum sensibly appears to me to have: and yet, if my sense-datum is identical with the surface we are both of us seeing, his must be identical with it also. My sense-datum can, therefore, be identical with this surface only on condition that it is identical with his sense-datum; and, since his sense-datum sensibly appears to him to have qualities incompatible with those which mine sensibly appears to me to have, his sense-datum can be identical with mine only on condition that the sense-datum in question either has not got the qualities which it sensibly appears to me to have, or has not got those which it sensibly appears to him to have.

130

I do not, however, think that this is a fatal objection to this first type of view. A far more serious objection seems to me to be that, when we see a thing double (have what is called 'a double image' of it), we certainly have *two* sense-data each of which is *of* the surface seen, and which cannot therefore both be identical with it; and that yet it seems as if, if any sense-datum is ever identical with the surface *of* which it is a sense-datum, each of these so-called 'images' must be so. It looks, therefore, as if every sense-datum is, after all, only 'representative' of the surface, *of* which it is a sense-datum.

(2) But, if so, what relation has it to the surface in question? This second type of view is one which holds that when I know 'This is part of the surface of a human hand', what I am knowing with regard to the sense-datum which is *of* that surface, is, *not* that it is *itself* part of the surface of a human hand, but something of the following kind. There is, it says, *some* relation, R, such that what I am knowing with regard to the sense-datum is either 'There is one thing and only one thing, of which it is true both that it is a part of the surface of a human hand, and that it has R to this sense-datum', or else 'There are a set of things, of which it is true both that that set, taken collectively, *are* part of the surface of a human hand, and also that each member of the set has R to this sense-datum, and that nothing which is not a member of the set has R to it'.

Obviously, in the case of this second type, many different views are possible, differing according to the view they take as to what the relation R is. But there is only one of them, which seems to me to have any plausibility; namely that which holds that R is an ultimate and unanalysable relation, which might be expressed by saying that '*x*R*y*' means the same as '*y* is an appearance or manifestation of *x*'. I.e. the analysis which this answer would give of 'This is part of the surface of a human hand' would be 'There is one and only one thing of which it is true both that it is part of the surface of a human hand, and that this sense-datum is an appearance or manifestation of it'.

To this view also there seem to me to be very grave objections, chiefly drawn from a consideration of the questions how we can possibly *know* with regard to any of our sense-data that there is one thing and one thing only which has to them such a supposed ultimate relation; and how, if we do, we can possibly *know* anything further about such things, e.g., of what size or shape they are.

(3) The third type of answer, which seems to me to be the only possible alternative if (1) and (2) are rejected, is the type of answer which J.S. Mill seems to have been implying to be the true one when he said that material things are 'permanent possibilities of sensation'. He seems to have thought that when I know such a fact as 'This is part of the surface of a human hand', what I am knowing with regard to the sense-datum which is the principal subject of that fact, is not that it is itself part of the surface of a human hand, nor yet, with regard to any relation, that *the* thing which has to it that relation is part of the surface of a human hand, but a whole set of hypothetical facts each of which is a fact of the form 'If *these* conditions had been fulfilled, I should have been perceiving a sense-datum intrinsically related to *this* sense-datum in *this* way', 'If *these* (other) conditions had been fulfilled, I should have been perceiving a sense-datum intrinsically related to *this* sense-datum in *this* (other) way', etc., etc.

With regard to this third type of view as to the analysis of propositions of the kind we are considering, it seems to me, again, just *possible* that it is a true one; but to hold (as Mill himself and others seems to have held) that it is *certainly*, or nearly certainly, true, seems to me as great a mistake, as to hold with regard either to (1) or to (2), that they are *certainly*, or nearly certainly, true. There seem to me to be very grave objections to it; in particular the three, (*a*) that though, in general, when I know such a fact as 'This is a hand', I certainly do know some hypothetical facts of the form 'If *these* conditions had been fulfilled, I should have been perceiving a sense-datum of *this* kind, which would have been a sense-datum of the same surface of which *this* is a sense-datum', it seems doubtful whether any conditions with regard to which I know this are not themselves conditions of the form 'If this and that *material thing* had been in those positions and conditions . . .', (*b*) that it seems again very doubtful whether there is any intrinsic relation, such that my knowledge that (under *these* conditions) I should have been perceiving a sense-datum of *this* kind, which would have been a sense-datum of the same surface of which *this* is a sense-datum, is equivalent to a knowledge, with regard to that relation, that I should, under those conditions, have been perceiving a sense-datum related by it to *this* sense-datum, and (c) that, if it were true, the sense in which a material surface is 'round' or 'square', would necessarily be utterly different from that in which our sense-data sensibly appear to us to be 'round' or 'square'.

V. Just as I hold that the proposition 'There are and have been material things' is quite certainly true, but that the question how this proposition is to be analysed is one to which no answer that has been hitherto given is anywhere near certainly true; so I hold that the proposition 'There are and have been many Selves' is quite certainly true, but that here again all the analyses of this proposition that have been suggested by philosophers are highly doubtful.

That I am now perceiving many different sense-data, and that I have at many times in the past perceived many different sense-data, I know for certain – that is to say, I know that there are mental facts of class (β), connected in a way which it is proper to express by saying that they are all of them facts about *me*; but how this kind of connexion is to be analysed, I do not know for certain, nor do I think that any other philosopher knows with any approach to certainty. Just as in the case of the proposition 'This is part of the surface of a human hand', there are several extremely different views as to its analysis, each of which seems to me *possible*, but none nearly certain, so also in the case of the proposition 'This, that and that sense-datum are all at present being perceived by *me*', and still more so in the case of the proposition '*I* am now perceiving this sense-datum, and *I* have in the past perceived sense-data of these other kinds'. Of the *truth* of these propositions there seems to me to be no doubt, but as to what is the correct analysis of them there seems to me to be the gravest doubt – the true analysis may, for instance, *possibly* be quite as paradoxical as is the third view given above under IV as to the analysis of 'This is part of the surface of a human hand'; but whether it *is* as paradoxical as this seems to me to be quite as doubtful as in that case. Many philosophers, on the other hand, seem to me to have assumed that there is little or no doubt as to the correct analysis of such propositions; and many of these, just reversing my position, have also held that the propositions themselves are not true.

8

IS EXISTENCE A PREDICATE?

I am not at all clear as to the meaning of this question. Mr Kneale says that existence is not a predicate. But what does he mean by the words 'Existence is not a predicate'?

In his second paragraph, he says that the word 'predicate' has two different senses, a logical sense and a grammatical one. If so, it would follow that the words 'Existence is not a predicate' may have two different meanings, according as the person who uses them is using 'predicate' in the logical or the grammatical sense. And I think it is clear that he means us to understand that when *he* says 'Existence is not a predicate', he is using 'predicate' in the logical sense, and not in the grammatical one. I think his view is that if anyone were to say 'Existence is a predicate', using 'predicate' in the grammatical sense, such a person would be perfectly right: I think he holds that existence really is a predicate in the grammatical sense. But, whether he holds this or not, I think it is clear that he does not wish to discuss the question whether it is or is not a predicate in the grammatical sense, but solely the question whether it is so in the logical one.

Now I think it is worth noticing that if we assert 'Existence is a predicate', using 'predicate' in the grammatical sense, our proposition is a proposition about certain *words*, to the effect that they are often used in a certain way; but not, curiously enough, about the word 'existence' itself. It is a proposition to the effect that the word 'exists' and other fine parts of the verb 'to exist', such as 'existed', 'will exist' or 'exist' (in the plural) are often the predicates (in some grammatical sense) of sentences in which

Originally published in *Aristotelian Society Supplementary Volume 15* (1936), pp. 175–88. Moore's paper is a reply to a paper in the same volume by W. Kneale (pp. 154–74).

they occur; but nobody means to say that the word 'existence' itself is often the predicate of sentences in which it occurs. And I think Mr Kneale implies that, similarly, the proposition which anyone would express, if he asserted 'Existence is a predicate', using 'predicate' in the logical sense, is again equivalent to a proposition, *not* about the word 'existence' itself, but about the word 'exists' and other finite parts of the verb 'to exist'. He implies that 'Existence is a predicate', with this use of 'predicate', is equivalent to the proposition that the word 'exists', and other finite parts of the verb, often do *'stand for* a predicate in the logical sense'. It would appear, therefore, that one difference between the two different meanings of 'Existence is a predicate' is as follows: namely that, if a person who says these words is using 'predicate' in the grammatical sense, he is *not* saying that the words, 'exists', etc., ever *'stand for* a predicate in the logical sense'; whereas, if he is using 'predicate' in the logical sense, he is saying that they do (often, at least) *'stand for* a predicate in the logical sense'. What Mr Kneale himself means by 'Existence is not a predicate' is apparently some proposition which he would express by saying: 'The words, "exists", etc., never *stand for* a predicate in the logical sense'.

What I am not clear about is as to what is meant by saying of a particular word (or particular phrase) in a particular sentence that it 'stands for a predicate in the logical sense'; nor, therefore, as to what is meant by saying of another particular word in another particular sentence that it does *not* 'stand for a predicate in the logical sense'. Mr Kneale does, indeed, tell us that a 'predicate in the logical sense' is the same as 'an attribute'; but, though I think that the meaning of the word 'attribute' is perhaps a little clearer than that of the phrase 'predicate in the logical sense', it still seems to me far from clear; I do not clearly understand what he would mean by saying that 'exists', etc., do not 'stand for attributes'. But, from examples which he gives, it is, I think, clear that he would say that in the sentence 'This is red' the word 'red', or the phrase 'is red' (I am not clear which), does 'stand for an attribute'; and also that in the sentence 'Tame tigers growl', 'growl' so stands, and in the sentence 'Rajah growls', 'growls' does. It is, therefore, presumably some difference between the way in which 'exists', etc., are used in sentences in which they occur, and the way in which 'is red' (or 'red') and 'growl' and 'growls' are used in these sentences, that

135

he wishes to express by saying that, whereas 'exists', etc., do *not* 'stand for attributes', these words in these sentences do. And if we can find what differences there are between the use of finite parts of the verb 'to exist', and the use of 'is red', 'growl' and 'growls', we may perhaps find what the difference is which he expresses in this way.

I. It will, I think, be best to begin with one particular use of 'exist' – the one, namely, which Mr Kneale illustrates by the example 'Tame tigers exist'. He clearly thinks that there is some very important difference between the way in which 'exist' is used here, and the way in which 'growl' is used in 'Tame tigers growl'; and that it is a difference which does not hold, e.g., between the use of 'scratch' in 'Tame tigers scratch' and the use of 'growl' in 'Tame tigers growl'. He would say that 'scratch' and 'growl' both 'stand for attributes', whereas 'exist' does not; and he would also say that 'Tame tigers exist' is a proposition of a different *form* from 'Tame tigers growl' whereas I think he would say that 'Tame tigers growl' and 'Tame tigers scratch' are *of the same form*. What difference between 'Tame tigers exist' and 'Tame tigers growl' can be the one he has in mind?

(1) That there is a difference between the way in which we use 'exist' in the former sentence and 'growl' in the latter, of a different kind from the difference between our usages of 'scratch' and 'growl' in the two sentences 'Tame tigers scratch' and 'Tame tigers growl', can, I think, be brought out in the following way.

The sentence 'Tame tigers growl' seems to me to be ambiguous. So far as I can see, it might mean 'All tame tigers growl', or it might mean merely 'Most tame tigers growl', or it might mean merely 'Some tame tigers growl'. Each of these three sentences has a clear meaning, and the meaning of each is clearly different from that of either of the two others. Of each of them, however, it is true that the proposition which it expresses is one which cannot possibly be true, unless some tame tigers do growl. And hence I think we can say of 'Tame tigers growl' that, whichever sense it is used in, it means something which cannot possibly be true unless some tame tigers do growl. Similarly I think it is clear that 'Tame tigers exist' means something which cannot possibly be true unless some tame tigers do exist. But I do not think that there is any ambiguity in 'Tame tigers exist' corresponding to that which I have pointed out in 'Tame tigers growl'. So far as I can see 'Tame tigers exist' and 'Some tame tigers exist' are merely two different ways of expressing exactly the same proposition. That is to say, it is not true that 'Tame tigers exist', might mean 'All tame tigers exist', or 'Most tame tigers exist', instead of merely 'Some tame tigers exist'. It always means just 'Some tame tigers exist', and nothing else whatever. I have said it is never used to mean 'All tame tigers exist', or 'Most tame tigers exist'; but I hope it will strike everyone that there is something queer about this proposition. It seems to imply that 'All tame tigers exist' and 'Most tame tigers exist' have a clear meaning, just as have 'All tame tigers growl' and 'Most tame tigers growl'; and that it is just an accident that we do not happen ever to use 'Tame tigers exist' to express either of those two meanings instead of the meaning 'Some tame tigers exist', whereas we do sometimes use 'Tame tigers growl' to mean 'All tame tigers growl' or 'Most tame tigers growl', instead of merely 'Some tame tigers growl'. But is this in fact the case? Have 'All tame tigers exist' and 'Most tame tigers exist' any meaning at all? Certainly they have not a clear meaning, as have 'All tame tigers growl' and 'Most tame tigers growl'. They are puzzling expressions, which certainly do not carry their meaning, if they have any, on the face of them. That this is so indicates, I think, that there is some important difference between the usage of 'exist' with which we are concerned, and the usage of such words as 'growl' or 'scratch'; but it does not make clear just what the difference is.

I think this can be made clear by comparing the expressions 'Some tame tigers don't growl' and 'Some tame tigers don't exist'. The former, whether true or false, has a perfectly clear meaning – a meaning just as clear as that of 'Some tame tigers do growl'; and it is perfectly clear that both propositions might be true together. But with 'Some tame tigers don't exist' the case is different. 'Some tame tigers exist' has a perfectly clear meaning: it just means 'There are some tame tigers'. But the meaning of 'Some tame tigers don't exist', if any, is certainly not equally clear. It is another queer and puzzling expression. Has it any meaning at all? And, if so, what meaning? If it has any, it would appear that it must mean the same as: 'There are some tame tigers, which don't exist'. But has *this* any meaning? And if so, what? Is it possible that there should be any tame tigers which

137

don't exist? I think the answer is that, if in the sentence 'Some tame tigers don't exist' you are using 'exist' with the same meaning as in 'Some tame tigers exist', then the former sentence as a whole has no meaning at all – it is pure nonsense. A meaning can, of course, be given to 'Some tame tigers don't exist'; but this can only be done if 'exist' is used in a different way from that in which it is used in 'Some tame tigers exist'. And, if this is so, it will follow that 'All tame tigers exist' and Most tame tigers exist', also have no meaning at all, if you are using 'exist' in the sense with which we are concerned. For 'All tame tigers growl' is equivalent to the conjunction 'Some tame tigers growl, and there is no tame tiger which does not growl'; and this has a meaning, because 'There is at least one tame tiger which does not growl' has one. If, therefore, 'There is at least one tame tiger which does not exist' has no meaning, it will follow that 'All tame tigers exist' also has none; because 'There is no tame tiger which does not exist' will have none, if 'There is a tame tiger which does not exist' has none. Similarly 'Most tame tigers growl' is equivalent to the conjunction 'Some tame tigers growl, and the number of those (if any) which do not growl is smaller than that of those which do' – a statement which has a meaning only because 'There are tame tigers which do not growl' has one. If, therefore, 'There are tame tigers which don't exist' has no meaning, it will follow that 'Most tame tigers exist' will also have none. I think, therefore, we can say that one important difference between the use of 'growl' in 'Some tame tigers growl' and the use of 'exist' in 'Some tame tigers exist', is that if in the former case we insert 'do not' before 'growl', without changing the meaning of 'growl', we get a sentence which is significant, whereas if, in the latter, we insert 'do not' before 'exist' without changing the meaning of 'exist', we get a sentence which has no meaning whatever; and I think we can also say that this fact explains why, with the given meaning of 'growl', 'All tame tigers growl' and 'Most tame tigers growl' are both significant, whereas, with the given meaning of 'exist', 'All tame tigers exist' and 'Most tame tigers exist' are utterly meaningless. And if by the statement that 'growl', in this usage, 'stands for an attribute', whereas 'exist', in this usage, does not, part of what is meant is that there is this difference between them, then I should agree that 'exist' in this usage, does not 'stand for an attribute'.

But is it really true that if, in the sentence 'Some tame tigers exist', we insert 'do not' before 'exist', without changing the meaning of 'exist', we get a sentence which has no meaning whatever? I have admitted that a meaning *can* be given to 'Some tame tigers do not exist'; and it may, perhaps, be contended by some people that the meaning which 'exist' has in this sentence, where it is significant, *is* precisely the same as that which it has in 'Some tame tigers exist'. I cannot show the contrary as clearly as I should like to be able to do; but I will do my best.

The meaning which such an expression as 'Some tame tigers do not exist' sometimes does have, is that which it has when it is used to mean the same as 'Some tame tigers are imaginary' or 'Some tame tigers are not real tigers'. That 'Some tame tigers are imaginary' may really express a proposition, whether true or false, cannot I think be denied. If, for instance, two different stories have been written, each of which is about a different imaginary tame tiger, it will follow that there are at least two imaginary tame tigers; and it cannot be denied that the sentence 'Two different tame tigers occur in fiction' is significant, though I have not the least idea whether what it means is true or false. I know that at least one unicorn occurs in fiction, because one occurs in *Alice Through the Looking Glass*; and it follows that there is at least one imaginary unicorn, and therefore (in a sense) at least one unicorn which does not exist and never did. Again, if it should happen that at the present moment two different people are each having an hallucination of a different tame tiger, it will follow that there are at the present moment two different imaginary tame tigers; and the statement that two such hallucinations are occurring now is certainly significant, though it may very likely be false. The sentence 'There are some tame tigers which do not exist' is, therefore, certainly significant, if it means only that there are some imaginary tigers, in either of the two senses which I have tried to point out. But what it means is that either some real people have written stories about imaginary tigers, or are having or have recently had hallucinations of tame tigers, or, perhaps, are dreaming or have dreamed of particular tame tigers. If nothing of this sort has happened or is happening to anybody, then there are no imaginary tame tigers. But if 'Some tame tigers do not exist' means all this, is it not clear that 'exist' has not, in this sentence, the same comparatively simple meaning as it has in 'Some tame tigers exist' or in 'No tame tigers exist'? Is it not clear that 'Some tame tigers do not exist', if it means all this, is not related to 'Some tame tigers exist', in the same simple way in which 'Some tame tigers do not grow!' is related to 'Some tame tigers growl'?

(2) There is, I think, also another important difference between this use of 'exist' and the use of 'growl', which may be brought out as follows.

Mr Russell has said[1] 'When we say "some men are Greeks", that means that the propositional function "x is a man and a Greek" is sometimes true'; and has explained just previously that by 'sometimes true' he means 'true in at least one instance'. With this explanation of what he means by 'sometimes true', I do not think that his statement as to the meaning of 'Some men are Greeks' is strictly correct; since I think that the use of the plural implies that 'x is a man and a Greek' is true in *more* than one instance, that is to say, in at least two instances. Let us suppose that he would accept this correction and say that what 'Some men are Greeks' means is not, strictly, that 'x is a man and a Greek' is true in at least one instance, but that it is true in at least two. He has further implied[2] that to say of a propositional function that it is true in at least two instances is the same thing as to say that at least two 'values' of it are true; and he has told us[3] that the 'values' of propositional functions are propositions. With these explanations, his view would appear to be that what 'Some men are Greeks' means is that at least two propositions, related to the propositional function 'x is a man and a Greek' in some way which he expresses by saying that they are 'values' of that function, are true. Now I cannot imagine what sort of propositions would be 'values' of 'x is a man and a Greek', except propositions of the following sort. There are propositions which we express by pointing at (or indicating in some other way) an object which we are seeing (or perceiving in some other way) and uttering the words 'This is a so and so' (or equivalent words in some other language). Let us suppose that the kind of propositions which would be 'values' of 'x is a man and a Greek' would be propositions of this sort, where the words used were '*This* is a man and a Greek'. Mr Russell's doctrine would then be that 'Some men are Greeks' means that at least two different *true* propositions of this sort could be made: that there must have been at least two different objects at which a man might have pointed and said truly 'This is a man and a Greek'. And, if this is his doctrine, it seems to me to be true. Surely 'Some men are Greeks' cannot possibly be true, unless there are at least two different objects, in the case of each of which a man might have seen it, pointed at it, and said with truth 'This is a man and a Greek'?

On this view 'Some tame tigers growl' means that at least two values of 'x is a tame tiger and growls' are true; and this means that there are at least two objects, in the case of each of which a man might have seen it, pointed at it, and said with truth 'This is a tame tiger and growls'. Now in this sentence 'This is a tame tiger and growls' it is clear that, except for the difference consisting in the fact that 'growls' is in the singular and 'growl' in the plural, the word 'growls' has the same meaning as has the word 'growl' in 'Some tame tigers growl'. We can say, then, that one feature about our use of 'growl' is that, if we consider a 'value' of the propositional function which is such that 'Some tame tigers growl' means that at least two values of it are true, then the singular of 'growl' can be used, with the same meaning, in the expression of such a value. And perhaps this may be part of what is meant by saying that 'growl' 'stands for an attribute'. It may perhaps be meant that to point at an object which you are seeing, and utter the words 'This object growls', is significant – that the words and gesture together with the object pointed at do really express a proposition, true or false.

But now consider 'Some tame tigers exist': is the same true of 'exist' in this sentence? Mr Russell says[4] 'We say that "men exist" or "a man exists" if the propositional function "x is human" is sometimes true'. And he goes on to protest that though the proposition 'Socrates is a man' is '*equivalent*' to 'Socrates is human', it 'is not the very same proposition'. For my part I doubt whether we ever do use 'is human' in such a way that 'Socrates is human' is equivalent to 'Socrates is a man'. I think Mr Russell is using 'is human' in a very special sense, in which nobody but he has ever used it, and that the only way of explaining how he is using it is to say that he is using it to mean precisely that which we ordinarily express by 'is a human being'. If this is so, and if we are allowed to distinguish, as I think we ought, between 'men exist' and 'a man exists', and to say that 'men exist' means, *not* '"x is a human being" is true in at least one instance', but '"x is a human being" is true in at least two instances', then I think his doctrine is true; provided, again,

141

that we are allowed to regard the sort of propositions which we express, e.g., by pointing at an object which we are seeing, and saying the words 'This is a human being', as being those which are values of 'x is a human being'. Surely 'Human beings exist' can be true if, and only if, there are at least two objects, such that, if a man were to see and point to either of them and utter the words 'This is a human being', he would be expressing a true proposition by what he did?

Now, if this is right, we see at once that the use of 'growl' in 'Some tame tigers growl' differs from that of 'exist' in 'Some tame tigers exist', in the respect that, while the first asserts that more than one value of 'x is a tame tiger *and growls*' is true, the second asserts, *not* that more than one value of 'x is a tame tiger *and exists*' is true, but merely that more than one value of 'x is a tame tiger' is true. Owing to this view of his that 'Some tame tigers exist' means the same as 'Some values of the propositional function "x is a tame tiger" are true', Mr Russell has been led to say:[5] 'Existence is essentially a property of a propositional function' and 'It is of propositional functions that you can assert or deny existence'[6] and that it is a fallacy to transfer 'to the individual that satisfies a propositional function a predicate which only applies to a propositional function';[7] so that, according to him, existence is, after all, in this usage, a 'property' or 'predicate', though not a property of individuals, but only of propositional functions! I think this is a mistake on his part. Even if it is true that 'Some tame tigers exist' means the same as 'Some values of "x is a tame tiger" are true' it does not follow, I think, that we can say that 'exist' means the same as 'is sometimes true', and 'some tame tigers' the same as 'x is a tame tiger': indeed, I think it is clear that we cannot say this; for certainly '"x is a tame tiger" exists' would not mean the same as 'Some tame tigers exist'. But what I think does follow from this interpretation of 'Some tame tigers exist' is another thing which Mr Russell himself holds, namely, that if a proposition which you express by pointing at something which you see and saying 'This is a tame tiger', is a 'value' of 'x is a tame tiger', then if, pointing at the same thing, you were to say the words 'This exists', and, if you were using 'exists' merely as the singular of 'exist' in the sense in which it is used in 'Some tame tigers exist', what you did would not express a proposition at all, but would be absolutely meaningless. That is to say, there is between

'Some tame tigers growl' and 'Some tame tigers exist', not only the difference that, whereas the first asserts that some values of 'x is a tame tiger *and growls*' are true, the second asserts only that some values of 'x is a tame tiger' are true; there is also the further and more important difference that, why the second asserts only that some values of 'x is a tame tiger' are true, is not because we happen to use 'This is a tame tiger' to mean the same as 'This is a tame tiger *and exists*', but because by pointing and saying 'This *exists*' we should express *no proposition at all*, so long as we were using 'exists' as the singular of the use of 'exist' with which we are concerned; whereas by pointing and saying 'This growls' we certainly should be expressing a proposition, even though we were using 'growls' merely as the singular of 'growl' with the meaning it has in 'Some tame tigers growl'. 'This is a tame tiger, *and exists*' would be not tautologous but meaningless.

This, I think, gives us a second true thing, which may perhaps be sometimes part of what is meant by saying that 'exist', in this usage, 'does not stand for an attribute'.

II. So far I have been solely concerned with the use of 'exist' in such sentences as 'Some tame tigers exist', and have tried to point out two differences between its use here and the use of 'growl' in 'Some tame tigers growl', which may perhaps be part of what is meant by saying that 'exist', in this usage, does not 'stand for an attribute', whereas 'growl' does. But I cannot help thinking that there are other significant uses of 'exists'; and I want, in particular, to try to point out two such, and to consider what, if anything, true can be meant by saying that in these usages also 'exists' does not 'stand for an attribute'.

(1) I have just said that to point at a thing which you see and say 'This exists' seems to me to be meaningless, if 'exists' is the singular of 'exist' in the sense in which it is used in 'Tame tigers exist'; but I cannot help thinking that in the case of anything to point at which and say 'This is a tame tiger' is significant, it is also significant to point at it and say 'This exists', *in some sense or other*. My reason for thinking this is that it seems to me that you can clearly say *with truth* of any such object 'This *might* not have existed', 'It is *logically possible* that this should not have existed'; and I do not see how it is possible that 'This might not have existed' should be true, unless 'This does in fact exist' is also

true, and therefore the words 'This exists' significant. If the sentence (a) 'It is logically possible that this should not have existed' expresses a true proposition, it seems to follow that the sentence (b) 'This does not exist', where 'this' refers to the same object to which it refers in (a), must express a proposition, though a false one; and, if so, the sentence 'This exists', which expresses its contradictory, must also be significant, and the proposition it expresses true. Now I cannot help thinking that in every case in which I point at an object which I am perceiving and say significantly 'This is a tame tiger', 'This is a book', etc., my proposition is in fact a proposition about some sense-datum, or some set of sense-data, which I am perceiving; and that part of what I am saying is that this sense-datum (or these sense-data) is 'of' a physical object. That is to say, I am saying of some sense-datum that it is 'of' a physical object in the sense in which it is true to say of an after-image which I see with my eyes shut that it is *not* 'of' a physical object. And I think that part, at least, of what we mean by 'This exists', where we are using 'this' in the same way as when we point and say 'This is a book', is 'This sense-datum is *of* a physical object', which seems to me to be certainly significant. If 'of' here stood for a relation, we might say that 'This is a book' was short for 'The thing which this sense-datum is "of" is a book', and therefore 'This exists' short for 'The thing which this sense-datum is "of" exists'; in which case the use of 'exists' in question would be that which in *Principia Mathematica* is symbolised by 'E!' and there would be the same sort of reason for saying that it does not 'stand for an attribute' as in the case of the 'exist' which occurs in 'Some tame tigers exist'. I do not believe, however, that 'of' here does stand for a relation, nor therefore that 'This' in 'This is a book' can be said to be short for the sort of phrase which Russell has called 'a definite description'; and, this being so, I am not at all clear as to what that is true could be meant by saying that 'exists', in this usage, 'does not stand for an attribute'. The only suggestion I can make is this. It seems to me that 'This exists' (in this usage) always forms part of what is asserted by 'This is a book', 'This is red', etc., etc., where 'this' is used in the manner with which we are now concerned; and possibly part of what is meant by saying that 'is a book', 'is red', etc., 'stand for attributes', is that *part but not the whole* of what is asserted by any 'value' of '*x* is a book', '*x* is red', etc., is 'This exists'. In that case 'exists' in 'This exists' would not 'stand for an attribute', solely because the whole of what it asserts, and not merely a part, is 'This exists'.

(2) Another reason why 'This exists', where 'this' is used as it is in 'This is a book', seems to me to be significant, is because it seems to me not only significant to say of a given sense-datum 'This *is* of a physical object' or 'This is *not* of a physical object', but also to say of the sense-datum itself 'This exists'. If this is so, we have to do with a new sense of 'exists', since certainly no part of the meaning of such an assertion with regard to a sense-datum is that it, or any other sense-datum, is 'of' a physical object. But my reason for holding that it is significant for me to say, for instance, of an after-image which I am seeing with my eyes shut, 'This exists', is similar to that which I gave in the last case: namely that it seems to me that in the case of every sense-datum which anyone ever perceives, the person in question could always say with truth of the sense-datum in question 'This might not have existed'; and I cannot see how this could be true, unless the proposition 'This does in fact exist' is also true, and therefore the words 'This exists' significant. That 'This exists' has any meaning in such cases, where, as Mr Russell would say, though falsely, we are using 'this' as a 'proper name' for something with which we are 'acquainted', is, I know, disputed; my view that it has, involves, I am bound to admit, the curious consequence that 'This exists', when used in this way, is always true, and 'This does not exist' always false; and I have little to say in its favour except that it seems to me so plainly true that, in the case of every sense-datum I have, it is logically possible that the sense-datum in question should not have existed – that there should simply have been no such thing. If, for instance, I am seeing a bright after-image with my eyes shut, it seems to me quite plainly conceivable that I should have had instead, at that moment, a uniform black field, such as I often have with my eyes shut; and, if I had had such a field, then that particular bright after-image simply would not have existed.

But, supposing 'This exists', in this usage, has a meaning, why should we not say that 'exists' here 'stands for an attribute'? I can suggest no reason why we should not, except the same which I suggested in the last case.

NOTES

1 B. Russell, *Introduction to Mathematical Philosophy* (George Allen & Unwin, London: 1919), p.159.
2 ibid. p.158.
3 ibid. p.156.
4 ibid. pp.171–2.
5 B. Russell, 'The Philosophy of Logical Atomism III', *Monist* 29 (1919), p.125. Reprinted in *Logic and Knowledge*, ed. R. Marsh (Allen & Unwin, London: 1956), p.232.
6 ibid. p.196 (*Logic and Knowledge*, p.233).
7 ibid. p.197 (*Logic and Knowledge*, p.233).

9

PROOF OF AN EXTERNAL WORLD

In the Preface to the second edition of Kant's *Critique of Pure Reason* some words occur, which, in Professor Kemp Smith's translation, are rendered as follows:

> It still remains a scandal to philosophy . . . that the existence of things outside of us . . . must be accepted merely on *faith*, and that, if anyone thinks good to doubt their existence, we are unable to counter his doubts by any satisfactory proof.*

It seems clear from these words that Kant thought it a matter of some importance to give a proof of 'the existence of things outside of us' or perhaps rather (for it seems to me possible that the force of the German words is better rendered in this way) of 'the existence of *the* things outside of us'; for had he not thought it important that a proof should be given, he would scarcely have called it a 'scandal' that no proof had been given. And it seems clear also that he thought that the giving of such a proof was a task which fell properly within the province of philosophy; for, if it did not, the fact that no proof had been given could not possibly be a scandal to *philosophy*.

Now, even if Kant was mistaken in both of these two opinions, there seems to me to be no doubt whatever that it is a matter of some importance and also a matter which falls

---

* B xxxix, note: Kemp Smith, p.34. The German words are 'so bleibt es immer ein Skandal der Philosophie . . ., das Dasein der Dinge ausser uns . . ., bloss auf *Glauben* annehmen zu müssen, und wenn es jemand einfällt es zu bezweifeln, ihm keinen genugtuenden Beweis entgegenstellen zu können'.

Originally published in *Proceedings of the British Academy* 25 (1939), pp.273–300.

properly within the province of philosophy, to discuss the question what sort of proof, if any, can be given of 'the existence of things outside of us'. And to discuss this question was my object when I began to write the present lecture. But I may say at once that, as you will find, I have only, at most, succeeded in saying a very small part of what ought to be said about it.

The words 'it . . . remains a scandal to philosophy . . . that we are unable . . .' would, taken strictly, imply that, at the moment at which he wrote them, Kant himself was unable to produce a satisfactory proof of the point in question. But I think it is unquestionable that Kant himself did not think that he personally was at the time unable to produce such a proof. On the contrary, in the immediately preceding sentence, he has declared that he has, in the second edition of his *Critique*, to which he is now writing the Preface, given a 'rigorous proof' of this very thing; and has added that he believes this proof of his to be 'the only possible proof'. It is true that in this preceding sentence he does not describe the proof which he has given as a proof of 'the existence of things outside of us' or of 'the existence of the things outside of us', but describes it instead as a proof of 'the objective reality of outer intuition'. But the context leaves no doubt that he is using these two phrases, 'the objective reality of outer intuition' and 'the existence of things (*or* 'the things') outside of us', in such a way that whatever is a proof of the first is also necessarily a proof of the second. We must, therefore, suppose that when he speaks as if *we* are unable to give a satisfactory proof, he does not mean to say that he himself, as well as others, is *at the moment* unable; but rather that, until he discovered the proof which he has given, both he himself and everybody else *were* unable. Of course, if he is right in thinking that he has given a satisfactory proof, the state of things which he describes came to an end as soon as his proof was published. As soon as that happened, anyone who read it was able to give a satisfactory proof by simply repeating that which Kant had given, and the 'scandal' to philosophy had been removed once for all.

If, therefore, it were certain that the proof of the point in question given by Kant in the second edition is a satisfactory proof, it would be certain that at least one satisfactory proof can be given; and all that would remain of the question which I said I proposed to discuss would be, firstly, the question as to what *sort* of a proof this of Kant's is, and secondly the question whether (contrary to Kant's own opinion) there may not perhaps be other proofs, of the same or of a different sort, which are also satisfactory. But I think it is by no means certain that Kant's proof is satisfactory. I think it is by no means certain that he did succeed in removing once for all the state of affairs which he considered to be a scandal to philosophy. And I think, therefore, that the question whether it is possible to give *any* satisfactory proof of the point in question still deserves discussion.

But what is the point in question? I think it must be owned that the expression 'things outside of us' is rather an odd expression, and an expression the meaning of which is certainly not perfectly clear. It would have sounded less odd if, instead of 'things outside of us' I had said 'external things', and perhaps also the meaning of this expression would have seemed to be clearer; and I think we make the meaning of 'external things' clearer still if we explain that this phrase has been regularly used by philosophers as short for 'things external to *our minds*'. The fact is that there has been a long philosophical tradition, in accordance with which the three expressions 'external things', 'things external to *us*', and 'things external to *our minds*' have been used as equivalent to one another, and have, each of them, been used as if they needed no explanation. The origin of this usage I do not know. It occurs already in Descartes; and since he uses the expressions as if they needed no explanation, they had presumably been used with the same meaning before. Of the three, it seems to me that the expression 'external to *our minds*' is the clearest, since it at least makes clear that what is meant is not 'external to *our bodies*'; whereas both the other expressions might be taken to mean this: and indeed there has been a good deal of confusion, even among philosophers, as to the relation of the two conceptions 'external things' and 'things external to *our bodies*'. But even the expression 'things external to our minds' seems to me to be far from perfectly clear; and if I am to make really clear what I mean by 'proof of the existence of things outside of us', I cannot do it by merely saying that by 'outside of us' I mean 'external to our minds'.

There is a passage (*Kritik der reinen Vernunft*, A373) in which Kant himself says that the expression 'outside of us' 'carries with it an unavoidable ambiguity'. He says that 'sometimes it

149

means something which exists *as a thing in itself* distinct from us, and sometimes something which merely belongs to external *appearance'*; he calls things which are 'outside of us' in the first of these two senses 'objects which might be called external in the transcendental sense', and things which are so in the second *'empirically external* objects'; and he says finally that, in order to remove all uncertainty as to the latter conception, he will distinguish empirically external objects from objects which might be called 'external' in the transcendental sense, 'by calling them outright things which are *to be met with in space'*.

I think that this last phrase of Kant's 'things which are to be met with in space', does indicate fairly clearly what sort of things it is with regard to which I wish to inquire what sort of proof, if any, can be given that there are any things of that sort. My body, the bodies of other men, the bodies of animals, plants of all sorts, stones, mountains, the sun, the moon, stars, and planets, houses and other buildings, manufactured articles of all sorts – chairs, tables, pieces of paper, etc., are all of them 'things which are to be met with in space'. In short, all things of the sort that philosophers have been used to call 'physical objects', 'material things', or 'bodies' obviously come under this head. But the phrase 'things that are to be met with in space' can be naturally understood as applying also in cases where the names 'physical object', 'material thing', or 'body' can hardly be applied. For instance, shadows are sometimes to be met with in space, although they could hardly be properly called 'physical objects', 'material things', or 'bodies'; and although in one usage of the term 'thing' it would not be proper to call a shadow a 'thing', yet the phrase 'things which are to be met with in space' can be naturally understood as synonymous with 'whatever can be met with in space', and this is an expression which can quite properly be understood to include shadows. I wish the phrase 'things which are to be met with in space' to be understood in this wide sense; so that if a proof can be found that there ever have been as many as two different shadows it will follow at once that there have been at least two 'things which were to be met with in space', and this proof will be as good a proof of the point in question as would be a proof that there have been at least two 'physical objects' of no matter what sort.

The phrase 'things which are to be met with in space' can, therefore, be naturally understood as having a very wide meaning – a meaning even wider than that of 'physical object' or 'body', wide as is the meaning of these latter expressions. But wide as is its meaning, it is not, in one respect, so wide as that of another phrase which Kant uses as if it were equivalent to this one; and a comparison between the two will, I think, serve to make still clearer what sort of things it is with regard to which I wish to ask what proof, if any, can be given that there are such things.

The other phrase which Kant uses as if it were equivalent to 'things which are to be met with in space' is used by him in the sentence immediately preceding that previously quoted in which he declares that the expression 'things outside of us' 'carries with it an unavoidable ambiguity' (A373). In this preceding sentence he says that an 'empirical object' 'is called *external*, if it is presented (*vorgestellt*) *in space*'. He treats, therefore, the phrase 'presented in space' as if it were equivalent to 'to be met with in space'. But it is easy to find examples of 'things', of which it can hardly be denied that they are 'presented in space', but of which it could, quite naturally, be emphatically denied that they are 'to be met with in space'. Consider, for instance, the following description of one set of circumstances under which what some psychologists have called a 'negative after-image' and others a 'negative after-sensation' can be obtained. 'If, after looking steadfastly at a white patch on a black ground, the eye be turned to a white ground, a grey patch is seen for some little time' (Foster's *Text-book of Physiology*,[1] iv, iii, 3, p.1266; quoted in Stout's *Manual of Psychology*,[2] 3rd edition, p.280). Upon reading these words recently, I took the trouble to cut out of a piece of white paper a four-pointed star, to place it on a black ground, to 'look steadfastly' at it, and then to turn my eyes to a white sheet of paper: and I did find that I saw a grey patch for some little time – I not only saw a grey patch, but I saw it *on* the white ground, and also this grey patch was of roughly the same shape as the white four-pointed star at which I had 'looked steadfastly' just before – it also was a four-pointed star. I repeated this simple experiment successfully several times. Now each of those grey four-pointed stars, one of which I saw in each experiment, was what is called an 'after-image' or 'after-sensation'; and can anybody deny that each of these after-images can be quite properly said to have been 'presented in space'? I saw each of them on a real white background, and, if so, each of them was 'presented' on a real white background. But though they were 'presented in space' everybody, I think, would feel that it was gravely misleading to say that they were 'to be met with in space'. The white star at which I 'looked steadfastly', the black ground on which I saw it, and the white ground on which I saw the after-images, were, of course, 'to be met with in space': they were, in fact, 'physical objects' or surfaces of physical objects. But one important difference between them, on the one hand, and the grey after-images, on the other, can be quite naturally expressed by saying that the latter were *not* 'to be met with in space'. And one reason why this is so is, I think, plain. To say that so and so was at a given time 'to be met with in space' naturally suggests that there are conditions such that *any one* who fulfilled them might, conceivably, have 'perceived' the 'thing' in question – might have seen it, if it was a visible object, have felt it, if it was a tangible one, have heard it, if it was a sound, have smelt it, if it was a smell. When I say that the white four-pointed paper star, at which I looked steadfastly, was a 'physical object' and was 'to be met with in space', I am implying that *anyone*, who had been in the room at the time, and who had normal eyesight and a normal sense of touch, might have seen and felt it. But, in the case of those grey after-images which I saw, it is not conceivable that anyone besides myself should have seen any one of them. It is, of course, quite conceivable that other people, if they had been in the room with me at the time, and had carried out the same experiment which I carried out, would have seen grey after-images *very like* one of those which I saw: there is no absurdity in supposing even that they might have seen after-images *exactly* like one of those which I saw. But there is an absurdity in supposing that any one of the after-images which I saw could also have been seen by anyone else: in supposing that two different people can ever see the *very same* after-image. One reason, then, why we should say that none of those grey after-images which I saw was 'to be met with in space', although each of them was certainly 'presented in space' to me, is simply that none of them could conceivably have been seen by anyone else. It is natural so to understand the phrase 'to be met with in space', that to say of anything which a man perceived that it was to be met with in space is to say that it might have been perceived by *others* as well as by the man in question.

Negative after-images of the kind described are, therefore, one example of 'things' which, though they must be allowed to be 'presented in space', are nevertheless *not* 'to be met with in space', and are *not* 'external to our minds' in the sense with which we shall be concerned. And two other important examples may be given.

The first is this. It is well known that people sometimes see things double, an occurrence which has also been described by psychologists by saying that they have a 'double image', or two 'images', of some object at which they are looking. In such cases it would certainly be quite natural to say that each of the two 'images' is 'presented in space': they are seen, one in one place, and the other in another, in just the same sense in which each of those grey after-images which I saw was seen at a particular place on the white background at which I was looking. But it would be utterly unnatural to say that, when I have a double image, each of the two images is 'to be met with in space'. On the contrary it is quite certain that *both* of them are not 'to be met with in space'. If both were, it would follow that somebody else might see the *very same* two images which I see; and, though there is no absurdity in supposing that another person might see a pair of images exactly similar to a pair which I see, there is an absurdity in supposing that anyone else might see the *same identical pair*. In every case, then, in which anyone sees anything double, we have an example of at least one 'thing' which, though 'presented in space' is certainly not 'to be met with in space'.

And the second important example is this. Bodily pains can, in general, be quite properly said to be 'presented in space'. When I have a toothache, I feel it *in* a particular region of my jaw or *in* a particular tooth; when I make a cut on my finger smart by putting iodine on it, I feel the pain in a particular place in my finger; and a man whose leg has been amputated may feel a pain *in* a place where his foot might have been if he had not lost it. It is certainly perfectly natural to understand the phrase 'presented in space' in such a way that if, in the sense illustrated, a pain is felt *in* a particular place, that pain is 'presented in space'. And yet of pains it would be quite unnatural to say that they are 'to be met with in space', for the same reason as in the case of after-images or double images. It is quite conceivable that another person should feel a pain exactly like one which I feel, but there is an absurdity in supposing that he could feel *numerically the same* pain which I feel. And pains are in fact a typical example of the sort of 'things' of which philosophers say that they are *not* 'external' to our minds, but 'within' them. Of any pain which *I* feel they would say that it is necessarily *not* external to my mind but *in* it.

And finally it is, I think, worth while to mention one other class of 'things', which are certainly not 'external' objects and certainly not 'to be met with in space', in the sense with which I am concerned, but which yet some philosophers would be inclined to say are 'presented in space', though they are not 'presented in space' in quite the same sense in which pains, double images, and negative after-images of the sort I described are so. If you look at an electric light and then close your eyes, it sometimes happens that you see, for some little time, against the dark background which you usually see when your eyes are shut, a bright patch similar in shape to the light at which you have just been looking. Such a bright patch, if you see one, is another example of what some psychologists have called 'after-images' and others 'after-sensations'; but, unlike the negative after-images of which I spoke before, it is seen when your eyes are shut. Of such an after-image, seen with closed eyes, some philosophers might be inclined to say that this image too was 'presented in space', although it is certainly not 'to be met with in space'. They would be inclined to say that it is 'presented in space', because it certainly is presented as at some little distance from the person who is seeing it: and how can a thing be presented as at some little distance from me, without being 'presented in space'? Yet there is an important difference between such after-images, seen with closed eyes, and after-images of the sort I previously described – a difference which might lead other philosophers to deny that these after-images, seen with closed eyes, are 'presented in space' at all. It is a difference which can be expressed by saying that when your eyes are shut, you are not seeing any part of *physical* space at all – of the space which is referred to when we talk of 'things which are to be met with in *space*'. An after-image seen with closed eyes certainly is presented in *a* space, but it may be questioned whether it is proper to say that it is presented in *space*.

It is clear, then, I think, that by no means everything which can naturally be said to be 'presented in space' can also be naturally said to be 'a thing which is to be met with in space'. Some of the 'things', which are presented in space, are very emphatically *not* to be met with in space: or, to use another phrase, which may be used to convey the same notion, they are emphatically *not* 'physical realities' at all. The conception 'presented in space' is therefore, in one respect, much wider than the conception 'to be met with in space': many 'things' fall under the first conception which do not fall under the second – many after-images, one at least of the pair of 'images' seen whenever anyone sees double, and most bodily pains, are 'presented in space', though none of them are to be met with in space. From the fact that a 'thing' is presented in space, it by no means follows that it is to be met with in space. But just as the first conception is, in one respect, wider than the second, so, in another, the second is wider than the first. For there are many 'things' to be met with in space, of which it is not true that they are presented in space. From the fact that a 'thing' is to be met with in space, it by no means follows that it is presented in space. I have taken 'to be met with in space' to imply, as I think it naturally may, that a 'thing' *might be* perceived; but from the fact that a thing *might be* perceived, it does not follow that it *is* perceived; and if it is not actually perceived, then it will not be presented in space. It is characteristic of the sorts of 'things', including shadows, which I have described as 'to be met with in space', that there is no absurdity in supposing with regard to any one of them which *is*, at a given time, perceived, both (1) that it might have existed at that very time, without being perceived; (2) that it might have existed at another time, without being perceived at that other time; and (3) that during the whole period of its existence, it need not have been perceived at any time at all. There is, therefore, no absurdity in supposing that many things, which were at one time to be met with in space, never were 'presented' at any time at all, and that many things which *are* to be met with in space now, are not now 'presented' and also never were and never will be. To use a Kantian phrase, the conception of 'things which are to be met with in space', embraces not only objects of actual experience, but also objects of *possible* experience; and from the fact that a thing is or was an object of *possible* experience, it by no means follows that it either was or is or will be 'presented' at all.

I hope that what I have now said may have served to make

clear enough what sorts of 'things' I was originally referring to as 'things outside us' or 'things external to our minds'. I said that I thought that Kant's phrase 'things that are to be met with in space' indicated fairly clearly the sorts of 'things' in question; and I have tried to make the range clearer still, by pointing out that this phrase only serves the purpose, if (*a*) you understand it in a sense, in which many 'things', e.g., after-images, double images, bodily pains, which might be said to be 'presented in space', are nevertheless *not* to be reckoned as 'things that are to be met with in space', and (*b*) you realise clearly that there is no contradiction in supposing that there have been and are 'to be met with in space' things which never have been, are not now, and never will be perceived, nor in supposing that among those of them which have at some time been perceived many existed at times at which they were not being perceived. I think it will now be clear to everyone that, since I do not reckon as 'external things' after-images, double images, and bodily pains, I also should not reckon as 'external things', any of the 'images' which we often 'see with the mind's eye' when we are awake, nor any of those which we see when we are asleep and dreaming; and also that I was so using the expression 'external' that from the fact that a man was at a given time having a visual hallucination, it will follow that he was seeing at that time something which was *not* 'external' to his mind, and from the fact that he was at a given time having an auditory hallucination, it will follow that he was at the time hearing a sound which was *not* 'external' to his mind. But I certainly have not made my use of these phrases, 'external to our minds' and 'to be met with in space', so clear that in the case of every kind of 'thing' which might be suggested, you would be able to tell at once whether I should or should not reckon it as 'external to our minds' and 'to be met with in space'. For instance, I have said nothing which makes it quite clear whether a reflection which I see in a looking-glass is or is not to be regarded as 'a thing that is to be met with in space' and 'external to our minds', nor have I said anything which makes it quite clear whether the sky is or is not to be so regarded. In the case of the sky, everyone, I think, would feel that it was quite inappropriate to talk of it as 'a thing that is to be met with in space'; and most people, I think, would feel a strong reluctance to affirm, without qualification, that reflections which people see in looking-glasses are 'to be met with in space'. And yet neither the sky nor reflections seen in mirrors are in the same position as bodily pains or after-images in the respect which I have emphasised as a reason for saying of these latter that they are *not* to be met with in space – namely that there is an absurdity in supposing that *the very same* pain which I feel could be felt by someone else or that *the very same* after-image which I see could be seen by someone else. In the case of reflections in mirrors we should quite naturally, in certain circumstances, use language which implies that another person may see the same reflection which we see. We might quite naturally say to a friend: 'Do you see that reddish reflection in the water there? I can't make out what it's a reflection of', just as we might say, pointing to a distant hill-side: 'Do you see that white speck on the hill over there? I can't make out what it is'. And in the case of the sky, it is quite obviously *not* absurd to say that other people see it as well as I.

It must, therefore, be admitted that I have not made my use of the phrase 'things to be met with in space', nor therefore that of 'external to our minds', which the former was used to explain, so clear that in the case of every kind of 'thing' which may be mentioned, there will be no doubt whatever as to whether things of that kind are or are not 'to be met with in space' or 'external to our minds'. But this lack of a clear-cut definition of the expression 'things that are to be met with in space', does not, so far as I can see, matter for my present purpose. For my present purpose it is, I think, sufficient if I make clear, in the case of many kinds of things, that I am so using the phrase 'things that are to be met with in space', that, in the case of each of these kinds, from the proposition that there are things of that kind it *follows* that there are things to be met with in space. And I have, in fact, given a list (though by no means an exhaustive one) of kinds of things which are related to my use of the expression 'things that are to be met with in space' in this way. I mentioned among others the bodies of men and of animals, plants, stars, houses, chairs, and shadows; and I want now to emphasise that I am so using 'things to be met with in space' that, in the case of each of these kinds of 'things', from the proposition that there are 'things' of that kind it *follows* that there are things to be met with in space: e.g., from the proposition that there are plants or that plants exist it *follows* that there are things to be met with in space, from the proposition that shadows exist, it *follows* that there are things to be met with in space, and so on, in the case of all the kinds of 'things' which I mentioned in my first list. That this should be clear is sufficient for my purpose, because, if it is clear, then it will also be clear that, as I implied before, if you have proved that two plants exist, or that a plant and a dog exist, or that a dog and a shadow exist, etc., etc., you will *ipso facto* have proved that there are things to be met with in space: you will not require *also* to give a separate proof that from the proposition that there are plants it *does* follow that there are things to be met with in space.

Now with regard to the expression 'things that are to be met with in space' I think it will readily be believed that I may be using it in a sense such that no proof is required that from 'plants exist' there follows 'there are things to be met with in space'; but with regard to the phrase 'things external to our minds' I think the case is different. People may be inclined to say: 'I can see quite clearly that from the proposition "At least two dogs exist at the present moment" there *follows* the proposition "At least two things are to be met with in space at the present moment", so that if you can prove that there are two dogs in existence at the present moment you will *ipso facto* have proved that two things at least are to be met with in space at the present moment. I can see that you do not also require a separate proof that from "Two dogs exist" "Two things are to be met with in space" *does* follow; it is quite obvious that there couldn't be a dog which wasn't to be met with in space. But it is not by any means so clear to me that if you can prove that there are two dogs or two shadows, you will *ipso facto* have proved that there are two things *external to our minds*. Isn't it possible that a dog, though it certainly must be "to be met with in space", might *not* be an external object – an object external to our minds? Isn't a separate proof required that anything that is to be met with in space must be external to our minds? Of course, if you are using "external" as a mere synonym for "to be met with in space", no proof will be required that dogs are external objects: in that case, if you can prove that two dogs exist, you will *ipso facto* have proved that there are some external things. But I find it difficult to believe that you, or anybody else, do really use "external" as a mere synonym for "to be met with in space"; and if you don't, isn't some proof required that whatever is to be met with in space must be external to our minds?'

Now Kant, as we saw, asserts that the phrases 'outside of us' or 'external' are in fact used in two very different senses; and with regard to one of these two senses, that which he calls the 'transcendental' sense, and which he tries to explain by saying that it is a sense in which 'external' means 'existing *as a thing in itself* distinct from us', it is notorious that he himself held that things which are to be met with in space are *not* 'external' in that sense. There is, therefore, according to him, *a* sense of 'external', a sense in which the word has been commonly used by philosophers – such that, if 'external' be used in that sense, then from the proposition 'Two dogs exist' it will *not* follow that there are some external things. What this supposed sense is I do not think that Kant himself ever succeeded in explaining clearly; nor do I know of any reason for supposing that philosophers ever have used 'external' in a sense, such that in *that* sense things that are to be met with in space are *not* external. But how about the other sense, in which, according to Kant, the word 'external' has been commonly used – that which he calls 'empirically external'? How is this conception related to the conception 'to be met with in space'? It may be noticed that, in the passages which I quoted (A373), Kant himself does not tell us at all clearly what he takes to be the proper answer to this question. He only makes the rather odd statement that, in order to remove all uncertainty as to the conception 'empirically external', he will distinguish objects to which it applies from those which might be called 'external' in the transcendental sense, by 'calling them outright things which are *to be met with in space*'. These odd words certainly suggest, as one possible interpretation of them, that in Kant's opinion the conception 'empirically external' is *identical* with the conception 'to be met with in space' – that he does think that 'external', when used in this second sense, is a mere synonym for 'to be met with in space'. But, if this is his meaning, I do find it very difficult to believe that he is right. Have philosophers, in fact, ever used 'external' as a mere synonym for 'to be met with in space'? Does he himself do so?

I do not think they have, nor that he does himself; and, in order to explain how they have used it, and how the two conceptions 'external to our minds' and 'to be met with in space' are related to one another, I think it is important expressly to call attention to a fact which hitherto I have only referred to incidentally: namely the fact that those who talk of certain things as 'external to' our minds, do, in general, as we should naturally expect, talk of other 'things', with which they wish to contrast the first, as 'in' our minds. It has, of course, been often pointed out that when 'in' is thus used, followed by 'my mind', 'your mind', 'his mind', etc., 'in' is being used metaphorically. And there are some metaphorical uses of 'in', followed by such expressions, which occur in common speech, and which we all understand quite well. For instance, we all understand such expressions as 'I had you in mind, when I made that arrangement' or 'I had you in mind, when I said that there are some people who can't bear to touch a spider'. In these cases 'I was thinking of you' can be used to mean the same as 'I had you in mind'. But it is quite certain that this particular metaphorical use of 'in' is not the one in which philosophers are using it when they contrast what is 'in' my mind with what is 'external' to it. On the contrary, in their use of 'external', you will be external to my mind even at a moment when I have you in mind. If we want to discover what this peculiar metaphorical use of '*in* my mind' is, which is such that nothing, which is, in the sense we are now concerned with, 'external' to my mind, can ever be 'in' it, we need, I think, to consider instances of the sort of 'things' which they would say are 'in' my mind in this special sense. I have already mentioned three such instances, which are, I think, sufficient for my present purpose: any bodily pain which I feel, any after-image which I see with my eyes shut, and any image which I 'see' when I am asleep and dreaming, are typical examples of the sort of 'thing' of which philosophers have spoken as '*in* my mind'. And there is no doubt, I think, that when they have spoken of such things as my body, a sheet of paper, a star – in short 'physical objects' generally – as 'external', they have meant to emphasize some important difference which they feel to exist between such things as these and such 'things' as a pain, an after-image seen with closed eyes, and a dream-image. But *what* difference? What difference do they feel to exist between a bodily pain which I feel or an after-image which I see with closed eyes, on the one hand, and my body itself, on the other – what difference which leads them to say that whereas the bodily pain and the after-image are 'in' my mind, my body itself is *not* 'in' my mind – not even when I am feeling it and seeing it or thinking of it? I have already said that one difference which there is between the two, is that my body is to be met with in space, whereas the bodily pain and the after-image are not. But I think it would be quite wrong to say that this is *the* difference which has led philosophers to speak of the two latter as 'in' my mind, and of my body as *not* 'in' my mind.

The question what the difference is which has led them to speak in this way, is not, I think, at all an easy question to answer; but I am going to try to give, in brief outline, what I *think* is a right answer.

It should, I think, be noted, first of all, that the use of the word 'mind', which is being adopted when it is said that any bodily pains which I feel are 'in my mind', is one which is not quite in accordance with any usage common in ordinary speech, although we are very familiar with it in philosophy. Nobody, I think, would say that bodily pains which I feel are 'in my mind', unless he was also prepared to say that it is *with* my mind that I feel bodily pains; and to say this latter is, I think, not quite in accordance with common non-philosophic usage. It is natural enough to say that it is with my mind that I remember, and think, and imagine, and feel *mental* pains – e.g., disappointment, but not, I think, quite so natural to say that it is with my mind that I feel *bodily* pains, e.g., a severe headache; and perhaps even less natural to say that it is with my mind that I see and hear and smell and taste. There is, however, a well-established philosophical usage according to which seeing, hearing, smelling, tasting, and having a bodily pain are just as much *mental* occurrences or processes as are remembering, or thinking, or imagining. This usage was, I think, adopted by philosophers, because they saw a real resemblance between such statements as 'I saw a cat', 'I heard a clap of thunder', 'I smelt a strong smell of onions', 'My finger smarted horribly', on the one hand, and such statements as 'I remembered having seen him', 'I was thinking out a plan of action', 'I pictured the scene to myself', 'I felt bitterly disappointed', on the other – a resemblance which puts all these statements in one class together, as contrasted with other statements in which 'I' or 'my' is used, such as, e.g., 'I was less than four feet high', 'I was lying on my back', 'My hair was very long'. What is the resemblance in question? It is a resemblance which might be expressed by saying that all the first eight statements are the sort of statements which furnish data for psychology, while the three latter are not. It is also a resemblance which may be expressed, in a way now common among philosophers, by saying that in the case of all the first eight statements, if we make the statement more specific by adding a date, we get a statement such that, if it is true, then it *follows* that I was 'having an experience' at the date in question, whereas this does not hold for the three last statements. For instance, if it is true that I saw a cat between 12 noon and 5 minutes past, today, it *follows* that I was 'having some experience' between 12 noon and 5 minutes past, today; whereas from the proposition that I was less than four feet high in December 1877, it does not *follow* that I had any experiences in December 1877. But this philosophic use of 'having an experience' is one which itself needs explanation, since it is not identical with any use of the expression that is established in common speech. An explanation, however, which is, I think, adequate for the purpose, can be given by saying that a philosopher, who was following this usage, would say that I was at a given time 'having an experience' if and only if either (1) I was conscious at the time or (2) I was dreaming at the time or (3) something else was true of me at the time, which resembled what is true of me when I am conscious and when I am dreaming, in a certain very obvious respect in which what is true of me when I am dreaming resembles what is true of me when I am conscious, and in which what would be true of me, if at any time, for instance, I had a vision, would resemble both. This explanation is, of course, in some degree vague; but I think it is clear enough for our purpose. It amounts to saying that, in this philosophic usage of 'having an experience', it would be said of me that I was, at a given time, having *no* experience, if I was at the time neither conscious nor dreaming nor having a vision nor *anything else of the sort*; and, of course, this is vague in so far as it has not been specified what else would be *of the sort*: this is left to be gathered from the instances given. But I think this is sufficient: often at night when I am asleep, I am neither conscious nor dreaming nor having a vision nor *anything else of the sort* – that is to say, I am having no experiences. If this explanation of this philosophic usage of 'having an experience' is clear enough, then I think that what has been meant by saying that any pain which I feel or any after-image which I see with my eyes closed is '*in* my mind', can be explained by saying that what is meant is neither more nor less than that there would be a contradiction in supposing *that very same pain* or *that very same after-image* to have existed at a time at which I was having no experience; or, in other words, that from the proposition, with regard to any time, that *that* pain or *that* after-image existed at that time, it *follows* that I was having some experience at the time in question. And if so, then we can say that the felt difference between bodily pains which I feel and after-images which I see, on the one hand, and my body on the other, which has led philosophers to say that any such pain or after-image is '*in* my mind', whereas my body *never* is but is always 'outside of' or 'external to' my mind, is just this, that whereas there is a contradiction in supposing a pain which I feel or an after-image which I see to exist at a time when I am having no experience, there is no contradiction in supposing my body to exist at a time when I am having no experience; and we can even say, I think, that just this and nothing more is what they have meant by these puzzling and misleading phrases 'in my mind' and 'external to my mind'.

But now, if to say of anything, e.g., my body, that it is external to *my* mind, means merely that from a proposition to the effect that it existed at a specified time, there in no case follows the further proposition that *I* was having an experience at the time in question, then to say of anything that it is external to *our* minds, will mean similarly that from a proposition to the effect that it existed at a specified time, it in no case follows that any of *us* were having experiences at the time in question. And if by *our* minds be meant, as is, I think, usually meant, the minds of human beings living on the earth, then it will follow that any pains which animals may feel, any after-images they may see, any experiences they may have, though not external to *their* minds, yet are external to *ours*. And this at once makes plain how different is the conception 'external to our minds' from the conception 'to be met with in space'; for, of course, pains which animals feel or after-images which they see are no more to be met with in space than are pains which *we* feel or after-images which *we* see. From the proposition that there are external objects – objects that are not in any of *our* minds, it does *not* follow that there are things to be met with in space; and hence 'external to our minds' is not a mere synonym for 'to be met with in space': that is to say, 'external to our minds' and 'to be met with in space' are two different conceptions. And the true relation between these conceptions seems to me to be this. We have already seen that there are ever so many kinds of 'things', such that, in the case of each of these kinds, from the proposition that there is at least one thing of that kind there *follows* the proposition that there is at least one thing to be met with in space: e.g., this follows from 'There is at least one star', from 'There is at least one human body', from 'There is at least one shadow', etc. And I think we can say that of every kind of thing of which this is true, it is also true that from the proposition that there is at least one 'thing' of that kind there *follows* the proposition that there is at least one thing external to our minds: e.g., from 'There is at least one star' there follows not only 'There is at least one thing to be met with in space' but also 'There is at least one external thing', and similarly in all other cases. My reason for saying this is as follows. Consider any kind of thing, such that anything of that kind, if there is anything of it, must be 'to be met with in space': e.g., consider the kind 'soap-bubble'. If I say of anything which I am perceiving, 'That is a soap-bubble', I am, it seems to me, certainly implying that there would be no contradiction in asserting that it existed before I perceived it and that it will continue to exist, even if I cease to perceive it. This seems to me to be part of what is meant by saying that it is a real soap-bubble, as distinguished, for instance, from an hallucination of a soap-bubble. Of course, it by no means follows, that if it really is a soap-bubble, it did in fact exist before I perceived it or will continue to exist after I cease to perceive it: soap-bubbles are an example of a kind of 'physical object' and 'thing to be met with in space', in the case of which it is notorious that particular specimens of the kind often do exist only so long as they are perceived by a particular person. But a thing which I perceive would not be a soap-bubble unless its existence at any given time were *logically independent* of my perception of it at that time; unless that is to say, from the proposition, with regard to a particular time, that it existed at that time, it *never* follows that I perceived it at that time. But, if it is true that it would not be a soap-bubble, unless it *could* have existed at any given time without being perceived by me at that time, it is certainly also true that it would not be a soap-bubble, unless it *could* have existed at any given time, without its being true that I was having any experience of any kind at the time in question: it would not be a soap-bubble, unless, whatever time you take, from the proposition that it existed at that time it does *not* follow that I was having any experience at that time. That is to say, from the proposition with regard to anything which I am perceiving that it is a soap-bubble, there *follows* the proposition that it is external to *my* mind. But if, when I say that anything which I perceive is a soap-bubble, I am implying that it is external to *my* mind, I am, I think, certainly also implying that it is also external to all other minds: I am implying that it is not a thing of a sort such that things of that sort *can* only exist at a time when somebody is having an experience. I think, therefore, that from any proposition of the form 'There's a soap-bubble!' there does really *follow* the proposition 'There's an external object!' 'There's an object external to *all* our minds!' And, if this is true of the kind 'soap-bubble', it is certainly also true of any other kind (including the kind 'unicorn') which is such that, if there are any things of that kind, it follows that there are *some* things to be met with in space.

I think, therefore, that in the case of all kinds of 'things', which are such that if there is a pair of things, both of which are of one of these kinds, or a pair of things one of which is of one of them and one of them of another, then it will follow at once that there are some things to be met with in space, it is true also that if I can prove that there are a pair of things, one of which is of one of these kinds and another of another, or a pair both of which are of one of them, then I shall have proved *ipso facto* that there are at least two 'things outside of us'. That is to say, if I can prove that there exist now both a sheet of paper and a human hand, I shall have proved that there are now 'things outside of us'; if I can prove that there exist now both a shoe and sock, I shall have proved that there are now 'things outside of us', etc.; and similarly I shall have proved it, if I can prove that there exist now two sheets of paper, or two human hands, or two shoes, or two socks, etc. Obviously, then, there are thousands of different things such that, if, at any time, I can prove any one of them, I shall have proved the existence of things outside of us. Cannot I prove any of these things?

It seems to me that, so far from its being true, as Kant declares to be his opinion, that there is only one possible proof of the existence of things outside of us, namely the one which he has given, I can now give a large number of different proofs, each of which is a perfectly rigorous proof; and that at many other times I have been in a position to give many others. I can prove now, for instance, that two human hands exist. How? By holding up my two hands, and saying, as I make a certain gesture with the right hand, 'Here is one hand', and adding, as I make a certain gesture with the left, 'and here is another'. And if, by doing this, I have proved *ipso facto* the existence of external things, you will all see that I can also do it now in numbers of other ways: there is no need to multiply examples.

But did I prove just now that two human hands were then in existence? I do want to insist that I did; that the proof which I gave was a perfectly rigorous one; and that it is perhaps impossible to give a better or more rigorous proof of anything whatever. Of course, it would not have been a proof unless three conditions were satisfied; namely (1) unless the premiss which I adduced as proof of the conclusion was different from the conclusion I adduced it to prove; (2) unless the premiss which I adduced was something which I *knew* to be the case, and not merely something which I believed but which was by no means certain, or something which, though in fact true, I did not know to be so; and (3) unless the conclusion did really follow from the premiss. But all these three conditions were in fact satisfied by my proof. (1) The premiss which I adduced in proof was quite certainly different from the conclusion, for the conclusion was merely 'Two human hands exist at this moment'; but the premiss was something far more specific than this – something which I expressed by showing you my hands, making certain gestures, and saying the words 'Here is one hand, and here is another'. It is quite obvious that the two were different, because it is quite obvious that the conclusion might have been true, even if the premiss had been false. In asserting the premiss I was asserting much more than I was asserting in asserting the conclusion. (2) I certainly did at the moment *know* that which I expressed by the combination of certain gestures with saying the words 'There is one hand and here is another'. I *knew* that there was one hand in the place indicated by combining a certain gesture with my first utterance of 'here' and that there was another in the different place indicated by combining a certain gesture with my second utterance of 'here'. How absurd it would be to suggest that I did not know it, but only believed it, and that perhaps it was not the case! You might as well suggest that I do not know that I am now standing up and talking – that perhaps after all I'm not, and that it's not quite certain that I am! And finally (3) it is quite certain that the conclusion did follow from the premiss. This is as certain as it is that if there is one hand here and another here *now*, then it follows that there are two hands in existence *now*.

My proof, then, of the existence of things outside of us did satisfy three of the conditions necessary for a rigorous proof. Are there any other conditions necessary for a rigorous proof, such that perhaps it did not satisfy one of them? Perhaps there may be; I do not know; but I do want to emphasise that, so far as I can see, we all of us do constantly take proofs of this sort as absolutely conclusive proofs of certain conclusions – as finally settling certain questions, as to which we were previously in doubt. Suppose, for instance, it were a question whether there were as many as three misprints on a certain page in a certain book. A says there are, B is inclined to doubt it. How could A prove that he is right? Surely he *could* prove it by taking the book, turning to the page, and pointing to three separate places on it, saying 'There's one misprint here, another here, and another here': surely that is a method by which it *might* be proved! Of course, A would not have proved, by doing this, that there were at least three misprints on the page in question, unless it was certain that there was a misprint in each of the places to which he pointed. But to say that he *might* prove it in this way, is to say that it *might* be certain that there was. And if such a thing as that could ever be certain, then assuredly it was certain just now that there was one hand in one of the two places I indicated and another in the other.

I did, then, just now, give a proof that there were *then* external objects; and obviously, if I did, I could *then* have given many other proofs of the same sort that there were external objects *then*, and could now give many proofs of the same sort that there are external objects *now*.

But, if what I am asked to do is to prove that external objects have existed *in the past*, then I can give many different proofs of this also, but proofs which are in important respects of a different *sort* from those just given. And I want to emphasise that, when Kant says it is a scandal not to be able to give a proof of the existence of external objects, a proof of their existence in the past would certainly *help* to remove the scandal of which he is speaking. He says that, if it occurs to anyone to question their existence, we ought to be able to confront him with a satisfactory proof. But by a person who questions their existence, he certainly means not merely a person who questions whether any exist at the moment of speaking, but a person who questions whether any have *ever* existed; and a proof that some have existed in the past would certainly therefore be relevant to *part* of what such a person is questioning. How then can I prove that there have been external objects in the past? Here is one proof. I can say: 'I held up two hands above this desk not very long ago; therefore two hands existed not very long ago; therefore at least two external objects have existed at some time in the past, QED'. This is a perfectly good proof, provided I *know* what is asserted in the premiss. But I *do* know that I held up two hands above this desk not very long ago. As a matter of fact, in this case you all know it too. There's no doubt whatever that I did. Therefore I have given a perfectly conclusive proof that external objects have existed in the past; and you will all see at once that, if this is a conclusive proof, I could have given many others of the same sort, and could now give many others. But it is also quite obvious that this sort of proof differs in important respects from the sort of proof I gave just now that there were two hands existing *then*.

I have, then, given two conclusive proofs of the existence of external objects. The first was a proof that two human hands existed at the time when I gave the proof; the second was a proof that two human hands had existed at a time previous to that at which I gave the proof. These proofs were of a different sort in important respects. And I pointed out that I could have given, then, many other conclusive proofs of both sorts. It is also obvious that I could give many others of both sorts now. So that, if these are the sort of proof that is wanted, nothing is easier than to prove the existence of external objects.

But now I am perfectly well aware that, in spite of all that I have said, many philosophers will still feel that I have not given any satisfactory proof of the point in question. And I want briefly, in conclusion, to say something as to why this dissatisfaction with my proofs should be felt.

One reason why, is, I think, this. Some people understand 'proof of an external world' as including a proof of things which I haven't attempted to prove and haven't proved. It is not quite easy to say *what* it is that they want proved – *what* it is that is such that unless they got a proof of it, they would not say that they had a proof of the existence of external things; but I can make an approach to explaining what they want by saying that if I had proved the propositions which I used as *premisses* in my two proofs, then they would perhaps admit that I had proved the existence of external things, but, in the absence of such a proof (which, of course, I have neither given nor attempted to give), they will say that I have not given what they mean by a proof of the existence of external things. In other words, they want a proof of what I assert *now* when I hold up my hands and say 'Here's one hand and here's another'; and, in the other case, they want a proof of what I assert *now* when I say 'I did hold up two hands above this desk just now'. Of course, what they really want is not merely a proof of these two propositions, but something like a general statement as to how *any* propositions of this sort may be proved. This, of course, I haven't given; and I do not believe it can be given: if this is what is meant by proof of the existence of external things, I do not believe that any proof of the existence of external things is possible. Of course, in some cases what might be called a proof of propositions which seem like these can be got. If one of you suspected that one of my hands was artificial he might be said to get a proof of my proposition 'Here's one hand, and here's another', by coming up and examining the suspected hand close up, perhaps touching and pressing it, and so establishing that it really was a human hand. But I do not believe that any proof is possible in nearly all cases. How am I to prove now that 'Here's one hand, and here's another'? I do not believe I can do it. In order to do it, I should need to prove for one thing, as Descartes pointed out, that I am not now dreaming. But how can I prove that I am not? I have, no doubt, conclusive reasons for asserting that I am not now dreaming; I have conclusive evidence that I am awake: but that is a very different thing from being able to prove it. I could not tell you what all my evidence is; and I should require to do this at least, in order to give you a proof.

But another reason why some people would feel dissatisfied with my proofs is, I think, not merely that they want a proof of something which I haven't proved, but that they think that, if I cannot give such extra proofs, then the proofs that I have given are not conclusive proofs at all. And this, I think, is a definite mistake. They would say: 'If you cannot prove your premiss that here is one hand and here is another, then you do not know it.

But you yourself have admitted that, if you did not know it, then your proof was not conclusive. Therefore your proof was not, as you say it was, a conclusive proof'. This view that, if I cannot prove such things as these, I do not know them, is, I think, the view that Kant was expressing in the sentence which I quoted at the beginning of this lecture, when he implies that so long as we have no proof of the existence of external things, their existence must be accepted merely on *faith*. He means to say, I think, that if I cannot prove that there is a hand here, I must accept it merely as a matter of faith – I cannot know it. Such a view, though it has been very common among philosophers, can, I think, be shown to be wrong – though shown only by the use of premises which are not known to be true, unless we do know of the existence of external things. I can know things, which I cannot prove; and among things which I certainly did know, even if (as I think) I could not prove them, were the premises of my two proofs. I should say, therefore, that those, if any, who are dissatisfied with these proofs merely on the ground that I did not know their premises, have no good reason for their dissatisfaction.

NOTES

1 Sir M. Foster, *Text-book of Physiology*, fifth edition, 4 vols (London: 1888).
2 G.F. Stout, *Manual of Psychology*, third edition (W.B. Clove, London: 1913).

10

CERTAINTY

I am at present, as you can all see, in a room and not in the open air; I am standing up, and not either sitting or lying down; I have clothes on, and am not absolutely naked; I am speaking in a fairly loud voice, and am not either singing or whispering or keeping quite silent; I have in my hand some sheets of paper with writing on them; there are a good many other people in the same room in which I am; and there are windows in that wall and a door in this one.

Now I have here made a number of different assertions; and I have made these assertions quite positively, as if there were no doubt whatever that they were true. That is to say, though I did not expressly say, with regard to any of these different things which I asserted, that it was not only true but also *certain*, yet by asserting them in the way I did, I *implied*, though I did not say, that they were in fact certain – implied, that is, that I myself knew for certain, in each case, that what I asserted to be the case was, at the time when I asserted it, in fact the case. And I do not think that I can be justly accused of dogmatism or over-confidence for having asserted these things positively in the way that I did. In the case of some kinds of assertions, and under some circumstances, a man can be justly accused of dogmatism for asserting something positively. But in the case of assertions such as I made, made under the circumstances under which I made them, the charge would be absurd. On the contrary, I should have been guilty of absurdity if, under the circumstances, I had *not* spoken positively about these things, if

This is a revised version of the Howison Lecture, delivered at the University of California at Berkeley in 1941. It was originally published in *Philosophical Papers* (George Allen & Unwin, London: 1959).

I spoke of them at all. Suppose that now, instead of saying 'I am inside a building', I were to say 'I *think* I'm inside a building, but perhaps I'm not: it's not *certain* that I am', or instead of saying 'I have got some clothes on', I were to say 'I think I've got some clothes on, but it's just possible that I haven't'. Would it not sound rather ridiculous for me now, under these circumstances, to say 'I *think* I've got some clothes on' or even to say 'I not only think I have, I know that it is very likely indeed that I have, but I can't be quite sure'? For some persons, under some circumstances, it might not be at all absurd to express themselves thus doubtfully. Suppose, for instance, there were a blind man, suffering in addition from general anaesthesia, who knew, because he had been told, that his doctors from time to time stripped him naked and then put his clothes on again, although he himself could neither see nor feel the difference: to such a man there might well come an occasion on which he would really be describing correctly the state of affairs by saying that he *thought* he'd got some clothes on, or that he knew that it was very likely he had, but was not quite sure. But for me, now, in full possession of my senses, it would be quite ridiculous to express myself in this way, because the circumstances are such as to make it quite obvious that I don't merely think that I have, but know that I have. For me now, it would be absurd to say that I *thought* I wasn't naked, because by saying this I should imply that I didn't know that I wasn't, whereas you can all see that I'm in a position to know that I'm not. But if *now* I am not guilty of dogmatism in asserting positively that I'm not naked, certainly I was not guilty of dogmatism when I asserted it positively in one of those sentences with which I began this lecture. I knew then that I had clothes on, just as I know now that I have.

Now those seven assertions with which I began were obviously, in some respects, not all of quite the same kind. For instance: while the first six were all of them (among other things) assertions about myself, the seventh, namely that there were windows in that wall, and a door in this one, was not about myself at all. And even among those which were about myself there were obvious differences. In the case of two of these – the assertion that I was in a room, and the assertion that there were a good many other people in the same room with me – it can quite naturally be said that each gave a partial answer to the question what sort of *environment* I was in at the time when I made them. And in the case of three others – the assertions that I had clothes on, that I was speaking in a fairly loud voice, and that I had in my hand some sheets of paper – it can also be said, though less naturally, that they each gave a partial answer to the same question. For, if I had clothes on, if I was in a region in which fairly loud sounds were audible, and if I had some sheets of paper in my hand, it follows, in each case that the surroundings of my body were, in at least one respect, different from what they would have been if that particular thing had not been true of me; and the term 'environment' is sometimes so used that any true statement from which it follows that the surroundings of my body were different, in any respect, from what they might have been is a statement which gives *some* information, however little, as to the kind of environment I was in. But though each of these five assertions can thus, in a sense, be said to have given, if true, *some* information as to the nature of my environment at the time when I made it, one of them, the assertion that I was speaking in a fairly loud voice, did not *only* do this: it also, if true, gave some information of a very different kind. For to say that I was speaking in a fairly loud voice was not only to say that there were audible in my neighbourhood fairly loud sounds, and sounds of which it was also true that they were words; it was also to say that some sounds of this sort were *being made by me* – a causal proposition. As for the sixth of the assertions which I made about myself – the assertion that I was standing up – that can hardly be said to have given any information as to the nature of my environment at the time when I made it: it would be naturally described as giving information only as to the posture of my body at the time in question. And as for the two assertions I made which were not about myself at all – the assertions that there were windows in that wall and a door in this one – though they were, in a sense, assertions about my environment, since the two walls about which I made them were, in fact, in my neighbourhood at the time; yet in making them I was not expressly asserting that they were in my neighbourhood (had I been doing so, they would have been assertions about myself) and what I expressly asserted was something which might have been true, even if they had not been in my neighbourhood. In this respect they were unlike my assertion that I was in a room, which could not have been true, unless some walls had been in my neighbourhood. From the proposition that there is a door in that wall it does not follow that that wall is in my neighbourhood; whereas from the proposition that I am in a room, it does follow that a wall is in my neighbourhood.

But in spite of these, and other, differences between those seven or eight different assertions, there are several important respects in which they were all alike.

(1) In the first place: All of those seven or eight different assertions, which I made at the beginning of this lecture, were alike in this respect, namely, that every one of them was an assertion, which, though it wasn't in fact false, yet *might have been false*. For instance, consider the time at which I asserted that I was standing up. It is certainly true that at that very time I *might* have been sitting down, though in fact I wasn't; and if I *had* been sitting down at that time, then my assertion that I was standing up would have been false. Since, therefore, I might have been sitting down at that very time, it follows that my assertion that I was standing up was an assertion which *might have been false*, though it wasn't. And the same is obviously true of all the other assertions I made. At the time when I said I was in a room, I might have been in the open air; at the time when I said I had clothes on, I might have been naked; and so on, in all the other cases.

But from the fact that a given assertion might have been false, it always follows that the negation or contradictory of the proposition asserted is not a self-contradictory proposition. For to say that a given proposition might have been false is equivalent to saying that its negation or contradictory might have been true; and from the fact that a given proposition might have been true, it always follows that the proposition in question is not self-contradictory, since, if it were, it could not possibly have been true. Accordingly all those things which I asserted at the beginning of this lecture were things of which the *contradictories were not self-contradictory*. If, for instance, when I said, 'I am standing up' I had said instead 'It is not the case that I am standing up', which would have been the contradictory of what I did say, it would have been correct to say 'That is not a self-contradictory proposition, though it is a false one'; and the same is true in the case of all the other propositions that I asserted. As a short expression for the long expression 'proposition which is not self-contradictory and of which the contradictory is not self-contradictory' philosophers have often used the technical term 'contingent proposition'. Using the term 'contingent' in this sense, we can say, then, that one respect in which all those seven propositions which I asserted at the beginning of this lecture resembled one another was that *they were all of them contingent*.

And before I go on to mention some other respects in which they were all alike, I think I had better now at once say some things about the consequences of this first fact that they were all of them contingent – things which are very relevant to a proper understanding of the use of the word which forms the title of this lecture, the word 'certainty'.

The first thing I want to say about the consequences of the fact that all those propositions were contingent is this: namely, that from the mere fact that they were all of them contingent, it does not follow that they were not all *known to be true* – nay more, it does not follow, in the case of any particular person whatever, that *that* person did not know them to be true. Some philosophers have in fact suggested that no contingent proposition is ever, as a matter of fact, known to be true. And I am not *now* disputing that suggestion, though I do in fact hold it to be false, and intend, in the course of this lecture to dispute it. All that I am asserting *now* is that, even if it is a fact that no contingent proposition is ever known to be true, yet in no case does this *follow* from the mere fact that it is contingent. For instance, that I am now standing up is a contingent proposition; but from the mere fact that it is so, from that fact *alone*, it certainly does not *follow* that I do not know that I am standing up. If it is to be shown – as many philosophers think they can show – that I do *not* know now that I am standing up, some other argument must be brought forward for this contention, over and above the mere fact that this proposition is contingent; for from this fact, by itself, it certainly does not *follow* that I don't know that I am standing up. I say that this is certain, and I do not know that anyone would dispute it. But if I were asked to defend my assertion, I do not know that I could give any better defence than merely to say that the conjunctive proposition 'I know that I am at present standing up, and yet the proposition that I am is contingent' is certainly not itself self-contradictory, even if it is false. Is it not obvious that if I say 'I know that I am at present standing up, although the proposition that I am is contingent', I am certainly not contradicting myself, even if I *am* saying something which is false?

The second thing I want to say about the consequences of the fact that all those seven propositions were contingent is something which follows from the first: namely that from the fact that they were contingent it does not follow, in the case of any single one among them, that it was *possible* that the proposition in question was false. To take, for instance, again, the proposition that I was then standing up: from the fact that this proposition was contingent, it does not follow that, if I had said 'It is possible that it is not the case that I am standing up', I should have been saying something true. That this is so follows from my former contention that the contingency of the proposition in question does not entail that it was not known to be true, because one, at least, of the ways in which we use expressions of the form 'It is possible that p' is such that the statement in question cannot be true if the person who makes it knows for certain that p is false. We very, very often use expressions of the form 'It is possible that p' in such a way that by using such an expression we are making an assertion of our own ignorance on a certain point – an assertion namely that we do not *know* that p is false. This is certainly one of the very commonest uses of the word 'possible'; it is a use in which what it expresses is often expressed instead by the use of the word 'may'. For instance, if I were to say 'It is possible that Hitler is dead at this moment' this would naturally be understood to mean exactly the same as if I said 'Hitler *may* be dead at this moment'. And is it not quite plain that if I did assert that Hitler *may* be dead at this moment part at least of what I was asserting would be that I personally did not know for certain that he was not dead? Consequently if I were to assert now 'It is possible that I am not standing up' I should naturally be understood to be asserting that I do not know for certain that I am. And hence, if I do know for certain that I am, my assertion that it is possible that I'm not would be false. Since therefore from the fact that 'I am standing up' is a contingent proposition it does not follow that I do not know that I am, it also does not follow from this fact that it is possible that I am *not*. For if from the contingency of this proposition it did follow that it is possible that I am not standing up, it would also follow that I do not know that I *am* standing up: since from

'It is possible that I am not standing up' there follows 'I do not know that I am standing up'; and if *p* entails *q*, and *q* entails *r*, it *follows* that *p* entails *r*. Since, therefore, our *p* ('the proposition "I am standing up" is contingent') does not entail our *r* ('I do not know that I am standing up'), and since our *q* ('It is possible that I am not standing up') *does* entail our *r*, it follows that our *p* does not entail our *q*: that is to say, the fact that the proposition 'I am standing up' is contingent does not entail the consequence that it is possible that it is false that I am standing up. In no case whatever from the mere fact that a proposition *p* is contingent does it *follow* that it is *possible* that *p* is false. But this, of course, is not to deny that it may, *as a matter of fact*, be true of every contingent proposition that it is possible that it is false. This *will* be true, if no contingent proposition is ever known to be true. But even if this is so, it still remains true that from the mere fact that a proposition is contingent it never *follows* that it *may* be false; this remains true because from the mere fact that a proposition is contingent it never follows that it is not known to be true, and never follows, either, in the case of any particular person, that that person does not know it to be true.

In the above paragraph I confined myself to saying that there is at least one common use of expressions of the form 'It is possible that *p*', such that any person who makes such an assertion is asserting that he personally does not know that *p* is false; and hence the only conclusion to which I am so far entitled is that the mere fact that a given proposition *p* is contingent does not entail the consequence that what is expressed by 'it is possible that not-*p*' will be true, *when 'possible' is used in the way in question*. And it may be thought that there is another use of 'possible' such that from '*p* is contingent' there does follow 'it is possible that *p* is false'. The fact is that the expression 'logically possible' has often been used by philosophers in such a way that many might be tempted to think that it is a mere synonym for 'not self-contradictory'. That it is not a mere synonym for this can, I think, be seen from the fact that the expression 'it is not self-contradictory that I am not standing up' is not English at all, whereas the expression 'It is logically possible that I am not standing up' certainly is English, though it may be doubted whether what it expresses is true. If, however, we consider the expression 'the proposition that I am not standing up is not self-contradictory' I think it would not be incorrect to say that the words 'logically possible' are so used that *in this expression* they could be substituted for 'not self-contradictory' without changing the meaning of the whole expression; and that the same is true whatever other proposition you might take instead of the proposition that I am not standing up. If this be so, then it follows that, in the case of any proposition whatever, from the proposition that that proposition is not self-contradictory it will follow that the proposition in question is also logically possible (and *vice versa*); in other words, for any *p*, '*p* is not self-contradictory' entails '*p* is logically possible'. But this being so, it is very natural to think that it follows that you can also take a further step and say truly that, for any *p*, '*p* is not self-contradictory' entails 'It is logically possible that *p*'; for surely from '*p* is logically possible' it must follow that 'it is logically possible that *p*'. Certainly it is very natural to think this; but for all that, I think it is a mistake to think so. To think that '*p* is logically possible' must entail 'It is logically possible that *p*' is certainly a mere mistake which does not do justice to the subtlety of the differences there may be in the way we use language. And I think it is actually a mistake to say that '*p* is not self-contradictory' entails 'It is logically possible that *p*', even though it does entail '*p* is logically possible'. Consider the following facts. 'It is logically possible that I *should have been* sitting down now' certainly does entail 'The proposition that I am sitting down now is not self-contradictory'. But if this latter proposition did entail 'It is logically possible that I *am* sitting down now' then it would follow that 'It is logically possible that I *should have been* sitting down now' entails 'It is logically possible that I *am* sitting down now'. But does it? Certainly it would be quite unnatural for me, who know that I am standing up, to say the latter, whereas it would be quite natural for me to say the former; and I think perhaps we can go further and say that if I said the latter I should be saying something untrue, whereas if I said the former I should be saying something true; just as if I said 'I *might have been* sitting down now', I should be saying something true, whereas if I said 'I *may* be sitting down now', I should be saying something false. In short I think that even the expression 'It is *logically* possible that so-and-so *is* the case' retains the characteristic which we have seen to belong to one ordinary use of the expression 'It is possible that so-and-so *is* the case', namely that it can only be said *with truth* by a person who does not know that the so-and-so in question is *not* the case. If I were to say now 'It is logically possible that I am sitting down' I should be implying that I don't know that I'm not, and therefore implying something which, if I do know that I'm not, is false. I think that perhaps philosophers have not always paid sufficient attention to the possibility that from the mere fact that a given proposition, *p*, is not self-contradictory, it perhaps does not follow that any person whatever can say with truth 'It is logically possible that *p is* true'. In the case of a non-self-contradictory proposition such as the proposition that I am at present sitting down, if there be a person, for instance some friend of mine in England, who does not know that this proposition is false, then, in his case, from the *conjunction* of the fact that the proposition is not self-contradictory with the fact that he does not know it to be false, it does follow that he could say with truth 'It is logically possible that Moore is at present sitting down'; but if there be another person, myself for instance, who does know that the proposition is false, it is by no means clear that from the mere fact that the proposition is not self-contradictory – from that fact *alone* – it follows that *I* can truly say 'It is logically possible that I am at present sitting down'. From the conjunction of the fact that the proposition is logically possible with the fact that I know it to be false, it does follow that I can truly say 'It is logically possible that I *should have been* sitting down at this moment'; but from the fact that I can truly say this, it certainly does not follow that I can *also* truly say 'It is logically possible that I *am* sitting down'; and it is certain that in fact the two are incompatible: that, if I can truly say 'It is logically possible that I *should have been* sitting down now' then it follows that I *cannot* truly say 'It is logically possible that I *am* sitting down now'. Perhaps, however, our use of the expression 'It is logically possible that so-and-so *is* the case' is not clearly enough fixed to entitle us to say this. What is important is to insist that if 'It is logically possible that *p is* true' is used in such a way that it does follow from '*p* is not self-contradictory', *by itself*, then from 'It is logically possible that *p is* true', it does not follow that *p* is not known to be false. And if a philosopher does choose to use 'It is logically possible that *p* is true' in such an unnatural way as this, there will be a danger that he will sometimes forget that that is the way in which he has chosen to use it, and will fall into the fallacy of thinking that from 'It is logically possible that *p is* true' there *does* follow '*p* is not known to be false'.

The third thing which I wish to say about the consequences of the fact that those seven assertions with which I began this paper were assertions of contingent propositions, is this: that this fact is quite compatible with its being true that every one of those seven things that I asserted was not only true but *absolutely certain*. That this is so again follows from the fact that the mere contingency of a given proposition, *p*, never entails, in the case of any person whatever, that that person does not know *p* to be true. It follows from this fact, because if any person whatever does at a given time know that a given proposition *p* is true, then it follows that that person could say with truth at that time 'It is absolutely certain that *p*'. Thus if I do know now that I am standing up, it follows that I can say with truth 'It is absolutely certain that I am standing up'. Since, therefore, the fact that this proposition is contingent is compatible with its being true that I know that I am standing up, it follows that it must also be compatible with its being true that it is absolutely certain that I am standing up.

I think that possibly some people might be inclined to object to what I have just said on the following ground. I have just said that if a person can ever say with truth, with regard to any particular proposition *p*, 'I know that *p* is true', it follows that he can also truly say 'It is absolutely certain that *p* is true'. But an objector might perhaps say: 'I admit that if a person could ever truly say "I know *with absolute certainty* that *p* is true" then it would follow that he could also truly say "It *is* absolutely certain that *p* is true". But what you said was not "know with absolute certainty" but "know"; and surely there must be some difference between "knowing" and "knowing with absolute certainty", since, if there were not, we should never be tempted to use the latter expression. I doubt, therefore, whether a mere "I know that *p*" does entail "It is absolutely certain that *p*"'. To this objection I should reply: I do not think that the only possible explanation of the fact that we sometimes say 'I know with absolute certainty that so-and-so' and sometimes merely 'I know that so-and-so' is that the latter can be properly used to express something which may be true even when what is expressed by the former is not true: I doubt therefore whether 'I know that *p*' does not always entail 'I know with absolute certainty that *p*'.

But even if 'I know that p' can be sometimes properly used to express something from which 'I know with absolute certainty that p' does *not* follow, it is certainly also sometimes used in such a way that if I don't know with absolute certainty that p, then it follows that I don't know that p. And I have been and shall be only concerned with uses of 'know' of the latter kind, i.e., with such that 'I know that p' does entail 'I know with absolute certainty that p'. And similarly, even if there are proper uses of the word 'certain', such that a thing can be 'certain' without being 'absolutely certain', there are certainly others (or at least one other) such that if a thing is not absolutely certain it cannot be truly said to be certain; and I have been and shall be concerned only with uses of 'certain' of this latter kind.

Another comment which might be made upon what I have said is that, even if there is *one* use of 'absolutely certain' such that, as I said, it is never logically impossible that a contingent proposition should be absolutely certain, yet there is another use of 'absolutely certain' such that this *is* logically impossible – a sense of 'absolutely certain', that is to say, in which only propositions whose contradictories are self-contradictory can be absolutely certain. Propositions whose contradictories are self-contradictory have sometimes been called 'necessary truths', sometimes '*a priori* propositions', sometimes 'tautologies'; and it is sometimes held that the sense in which such propositions can be 'certain', and therefore also the sense in which they can be 'known to be true', must be different from the sense (if any) in which contingent propositions are sometimes 'certain' and 'known to be true'. That this may be so, I do not wish to deny. So far as I can see, it may be the case that, if I say, 'I know that' or 'It is certain that' 'it is not the case that there are any triangular figures which are not trilateral', or 'I know that' or 'It is certain that' 'it is not the case that there are any human beings who are daughters and yet are not female', I am using 'know that' and 'it is certain that' in a different sense from that in which I use them if I say 'I know that' or 'It is certain that' 'I have some clothes on'; and it may be the case that only necessary truths can be known or be certain in the former sense. Accordingly, my statements that from the fact that a given proposition, p, is contingent it does not follow that p is not known and is not certain, should be understood to mean only that there is at least one sense in which 'known' and 'certain' can be properly used, such that this does not follow; just as all that I asserted positively before about the phrase 'It is possible that' was that there is at least one sense in which this phrase can be properly used, such that 'p is contingent' does not entail 'It is possible that p is false'.

Finally, there is one slightly puzzling point about our use of the phrases 'it is possible that' and 'it is certain that', which might lead some people to suspect that some of the things I have been saying about the consequences which follow from the fact that a given proposition is contingent are false, and which therefore I think I had better try to clear up at once.

There are four main types of expression in which the word 'certain' is commonly used. We may say 'I feel certain that . . .', or we may say 'I am certain that . . .', or we may say 'I know for certain that . . .', or finally we may say 'It *is* certain that . . .'. And if we compare the first of these expressions with the two last, it is, of course, very obvious, and has been pointed out again and again, that whereas 'I feel certain that p' may quite well be true in a case in which p is not true – in other words that from the mere fact that I feel certain that so-and-so is the case it never follows that so-and-so is in fact the case – there is at least one common use of 'I know for certain that p' and 'It is certain that p' such that these things can't be true unless p is true. This difference may be brought out by the fact that, e.g., 'I felt certain that he would come, but in fact he didn't' is quite clearly not self-contradictory; it is quite clearly logically possible that I should have felt certain that he would come and that yet he didn't; while, on the other hand, 'I knew for certain that he would come, but he didn't' or 'It was certain that he would come but he didn't' are, for at least one common use of those phrases, self-contradictory: the fact that he didn't come *proves* that I didn't *know* he would come, and that it wasn't certain that he would, whereas it does not prove that I didn't *feel* certain that he would. In other words, 'I feel certain that p' does not *entail* that p is true (although by saying that I feel certain that p, I do *imply* that p is true), but 'I know that p' and 'It is certain that p' do entail that p is true; they can't be true, unless it is. As for the fourth expression 'I *am* certain that . . .' or 'I am quite sure that . . .' (it is perhaps worth noting that in the expressions 'I feel certain that . . .' and 'I am certain that . . .' the word 'sure' or the words 'quite sure' can be substituted for the word 'certain' without change of meaning, whereas in the expressions 'I know for certain that . . .' or 'it is certain that . . .' this is not the case) these expressions are, I think, particularly liable to give rise to fallacious reasoning in philosophical discussions about certainty, because, so far as I can see, they are sometimes used to mean the same as 'I feel certain that . . .' and sometimes, on the contrary, to mean the same as 'I know for certain that'. For instance, the expression 'I was quite sure that he would come, but yet he didn't' *can*, it seems to me, be naturally used in such a way that it is not self-contradictory – which can only be the case if it is in that case merely another way of saying 'I felt quite sure that he would come . . .'; but if on the other hand a philosopher were to say to me now (as many would say) 'You can't be quite sure that you are standing up', he would certainly not be asserting that I can't *feel* certain that I am – a thing which he would not at all wish to dispute – and he certainly would be asserting that, even if I do feel certain that I am, I don't or can't *know for certain* that I am.

There is, therefore, a clear difference in meaning between 'I feel certain that . . .' on the one hand, and 'I know for certain that . . .' or 'It is certain that . . .' on the other. But the point with which I am at present concerned is whether there is not also a difference of importance between each of these expressions 'I feel certain that . . .', 'I am certain that . . .', and 'I know for certain that . . .', on the one hand, and 'It *is* certain that . . .' on the other. The first three expressions are obviously, in spite of the important difference I have just pointed out between the first and the last of them, alike in one important respect – a respect which may be expressed by saying that their meaning is relative to the person who uses them. They are alike in this respect, because they all contain the word 'I'. In the case of every sentence which contains this word, its meaning obviously depends on who it is that says that sentence; if I say 'I am hot', what I assert by saying this is obviously something different from what any other person would be asserting by saying exactly the same words; and it is obvious that what I assert by saying so may quite well be true even though what another person asserts by saying exactly the same words at exactly the same time is false. 'I am hot' said by me at a given time, does not contradict 'I am not hot' said by you at exactly the same time: both may perfectly well be true. And in the same way, if I say 'I feel certain that there are windows in that wall' or 'I know for certain that there are windows', I, by saying this, am making an assertion different from, and logically independent of, what another person would be asserting by saying exactly the same words at the same time: from the fact that I feel certain of or know for certain a given thing it *never* follows, in the case of any other person whatever, that he feels certain of or knows the thing in question, nor from the fact that he does does it ever follow that *I* do. But if we consider, by contrast, the expression 'It *is* certain that there are windows in that wall', it looks, at first sight, as if the meaning of this expression was *not* relative to the person who says it: as if it were a quite impersonal statement and should mean the same whoever says it, provided it is said at the same time and provided the wall referred to by the words 'that wall' is the same. It is, indeed, obvious, I think, that a thing can't be certain, unless it is *known*: this is one obvious point that distinguishes the use of the word 'certain' from that of the word 'true'; a thing that nobody knows may quite well be true, but cannot possibly be certain. We can, then, say that it is a necessary condition for the truth of 'It is certain that p' that somebody should know that p is true. But the meaning of 'Somebody knows that p is true' is certainly not relative to the person who says it: it is as completely impersonal as 'The sun is larger than the moon', and if two people say it at the same time, then, if the one by saying it is saying something true, so must the other be. If, therefore, 'It is certain that p' meant merely 'Somebody knows that p is true', then the meaning of 'It is certain that p' would *not* be relative to the person who says it, and there would then be an important difference between it, on the one hand, and 'I feel certain that p' or 'I know for certain that p' on the other, since the meaning of these two *is* relative to the person who says them. But though 'Somebody knows that p is true' is a necessary condition for the truth of 'It is certain that p', it can be easily seen that it is *not* a sufficient condition; for if it were, it would follow that in any case in which somebody did know that p was true, it would always be false for anybody to say 'It is not certain that p'. But in fact it is quite evident that if I say now 'It is not certain that Hitler is still alive', I am not thereby committing myself to the statement that nobody knows that Hitler is still alive: my statement is quite consistent with its being true that Hitler is still alive, and that he himself and other persons know that he is so. The fact is, then, that all that follows from 'Somebody knows that p is true' is that *somebody* could say with truth 'It is certain that p': it does not follow that more than one person could; nor does it follow that there are not some who could say with truth 'It is *not* certain that p'. Two different people, who say, at the same time about the same proposition, p, the one 'It is certain that p is true', the other 'It is not certain that p is true', may both be saying what is true and not contradicting one another. It follows, therefore, that, in spite of appearances, the meaning of 'It *is* certain that p' *is* relative to the person who says it. And this, I think, is because, as I have implied above, if anybody asserts 'It is certain that p' part of what he is asserting is that he himself knows that p is true; so that, even if many other people do know that p is true, yet his assertion will be false, if he himself does not know it. If, on the other hand, a person asserts 'It is *not* certain that p' his assertion will not necessarily be true merely because he personally does not know that p is true, though it will necessarily be false if he personally does know that p is true. If I say 'It is certain that p', that I should know that p is true is both a necessary and sufficient condition for the truth of my assertion. But if I say 'It is *not* certain that p', then that I should *not* know that p is true, though it is a necessary, is not a sufficient condition for the truth of my assertion. And similarly the expression 'It is possible that p is true' is, though it looks as if it were impersonal, really an expression whose meaning is relative to the person who uses it. If I say it, that I should not know that p is false, is a necessary, though not a sufficient, condition for the truth of my assertion; and hence if two people say it at the same time about the same proposition it is perfectly possible that what the one asserts should be true, and what the other asserts false: since, if one of the two knows that p is false, his assertion will necessarily be false; whereas, if the other does not know that p is false, his assertion may be, though it will not necessarily be, true. On the other hand, if it were right to use the expression 'It is *logically* possible that p' as equivalent to 'p is not self-contradictory', then the meaning of 'It is *logically* possible that p' would *not* be relative to the person who says it.

To sum up this digression. What I have said about the consequences of the fact that all those seven propositions with which I opened this lecture were contingent, is firstly (1) that this fact does *not* entail the consequence that I did not, when I made them, know them to be true; (2) that it does *not* entail the consequence that I could then have said with truth about any of them 'It is possible that this is false'; and (3) that it does not entail the consequence that I could then have said with truth about any of them 'It is not absolutely certain that this is true'. It follows that by asserting that those seven propositions were contingent, I have not committed myself to the view that they were not known to be true or that it was not absolutely certain they were. But on the other hand, even if I am right in saying that these consequences do *not* follow from the mere fact that they were contingent, it, of course, does not follow from this that I *did* know them to be true, when I asserted them, or that they were absolutely certain. The questions whether, when I first said that I was standing up, I did know that I was, and whether, therefore, it was absolutely certain that I was, still remain completely open.

(2) A second respect, in addition to the fact that they were all of them contingent, in which all those seven propositions resembled one another, was this: In the case of every one of them part at least of what I was asserting, in asserting it, was something from which nothing whatever about the state or condition of my own mind followed – something from which no psychological proposition whatever about myself followed. Every one of them asserted something which might have been true, no matter what the condition of my mind had been either at that moment or in the past. For instance, that I was then inside a room is something which might have been true, even if at the time I had been asleep and in a dreamless sleep, and no matter what my character or disposition or mental abilities might have been: from that fact alone no psychological proposition whatever about myself followed. And the same is true of part at least of what I asserted in each of the other six propositions. I am going to refer to this common feature of all those seven propositions, by saying that they were all of them propositions which implied the existence of *an external world* – that is to say, of a world *external to my mind*. These phrases 'external world' and 'external to my mind' have often been used in philosophy; and I think that the way in which I am now proposing to use them is in harmony with the way in which they generally (though not always) have been used. It is indeed not obvious that my assertion that I was standing up implied the existence of anything

external to *my body*; but it has generally been clear that those who spoke of a world *external* to any given individual, meant by that a world external to that individual's *mind*, and that they were using the expression 'external to a mind' in some meta-phorical sense such that my body *must* be external to my mind. Accordingly a proposition which implies the existence of my body does, for that reason alone, with this use of terminology, imply the existence of a world *external to my mind*; and I think that the reason why it is said to do so is because from the existence of my body at a given time nothing whatever logically follows as to the state or condition of my mind at that time. I think, therefore, that I am not saying anything that will be misleading to those familiar with philosophical terminology, if I say, for the reason given, that each of those seven assertions implied the existence of something external to my mind; and that hence, if I did know any one of them to be true, when I asserted it, the existence of an external world was at that time absolutely certain. If, on the other hand, as some philosophers have maintained, the existence of an external world is never absolutely certain, then it follows that I cannot have known any one of these seven propositions to be true.

(3) A third characteristic which was common to all those seven propositions was one which I am going to express by saying that I had for each of them, at the time when I made it, *the evidence of my senses*. I do not mean by this that the evidence of my senses was the *only* evidence I had for them: I do not think it was. What I mean is that, at the time when I made each, I was seeing or hearing or feeling things (or, if that will make my meaning clearer, 'having visual, auditory, tactile or organic sensations'), or a combination of these, such that to see or hear or feel those things *was* to have evidence (not necessarily *conclusive* evidence) for part at least of what I asserted when I asserted the prop-osition in question. In other words, in all seven cases, what I said was at least partly *based* on 'the then present evidence of my senses'.

(4) Fourth and finally, I think that all those seven assertions shared in common the following characteristic. Consider the class of all propositions which resemble them in the second respect I mentioned, namely, that they imply the existence of something external to the mind of the person who makes them. It has been and still is held by many philosophers that no

proposition which has this peculiarity is ever known to be true – is ever quite certain. And what I think is true of those seven propositions with which I began this lecture is this: namely, that, if I did not know them to be true when I made them, then those philosophers are right. That is to say, if those propositions were not certain, then nothing of the kind is ever certain: if *they* were not certain, then no proposition which implies the existence of anything external to the mind of the person who makes it is ever certain. Take any one of the seven you like: the case for saying that I *knew* that one to be true when I made it is as strong as the case ever is for saying of any proposition which implies the existence of something external to the mind of the person who makes it, that *that* person knows it to be true.

This, it will be seem, is not a matter of logic. Obviously it is logically possible, for instance, that it should have been false then that I knew I was standing up and yet should be true now that I know I am standing up. And similarly in the other cases. But though this is logically possible – though the proposition 'I know that I am standing up now, but I did not know then that I was' is certainly not self-contradictory – yet it seems to me that it is certainly false. If I didn't know then that I was standing up, then certainly I know nothing of the sort now, and never have known anything of the sort; and, not only so, but nobody else ever has. And similarly, conversely (though this also is not a matter of logic), if I did know then that I was standing up then I certainly also know that I am standing up now, and have in the past constantly known things of the sort; and, not only so, but millions of other people have constantly known things of the sort: we all of us constantly do. In other words, those seven propositions of mine seem to be as good test-cases as could have been chosen (*as* good as, but also no better than thousands of others) for deciding between what seems to me to be the only real (though far from the only logically possible) alternatives – namely the alternative that none of us ever knows for certain of the existence of anything external to his own mind, and the alternative that all of us – millions of us – constantly do. And it was because they seemed to me to be as good test-cases as could be chosen for deciding this that I chose them.

But can we decide between these two alternatives?

I feel that the discussion of this question is frightfully difficult; and I feel sure that better and more decisive things could be said about it than I shall be able to say. All that I can do is to discuss, and that very inadequately, just one of the types of argument which have sometimes been alleged to show that nobody ever has known for certain anything about a world external to his mind.

Suppose I say now: 'I know for certain that I am standing up; it is absolutely certain that I am; there is not the smallest chance that I am not'. Many philosophers would say: 'You are wrong: you do not know that you are standing up; it is *not* absolutely certain that you are; there is *some* chance, though perhaps only a very small one, that you are not'. And one argument which has been used as an argument in favour of saying this, is an argument in the course of which the philosopher who used it would assert: 'You do not know for certain that you are not dreaming; it is not absolutely certain that you are not; there is *some* chance, though perhaps only a very small one, that you are'. And from this, that I do not know for certain that I am not dreaming, it is supposed to follow that I do not know for certain that I am standing up. It is argued: If it is not certain that you are not dreaming, then it is not certain that you are standing up. And that *if* I don't know that I'm not dreaming, I also don't know that I'm not sitting down, I don't feel at all inclined to dispute. From the hypothesis that I am dreaming, it would, I think, certainly follow that I don't *know* that I am standing up; though I have never seen the matter argued, and though it is not at all clear to me how it is to be proved that it would follow. But, on the other hand, from the hypothesis that I am dreaming, it certainly would not follow that I am *not* standing up; for it is certainly logically possible that a man should be fast asleep and dreaming, while he is standing up and not lying down. It is therefore logically possible that I should both be standing up and also at the same time dreaming that I am; just as the story, about a well-known Duke of Devonshire, that he once dreamt that he was speaking in the House of Lords and, when he woke up, found that he *was* speaking in the House of Lords, is certainly logically possible. And if, as is commonly assumed, when I am dreaming that I am standing up it may also be correct to say that I am *thinking* that I am standing up, then it follows that the hypothesis that I am now dreaming is quite consistent with the hypothesis that I am both thinking that I am standing up and also actually standing up. And hence, if, as seems to me to be

189

certainly the case and as this argument assumes, from the hypothesis that I am now dreaming it *would* follow that I don't know that I am standing up, there follows a point which is of great importance with regard to our use of the word 'knowledge', and therefore also of the word 'certainty' – a point which has been made quite conclusively more than once by Russell, namely that from the conjunction of the two facts that a man thinks that a given proposition *p* is true, and that *p* is in fact true, it does *not* follow that the man in question *knows* that *p* is true: in order that I may be justified in saying that I know that I am standing up, something more is required than the mere conjunction of the two facts that I both think I am and actually am – as Russell has expressed it, true belief is not identical with knowledge; and I think we may further add that even from the conjunction of the two facts that I feel certain that I am and that I actually am it would not follow that I know that I am, nor therefore that it *is* certain that I am. As regards the argument drawn from the fact that a man who dreams that he is standing up and happens at the moment actually to be standing up will nevertheless not *know* that he is standing up, it should indeed be noted that from the fact that a man is dreaming that he is standing up, it certainly does not *follow* that he *thinks* he is standing up; since it does sometimes happen in a dream that we *think* that it is a dream, and a man who thought this certainly might, although he was dreaming that he was standing up, yet *think* that he was not, although he could not *know* that he was not. It is not therefore the case, as might be hastily assumed, that, if I dream that I am standing up at a time when I am in fact lying down, I am necessarily *deceived*: I should be deceived only if I thought I was standing when I wasn't; and I may dream that I am, without thinking that I am. It certainly does, however, often happen that we do dream that so-and-so is the case, without at the time thinking that we are only dreaming; and in such cases, I think we may perhaps be said to *think* that what we dream is the case *is* the case, and to be deceived if it is not the case; and therefore also, in such cases, if what we dream to be the case happens also to *be* the case, we may be said to be thinking truly that it is the case, although we certainly do not *know* that it is.

I agree, therefore, with that part of this argument which asserts that if I don't know now that I'm not dreaming, it follows that I don't *know* that I am standing up, even if I both actually am and think that I am. But this first part of the argument is a consideration which cuts both ways. For, if it is true, it follows that it is also true that if I *do* know that I am standing up, then I do know that I am not dreaming. I can therefore just as well argue: since I do know that I'm standing up, it follows that I do know that I'm not dreaming; as my opponent can argue: since you don't know that you're not dreaming, it follows that you don't know that you're standing up. The one argument is just as good as the other, unless my opponent can give better reasons for asserting that I don't know that I'm not dreaming, than I can give for asserting that I do know that I am standing up.

What reasons can be given for saying that I don't know for certain that I'm not at this moment dreaming?

I do not think that I have ever seen clearly stated any argument which is supposed to show this. But I am going to try to state, as clearly as I can, the premisses and the reasonings from them, which I think have led so many philosophers to suppose that I really cannot now know for certain that I am not dreaming.

I said, you may remember, in talking of the seven assertions with which I opened this lecture, that I had 'the evidence of my senses' for them, though I also said that I didn't think this was the only evidence I had for them, nor that this by itself was necessarily conclusive evidence. Now if I had *then* 'the evidence of my senses' in favour of the proposition that I was standing up, I certainly have *now* the evidence of my senses in favour of the proposition that I *am* standing up, even though this may not be all the evidence that I have, and may not be conclusive. But have I, in fact, the evidence of my senses *at all* in favour of this proposition? One thing seems to me to be quite clear about our use of this phrase, namely, that, if a man at a given time is only dreaming that he is standing up, then it follows that he has *not* at that time the evidence of his senses in favour of that proposition: to say 'Jones last night was *only* dreaming that he was standing up, and yet all the time he had the evidence of his senses that he was' is to say something self-contradictory. But those philosophers who say it is possible that I am now dreaming, certainly mean to say also that it is possible that I am *only* dreaming that I am standing up; and this view, we now see, entails that it is possible that I have *not* the evidence of my senses that I am. If, therefore, they are right, it follows that it is not certain even that I have the evidence of my senses that I am; it follows that it is not certain that I have *the evidence of my senses* for anything at all. If, therefore, I were to say now, that I certainly have the evidence of my senses in favour of the proposition that I am standing up, even if it's not certain that I am standing up, I should be begging the very question now at issue. For if it is not certain that I am not dreaming, it is not certain that I even have the evidence of my senses that I am standing up.

But, now, even if it is not certain that I have at this moment the evidence of my senses for anything at all, it is quite certain that I *either* have the evidence of my senses that I am standing up *or* have an experience which is *very like* having the evidence of my senses that I am standing up. *If* I am dreaming, this experience consists in having dream-images which are at least very like the sensations I should be having if I were awake and had the sensations, the having of which would constitute 'having the evidence of my senses' that I am standing up. Let us use the expression 'sensory experience', in such a way that this experience which I certainly am having will be a 'sensory experience', whether or not it merely consists in the having of dream-images. If we use the expression 'sensory experience' in this way, we can say, I think, that, if it is not certain that I am not dreaming now, then it is not certain that *all* the sensory experiences I am now having are not mere dream-images.

What then are the premisses and the reasonings which would lead so many philosophers to think that all the sensory experiences I am having now *may* be mere dream-images – that I do not know for certain that they are not?

So far as I can see, one premiss which they would certainly use would be this: 'Some at least of the sensory experiences which you are having now are similar in important respects to dream-images which actually have occurred in dreams'. This seems a very harmless premiss, and I am quite willing to admit that it is true. But I think there is a very serious objection to the procedure of using it as a premiss in favour of the derived conclusion. For a philosopher who does use it as a premiss, is, I think, in fact *implying*, though he does not expressly say, that he himself knows it to be true. He is *implying* therefore that he himself knows that dreams have occurred. And, of course, I think

192

he would be right. All the philosophers I have ever met or heard of certainly did know that dreams have occurred: we all know that dreams *have* occurred. But can he consistently combine this proposition that he knows that dreams have occurred, with his conclusion that he does not know that he is not dreaming? Can anybody possibly know that dreams have occurred, if, at the time, he does not himself know that he is not dreaming? If he *is* dreaming, it may be that he is only dreaming that dreams have occurred; and if he does not know that he is not dreaming, can he possibly know that he is *not* only dreaming that dreams have occurred? Can he possibly know therefore that dreams *have* occurred? I do not think that he can; and therefore I think that anyone who uses this premiss and also asserts the conclusion that nobody ever knows that he is not dreaming, is guilty of an inconsistency. By using this premiss he implies that he himself knows that dreams have occurred; while, if his conclusion is true, it follows that he himself does not know that he is not dreaming, and therefore does not know that he is not only dreaming that dreams have occurred.

However, I admit that the premiss is true. Let us now try to see by what sort of reasoning it might be thought that we could get from it to the conclusion.

I do not see how we can get forward in that direction at all, unless we first take the following huge step, unless we say, namely: since there have been dream-images similar in important respects to some of the sensory experiences I am now having, it is logically possible that there should be dream-images *exactly like all* the sensory experiences I am now having, and logically possible, therefore, that all the sensory experiences I am now having *are* mere dream-images. And it might be thought that the validity of this step could be supported to some extent by appeal to matters of fact, though only, of course, at the cost of the same sort of inconsistency which I have just pointed out. It might be said, for instance, that some people have had dream-images which were *exactly like* sensory experiences which they had when they were awake, and that therefore it must be logically possible to have a dream-image exactly like a sensory experience which is *not* a dream-image. And then it may be said: If it is logically possible for some dream-images to be exactly like sensory experiences which are not dream-images, surely it must be logically possible for *all* the dream-images occurring in a dream at a given time to be exactly like sensory experiences which are not dream-images, and logically possible also for all the sensory experiences which a man has at a given time when he is awake to be exactly like all the dream-images which he himself or another man had in a dream at another time.

Now I cannot see my way to deny that it is logically possible that all the sensory experiences I am having now should be mere dream-images. And if this is logically possible, and if further the sensory experiences I am having now were the only experiences I am having, I do not see how I could possibly know for certain that I am not dreaming.[1]

But the conjunction of my memories of the immediate past with these sensory experiences *may* be sufficient to enable me to know that I am not dreaming. I say it *may* be. But what if our sceptical philosopher says: It is *not* sufficient; and offers as an argument to prove that it is not, this: It is logically possible *both* that you should be having all the sensory experiences you are having, and also that you should be remembering what you do remember, and *yet* should be dreaming. If this *is* logically possible, then I don't see how to deny that I cannot possibly know for certain that I am not dreaming: I do not see that I possibly could. But can any reason be given for saying that it *is* logically possible? So far as I know nobody ever has, and I don't know how anybody ever could. And so long as this is not done my argument, 'I know that I am standing up, and therefore I know that I am not dreaming', remains at least as good as his, 'You don't know that you are not dreaming, and therefore don't know that you are standing up'. And I don't think I've ever seen an argument expressly directed to show that it is not.

One final point should be made clear. It is certainly logically possible that I *should have* been dreaming now; I *might* have been dreaming now; and therefore the proposition that I *am* dreaming now is not self-contradictory. But what I am in doubt of is whether it is logically possible that I should *both* be having all the sensory experiences and the memories that I have and *yet* be dreaming. The conjunction of the proposition that I have these sense experiences and memories with the proposition that I am dreaming does seem to me to be very likely self-contradictory.

NOTE

1 The manuscript of 'Certainty' was recently acquired by the University Library, Cambridge. The passage reproduced below comes from the last two pages and constitutes Moore's original conclusion, which he then deleted, substituting the paragraphs which follow in the main text. Concerning these paragraphs Casimir Lewy, the original editor of this paper, wrote 'It should, I think, be mentioned that Moore was particularly dissatisfied with the last four paragraphs of this paper, and I believe that he was thinking primarily of these paragraphs when he wrote, in the Preface, that the paper contains bad mistakes' (*Philosophical Papers*, p.251, note 1).

But the sensory experiences I am having now are not the only experiences I am having. I also have memories of the immediate past, which are certainly not merely sensory experiences; and these seem to me to make a big difference. Let me try to explain why. Suppose that for an hour together I had had the experiences of lying naked on a white beach, in front of a blue sea, under a bright sun, and then suddenly had exactly all the sensory experiences I have now, while at the same time I remembered those utterly different experiences which I had been having just before. It is certainly logically possible that this should happen, except that perhaps I could not remember the experiences of the sea and bright sun without having some images which would count as sensory experiences, and which are not among those I have now, and that perhaps also in my memories of the immediate past now, there are also included some images, which should count as sensory experiences, and which would not be included among my sensory experiences in the supposed case. Suppose, however, that, with these exceptions, the extraordinary – almost miraculous – state of things I have tried to describe, had really happened. My sensory experiences would, *ex hypothesi*, except for the possible presence of some memory images which are not now present, and the possible absence of some which are *now* present, be exactly as they are now, but I should remember from the moment before being naked under a bright sun by a blue sea; what should I *know* in such a case? I should certainly *not* know what to think; I should be utterly astonished, and I should certainly not know for certain at the moment that I was not dreaming; it would very likely occur to me as a possible explanation of the extremely strange state of things that I might be dreaming.

What does this show? It shows, I think, that the mere fact that it is logically possible that all the sensory experiences I am now having might be dream-images is not sufficient to show that I really *may* be dreaming – that I do not know for certain that I'm not. For the conjunction of my memories of the immediate past with those sensory images may be sufficient to enable me to know that I am not dreaming.

But what if the philosopher who thinks he can show that I don't know that I am not dreaming, says that they *are* not in fact sufficient, and gives as an argument in favour of this that I may be merely dreaming that I remember that my past experiences for some time have been of standing up and speaking in a room etc., etc., and not actually remembering these things? I should reply, first, that this is not an argument for his position, but a mere reassertion of it; since his statement 'You *may* be merely dreaming that you remember' means only 'You don't know that you are not dreaming', which is just what he was asked to give reasons for.

But if he says: 'No, that is not what I meant: what I meant is that it is logically possible that you are merely dreaming that you remember'. I should reply that, if he merely means by this that this proposition that I am merely dreaming that I remember is not self-contradictory, then I fully admit that it is not; but that, as I said before, it does not follow from this that I do not know it to be false. What we want from him is some good reason for thinking that I don't know it to be false.

And here I am at an end. I do not know what good argument can be brought forward in favour of the view that I do not know that I remember having heard myself speak for some time past. Perhaps, someone will say: 'Here is a good argument: we sometimes think that we remember so and so, and then subsequently find out that what we thought we remembered was not the case: therefore we can never be certain in any particular case that we are remembering'. This seems to me to be as good an argument as the following: we sometimes think that a person we see is a man, and then subsequently find out that the person in question was a woman; therefore we can never be quite certain in any particular case that a person we see is a man – which surely is as bad an argument as any argument can be.

11

BEING CERTAIN THAT ONE IS IN PAIN[1]

I've given 'Certainty' as the title of this paper; but I'm not going to say anything at all about the certainty of Mathematics and Logic, nor, in general, the certainty of *necessary* propositions. What I shall be solely concerned with is certainty in the sense or senses in which contingent or empirical matters of fact can be said to be 'certain'; and I'm going to talk about the use of the phrase 'It's certain that . . .' or 'That's certain', rather than such phrases as 'I'm certain that . . .' or 'I feel certain that . . .'.

I'm going to start from something which Mr John Wisdom says in a paper called 'Philosophical Perplexity' in the *Proceedings of the Aristotelian Society* for 1936–7.[2] He says (p. 82): 'Statements about sense-experiences are certain *only because* it makes no sense to say that they *may be wrong*'. This is a statement which I at once feel inclined to question. Is it really the case that such statements as 'I've got a pain' are certain, when they are certain, *only because* of this? And Mr Wisdom himself seems to have expected that many people would be inclined to question it since he adds in a foot-note: 'This, I realise, stands very much in need of pacifying explanation'. And I gather that when he says of a statement that it needs 'pacifying explanation', he would, sometimes at least, admit that it is a false statement, but would maintain that nevertheless there is some good in it (p.77). Possibly, then, he would even agree with the objections I am going to urge against this statement of his.

When Mr Wisdom talks of 'statements about sense-experiences' he means by this term statements of a sort which he considers to differ in an important way from another sort of statement which he calls 'statements about material things'. He

197

introduces the expressions 'sense-statements' and 'thing-statements', as short for these two longer expressions; and throughout the rest of this paper I shall follow him in using these shorter expressions. When he writes the statement I have quoted, he has just been asserting that sense-statements and thing-statements do *not* differ in a certain way which he has pointed out, and do differ in another way; and this statement itself is, I think, intended to point out a difference between them: he would *not* say of thing-statements what he here says of sense-statements. I don't think he has attempted to *define* the expressions 'sense-statement' and 'thing-statement': he has only tried to make clear how he is using them by giving examples of each kind. As examples of sense-statements he has given (p.83) 'I see a pinkish patch', 'I feel a softish patch', 'I am in pain' and (p.81) 'I hear a buzzing'; and as examples of thing-statements 'There is cheese on the table' (p.78), 'That is cheese on the table' (p.80) and 'This is my thumb' (p.83). In the case of both kinds of statements he says (p.84) that we do sometimes 'in ordinary language' speak of statements of this sort as 'certain': that is to say, he holds that it's sometimes a proper way of saying something true to say such a thing as 'It's certain that I have a pain' as well as such a thing as 'It's certain that that stuff there is cheese'. There are people, I know, who would dispute the first; and others who would dispute the second: whether there are any who would dispute both at once, I don't know. As regards the first, in favour of the view that it's not good English to put 'It's certain that' before such expressions as 'I've got a pain', you may be asked: Have you heard anybody do it? And it may be further pointed out that if, when a child says 'I've got a head-ache', its mother or teacher asks 'Are you quite certain that you have?', this is generally equivalent to asking 'Aren't you telling a lie?', [and][3] not at all, as would sometimes be [the case with] the question 'Are you quite certain that there was cheese on the table?', to 'Aren't you perhaps making a mistake?'. Nevertheless I am inclined to agree with Mr Wisdom that there are circumstances in which, if you have got a pain, it is quite proper to say not merely 'I've got a pain', but also 'It's certain that I've got a pain', when the latter doesn't merely mean 'I wasn't lying when I told you so'. As to the other point, that you're sometimes expressing correctly something if you say such things as (pointing to something on the table) 'It's certain

that that is cheese', Mr Wisdom is much more emphatic, because one of the points he is mainly concerned to show, is, that
whereas some philosophers have held that such a statement is
always false, i.e., that any statement with regard to a thing-
statement to the effect that it is certain is always false, this
statement of theirs is very misleading. He says (p.80) he sometimes *knows for certain* that a thing he points at is cheese; and
therefore *knows in the strict sense* that he won't have to correct
himself tomorrow; and goes on to say (p.81) that it is often
absolutely certain that what he points at is cheese, and also that it
is often *senseless to doubt* that what he points at is cheese. About
all this, except the last ('senseless to doubt'), about which I feel
some hesitation, I quite agree with him. It is, I should say,
absolutely certain that this here is a piece of paper with writing on
it.

But if, as I agree is the case, some thing-statements are absolutely certain, it follows that one thing which Wisdom says about
the difference between sense-statements and thing-statements
is true – namely that they do not differ in *degree* of certainty
(p.82). Many philosophers have held that all sense-statements
are more certain than any thing-statements, or that all sense-
statements are certain and no thing-statements are: and neither
view can be right, if some thing-statements are *absolutely* certain.
What is suggested by the statement of Mr Wisdom's with which
I began is that what is true is rather that 'certain' is used in two
different *senses*; in one sense when 'It's certain that' is followed
by a sense-statement, e.g. 'It's certain that I'm in pain', in
another when it's followed by a thing-statement, e.g., 'It's certain that this is a thumb'. And this statement of his further
makes a suggestion as to what the meaning of 'It's certain that'
is, in the first case; but, so far as I know, he makes no suggestion
as to what the different meaning is in the second case. And the
question what is meant by 'It's certain that' in such statements
as 'It's certain that this is a thumb' or 'It's certain that this is a
piece of paper', is, I confess, one which puzzles me, though
perhaps it oughtn't. We can say, I think, that if *I* say it, I imply
by saying it that I know for certain that this is a piece of paper;
although, on the other hand, it might be true in a sense that it is
certain that this is a piece of paper, even though I did *not* know
it, provided somebody else knows it (but I think, in fact, anyone
who says 'it's certain that *p*' is saying, and not only implying,

199

'I know for certain that p', though this is often not all that he is saying – he's often saying that other people know it for certain too). And it is also true that it can't be certain that this is a piece of paper, unless it *is* a piece of paper; just as it can't be the case that I *know* that it's a piece of paper unless it *is* a piece of paper. 'It is certain that p', where p is a thing-statement, entails p; just as 'I know that p', where p is a thing-statement, entails p. But on the other hand 'It's certain that p' and 'I know that p' both seem to say something *more* than is said by p; since it must be admitted that p might be the case, without its being the case that p is certain, and without its being the case that I know that p. *What* more than p, or than that p is true, does 'It's certain that p' say? This is the question which puzzles me. But, on the other hand, we all understand perfectly well such a sentence as 'It's certain that this is a piece of paper'; and since we do, is there any need to ask or sense in asking what 'it's certain that' *means* in such a sentence?

But to return to the use of 'It's certain that' when followed by a sense-statement (if such a use exists): when Wisdom says 'Sense-statements are certain *only because* it makes no sense to say they may be wrong', it looks as if he were suggesting that, e.g., 'It's certain that I am in pain' means the same as 'It makes no sense to say "It may possibly be false that I'm in pain"'. But before I consider this suggestion about the use of 'certain', I want first to consider Wisdom's view that, in the case of every sense-statement it is in fact the case that it makes no sense to say that it may be wrong.

Wisdom says (p.81) that, if another person says 'I'm in pain', *we*, who hear him, 'may be "absolutely certain" that he's not mistaken about his pain, in the very special sense that "he is mistaken" makes no sense in this connection'. That is to say, he's saying that if one person A makes a sense-statement, then for another person B to say 'A's mistaken about that' makes no sense. He admits, of course, that for B to say that A's statement is *false* will make sense: what he is saying is that it will only make sense to say that A's statement is *false* because it will make sense to say that A is *lying*. What he is saying is that it won't make sense for B to say 'A is mistaken' or even 'A is perhaps mistaken'; i.e., to say 'A thinks he's got a pain, but he hasn't' or 'A thinks he's got a pain, but *perhaps* he hasn't'.

I think that this is true. And I think that if it is, then certain other things are also true. If it makes no sense for B to say of A 'A thinks he's got a pain but he hasn't' or 'A thinks he's got a pain, but perhaps he hasn't'; then I think we can also say that it makes no sense for A himself to say any of the following:

> I think I've got a pain
> I think I've got a pain, but perhaps I haven't
> I think I've not got a pain
> I think I've not got a pain, but perhaps I have
> I'm in doubt whether I've got a pain or not
> I don't know whether I've got a pain or not.

With regard to these last two expressions it must, of course, be admitted that they do make sense, if all that A meant by them is that, with regard to a certain sensation that he has, he's in doubt and doesn't know whether it *ought to be called* a pain or not. What seems to be true is that they don't make sense if A is *using* the word 'pain' in such a way that he is not making any assertion *about* the word; just as, when anyone says 'I've got a pain', he is not, as a rule, making any assertion about the word. I think, then, that to put 'I think that', 'I believe that' etc. before a sense-statement, does not make sense. But what is meant by saying that it doesn't make sense, and why doesn't it?

Wisdom seems to be intending to give an answer to the former question by saying (p.81) '"He says that that is cheese but perhaps he is mistaken" *has a use in English* [whereas] "He says he is in pain, but perhaps he is mistaken" *has no use in English*'. I.e. he seems to be saying 'does not make sense' means 'has no use in English'. But this explanation seems to me most unsatisfactory, because I don't understand the phrase 'has no use in English'. Does this phrase mean merely 'is never in fact used in English'? That may in fact be true; but I find it difficult to believe that it's all that I mean by saying that it doesn't make sense. Does it mean merely that it's not in accordance with English idiom to say 'I think I've got a pain'? This would be to assimilate it to 'Three men *was* ploughing in a field', which is a breach of English grammar. But it does not seem to me that 'I think I've got a pain' can be said to be ungrammatical; and on the other hand 'Three men was ploughing in a field', though ungrammatical, seems to me to have a very good sense just in the sense in which 'I think I've got a pain' hasn't. Or does 'has no use in English' mean 'is useless', 'never serves any purpose'?

I think this comes nearer to what Wisdom must have meant. He might perhaps say that it's sometimes useful to say 'I *think* there's some cheese', in order to avoid raising people's hopes too high, or to prevent them from blaming you, if it turns out that there's no cheese: but that 'I think I've got a pain' can never serve either of these purposes. I think it can't, and that it can never serve any purpose. But it seems to me that *why* it can't is just because we don't know what it would be like for a person to think he's got a pain as distinguished from knowing that he has one; whereas we do know what it is like for a person to think that some stuff on the table is cheese, as distinguished from knowing that it is. It's not because it serves no purpose, that we don't know what it would be like; but the other way about. To say that we don't know what it would be like is the same thing as to say it makes no sense to say 'I think I've got a pain'; and what this means is not *explained* by saying that it serves no purpose to say so. Wisdom himself expresses the matter lower down (p.81) by saying that a doubt with regard to such a matter as whether I'm in pain or not 'is unintelligible'; and points to the fact such a phrase as 'I am in pain, unless I'm mistaken', 'raises a titter', as showing that it's 'unintelligible'. But it seems to me that it's because it's unintelligible, that it serves no purpose; and not *vice versa*. And that to say 'it has no use in English' does not in the least explain what is meant by saying that it *is* unintelligible.

Another thing which Wisdom says (p.82), apparently to help us to see the sense in which 'I think I'm in pain' makes no sense, is this: he says 'Notice the connection between "He says he's in pain but I think he's mistaken" and "He cries 'Ow!' but I think he's mistaken"'. But this comparison seems to me very unsatisfactory also. The latter phrase evidently is nonsensical, but partly for a reason which doesn't apply to the former; namely that a person who said 'A cried "Ow!" but I think he was mistaken' would not have told us *what* he thought A was mistaken about, whereas a person who said 'A said he was in pain, but I think he was mistaken' would have done so. To say 'A said he was in pain' is to mention an assertion which A made, and 'was mistaken' means 'was mistaken in *that* assertion': but to say 'A cried "Ow!"' is *not* to mention any assertion which A made – hence here 'was mistaken' is meaningless, because no assertion made by A has been mentioned. I can, of course, see the following connexions between the phrases Wisdom asks us to compare. 'He said he was in pain, but he was lying' *is* like 'He cried "Ow!" but he wasn't really in pain'. When a person cries 'Ow!' in order to deceive – in order to make people think he's in pain when he isn't, then he is doing something very like *saying* that he's in pain when he isn't. But that 'He expresses a false *belief* by saying "Ow!"' or 'He cried "Ow!" because he *thought* he was in pain' make no sense, seems to me not at all to *explain* why and in what sense 'He expressed a false belief by saying "I'm in pain"' makes no sense.[4]

I do not, then, see any satisfactory answer to the question why or in what sense it makes no sense to say 'I think I'm in pain'. But yet it seems to me it certainly does make no sense.[5] All that I can say about the reason why it makes no sense to say 'I think I've got a pain, but perhaps I haven't' is that the reason must be of the same sort as the reason why it makes no sense to say 'This table is between that wall', as distinguished from 'This table is between this wall and that wall'; or to give another example, which I think has been given by Wittgenstein, [the reason must be of the same sort as][6] the reason why 'The good is more identical than the beautiful' makes no sense, whereas 'The good is identical with the beautiful' does make sense, though of course it's very doubtful whether it's true. What puzzles me is *why* 'This table is between that wall' makes no sense. But some things are, I think, obvious about it. It is obvious, I think, that it *makes no sense* to say 'So-and-so makes no sense', unless it is a *sentence* we are talking of. If I say 'This table is between that wall' makes no sense, I am saying that that sentence, these words make no sense. But I am not *merely* saying this. I am saying that these words, *if used as they are ordinarily used* in English – with their ordinary English meanings – make no sense; or rather I am mentioning their ordinary English meanings, and saying that these words with these meanings make no sense. You could not understand what I am saying unless you understood the words 'This table', 'is', 'between', 'that wall'. I am far from merely saying that that sentence (those words) makes no sense: indeed I don't know that it doesn't make sense: I don't know that there mayn't be some African language in which these very same sounds do make sense. What I am saying is certainly that these words with these meanings don't make sense. Now it is, of course, true that why they don't make sense is because 'between' is used in English for a relation which *requires at least three terms*. It might easily not have been: if we had used 'is between' to mean 'is less than a mile from', then 'This table is between that wall' would have made sense, because it would have meant 'This table is less than a mile from that wall' and *this* sentence, *if the words are used with their ordinary English meanings*, does make sense. But though it's true to say that why 'This table is between that wall' doesn't make sense, is because 'between' is used in English for a relation which *requires* at least three terms; this doesn't at all answer my question, because I want to know what's meant by saying that the relation for which 'between' is used in English *requires at least three terms*. For this seems to come to much the same thing as the original statement that statements of the form '*x* is between *y*' don't make sense in English; that in order to get one which does make sense we require one of the form '*x* is between *y* and *z*' (and what I want to know is why we require this). And what I can't see is that this is merely a statement as to how the word 'between' is actually used in English. It seems to be a statement not merely as to the word and its use but as to the relation for which the word stands, to the effect that that relation *can't* unite only two terms; and I don't see how this can possibly be identified with any statement about the use of language.

But now as to the connexion of this phrase 'it makes no sense to say' with the phrase 'it's certain that'. Wisdom's assertion that 'statements about sense-experiences are certain *only* because it makes no sense to say that they may be wrong', seems to suggest, as I said, that his view is that in the case of sense-statements like 'I'm in pain', the expression 'It's certain that I'm in pain' just means the same as 'It makes no sense to say "perhaps I'm not in pain"'. But this certainly won't do as it stands, because 'It's certain that I'm in pain' entails 'I'm in pain', whereas 'It makes no sense to say "Perhaps I'm not in pain"' certainly does *not* entail 'I am in pain'. We must, therefore, suppose, I think, that what Wisdom means to suggest is rather that 'It's certain that I'm in pain' means 'I'm in pain *and* it makes no sense to say "Perhaps I'm not"': in other words that he's suggesting that the question 'what *more* than that I am in pain, does "It's certain that I am in pain" say?' is to be answered by saying 'The extra thing asserted is "It makes no sense to say 'Perhaps I'm not in pain'"'.

But I'm not satisfied with this suggestion, because it seems to me that the use of 'certain' in 'It's certain I'm in pain' is much more like the use of 'certain' in 'It's certain that that's a piece of cheese' (or 'that this is a thumb'), than this would allow. It's quite certain that 'I think that's a piece of cheese, but perhaps it's not' does *sometimes* make sense; and hence when we say 'It's certain that that's a piece of cheese' we can't be saying 'It makes no sense to say "I think that's a piece of cheese"'. But when we say (if we ever do) 'It's certain that I've got a pain' it seems to me that part at least of what we're saying is of the same kind as what we say when we say 'It's certain that that's a piece of cheese'. I think that one thing that's common to the two usages is of the following sort. One way in which we use statements that so-and-so is certain, or not certain, is in deliberation as to what we'd better do. In considering the pros and cons for a course of action we often try to separate out the *certainties* relevant to a decision from the mere probabilities: the certainties being things we can *safely* count on. And for this purpose it seems to me that sense-statements may be reckoned as certainties in exactly the same sense as thing-statements. For instance, if the question is: Shall I attend the meeting of the philosophical society tonight? We might say: It's certain I've got this nasty pain; it's certain it only began half an hour ago; and it's certain that, when I've had it before, it's always lasted at least four hours and has made me quite incapable of following an argument while it lasted. Here the certainty that I've got the pain seems to me to play just the same sort of part in this deliberation as the certainty of thing-statements does in others: e.g., as the certainty that there's plenty of hot water in the boiler may play in a deliberation as to whether you shall have a bath: they're both things that can be *safely* counted on. But to say: I have a nasty pain, *and it makes no sense to say 'Perhaps I haven't'*; doesn't seem at all equivalent to saying: That I have this pain is one of the data which can be *safely* counted on in trying to decide what it's wise to do.

I do not see therefore what the fact that it makes no sense to say 'I think I have a pain' has to do with the way in which we are using 'certain' if we say 'It's certain that I have a pain'.

NOTES

1 This is the text of a paper read to the Moral Sciences Club on 21 April 1939 which is now among Moore's papers in the University Library, Cambridge. As the first sentence of the paper shows, Moore's title for the paper was 'Certainty', but since he also used that title for another paper which occurs in this collection, I have changed it to the present title.

2 Wisdom's paper is reprinted in his collection *Philosophy and Psychoanalysis* (Blackwell, Oxford: 1957). I have left Moore's page references to the original publication unchanged.

3 I have inserted the words in square brackets here, since without them the text reads very harshly.

4 Moore's text continues at this point with the words 'because obviously' – but the sentence remains unfinished, and the next sentence begins on the next line.

5 The rest of this paragraph is a long insertion by Moore into his text.

6 Another insertion by me, to make sense of Moore's text.

12

MOORE'S PARADOX[1]

I'm going to talk about the same subject about which W.[2] talked at the first meeting this term, because there are still things which puzzle me about it. I start from this: that it's perfectly absurd or nonsensical to say such things as 'I don't believe it's raining, but as a matter of fact it is' or (what comes to the same thing) 'Though I don't believe it's raining, yet as a matter of fact it really is raining'. I'm just assuming that it is absurd or nonsensical to say such things. But I want it noted that there is nothing nonsensical about *merely saying these words*. I've just said them; but I've not said anything nonsensical. And W. pointed out another proof that there isn't. He pointed out (I think) that there's nothing nonsensical in saying 'It's quite possible that though I don't believe it's raining, yet as a matter of fact it really is' or 'If I don't believe it's raining, but as a matter of fact it really is, then I am mistaken in my belief'. In all these cases the very same identical words are said, but they are said in a context with other words, so that there is nothing nonsensical about them.

So far as I can see, when we say it's absurd to *say* them, we don't mean that it's absurd merely to utter *the words*, but something like this: It's absurd to say them in the sort of way in which people utter sentences, when they are using these sentences to *assert* the proposition which these sentences express. I will call this 'saying them assertively'. I don't want to say that to utter sentences assertively is the same thing as making an assertion. And it's further to be noted that there's nothing absurd in saying in an assertive way 'I don't believe it's raining' and then immediately afterwards 'In fact it is raining'. Two cases show this. W. pointed out to me that a person might say out loud to somebody 'I don't believe it's raining' and then immediately afterwards in a whispered aside to another person say 'As a matter of fact it really is raining', and there would be nothing nonsensical about this: what is true about this case is that one or other of his two assertions would be a *lie*: but to say two things in immediate succession one of which is a lie, is quite a different thing from saying something nonsensical. There's nothing *absurd* about it. And another instance which shews[3] the same is that a person might say such a thing as 'I don't believe he is married; No: as a matter of fact he is married' – saying the two things both in an assertive way, in close succession, but as we should say correcting himself. We might say he's changed his mind: when he said the first he didn't believe the man was married, immediately afterwards, when he said the other, he had remembered he was and did believe it. One may, and often does, believe a thing one moment, and not believe it the next; or the other way about. And there's nothing absurd in saying immediately after one another in an assertion my two sentences.

The forms which I have chosen shew that neither of these two things is the case. 'I don't believe it's raining, but as a matter of fact it is' or 'Though I don't believe it's raining, yet as a matter of fact it is' shew that we are not considering a case where one of the two things is said to one person and the other in an aside to another; not yet a case of change of mind. Nobody would express a change of mind in this way.

To say *these* in an assertive way really is absurd.

But now

(2)[4] It's *paradoxical* that it should be absurd to say them. Why? Two different reasons may be given.

(a) It's quite clear that though it's absurd to say 'I don't believe it's raining but as a matter of fact it is', there's no absurdity whatever in saying of a past occasion 'I didn't believe it was raining, but as a matter of fact it was'. This is in itself paradoxical: because, as a rule, if it's not absurd to say 'It was raining' it's also not absurd to say 'It is raining'. But also though it's absurd for me to say this of myself *in the present*, it's not the least absurd for another person to say *what seems to express exactly the same proposition* either *to* me or *of* me. There would be nothing absurd in a person saying to me 'I quite accept your statement that you don't believe it's raining, but as a matter of fact it is', or in saying to a third person 'Moore doesn't believe it's raining, but as a matter of fact it is'. These are paradoxical because, as a rule, if it's not absurd for another person to say assertively a sentence expressing a given proposition to me or to a third person, it isn't absurd for me to say assertively a sentence expressing the same proposition.

(b) But this last point is connected with another way of putting the paradox, which seems to me the fundamental one. I've said that if another person were to say of me 'Moore doesn't believe it's raining, but as a matter of fact it is' these words of his express the same proposition as I might express by saying at the same time 'I don't believe it's raining, but as a matter of fact it is'. This does seem to me to be true; and if so, it follows that what is *meant* by a sentence which a person would utter if he said 'I don't believe it's raining, but as a matter of fact it is' is something which may quite well be true, something which isn't a contradiction. And this seems to me clearly the case even if I'm wrong in saying that the meaning of my sentence 'I don't believe . . ., but as a matter of fact . . .' is the same as that of the sentence used by another person who said at the same time 'Moore doesn't believe . . ., but as a matter of fact . . .'. The words 'I don't believe it's raining' when said by a particular person have a definite meaning in English: we can say that what they mean is something about his state of mind – what they mean can't be true unless his state of mind is one which can be properly described by saying he doesn't believe that; and so with 'as a matter of fact it is raining'. The meanings of the two sentences are such that both can be true at the same time. It is quite different from 'It's not raining, but as a matter of fact it is'. Here the meaning of the two sentences is such that they can't both be true. It is a paradox that it should be perfectly absurd to *utter assertively words* of which the *meaning* is something which may quite well be true – is not a contradiction.

(3) Why should it be absurd for me to say about myself a thing which it is not absurd for another person to say about me? Why should it be absurd to utter assertively a sentence which has the same meaning as one which another person may utter about me without any absurdity, and which therefore may quite well express a truth?

Now though, according to me, there's no difference between what's *meant* by the sentence he utters assertively and what's *meant* by the sentence I utter assertively, and both express what may perfectly well be true; there is a difference between what I *imply* by uttering assertively the words 'it's raining' and what you *imply* by uttering the same words at the same time in the same place. Namely I *imply* that I believe it's raining and *not* that you do; you imply that you do, and not that I do. Of course it isn't true that the proposition expressed by my words *implies* that I believe it: from the proposition that it's raining it certainly doesn't follow that I believe it is. Nor is it true that from the proposition that I utter the words assertively it *follows* that I believe it: I might be lying. But yet it seems to me it's quite in accordance with ordinary language to say that by uttering these words I do *imply* that I believe it. Suppose we hear a man asserting one day that the so-called works of Shakspeare were really written by Bacon; and suppose meeting him that we say 'So you believe that Shakspeare's works were written by Bacon'. And suppose he answers 'No, I don't'. We might feel some surprise, and say 'Have you changed your mind since yesterday? You certainly implied yesterday that you did believe it'. And suppose he answered 'Yes, I *have* changed my mind since yesterday: yesterday I did believe that Bacon wrote Shakspeare, and I don't believe it now. But I entirely deny your proposition that I *implied* yesterday that I believed it. All that I did yesterday was to assert that Bacon did write Shakspeare's works, and by doing this I didn't in the least imply that I believed he did'. I think it's quite plain such a man would be grossly misusing language in saying that he hadn't implied that he believed it; even though it's perfectly true that the proposition that he believed it doesn't follow from what he asserted, and also doesn't follow from the fact that he asserted it.

But if so, what I imply by saying this contradicts what is meant by my saying that I don't believe it: so that there is a contradiction between what I implied and something that I said, though none between the two things I said. And I suggest that this is why it is absurd for me to say it, even though there's no contradiction between the two things I said. But now the question may be raised: What's meant by saying that I imply it? The only answer I can see to this is that it is something which follows from the following empirical fact: *viz.* that in the immense majority of cases in which a person says a thing assertively, he does *believe* the proposition which his words express.

Because this is so, a person's saying certain words assertively *tends* to make his hearer believe that he does believe the proposition expressed. We can't say it *always* makes us believe this, for if a person is a notorious liar, and the thing in question is a kind of thing about which he is apt to lie, we shan't think he believes it; and even if he isn't, we may have special reason to think he's lying in this instance. We can't therefore say that saying a thing assertively always does make the hearer believe that the speaker believes it. But it does *tend* to, and I think this may be all that's meant by saying his saying so-and-so *implies* that he believes that so-and-so.[5]

I don't see that there's any sense in which you can be said to be using language improperly by saying something assertively when you don't believe it. When you are lying, it doesn't follow that you are using language improperly.

But I feel there is a gap here.

I think the things I began with wouldn't be absurd to say, *unless* it was true that by saying a thing assertively we imply that we believe it. But I don't know that this fully explains why it is absurd.

I think the natural reaction to anybody saying this would be 'What a nonsensical thing to say! How can you *know* that it really is raining, when you don't believe it?'.

When a person says a thing assertively we often ask: 'How do you know that?' – as if by saying it he *implied* not only that he believed it but that he *knew* it. And *very* often we do. And I think it's again true that in the immense majority of cases where people assert a thing positively they do know it.

This introduces one last remark. W. pointed out that there is a similar absurdity in saying: 'Possibly it isn't raining, but as a matter of fact it is'. And this may be put in the form: 'It isn't certain that it's raining, but as a matter of fact it is'.

NOTES

1 This is an untitled and incomplete manuscript from the Moore papers in the University Library, Cambridge, which Moore never prepared for publication; the manuscript is rather messy and in some places Moore's handwriting is difficult to decipher. I tentatively date it from 1944. In several of his lecture courses from the 1930s Moore had briefly mentioned his 'paradox', and he described it in his 1942 reply to his critics in *The Philosophy of G.E. Moore* and in his 1944 essay 'Russell's Theory of Descriptions' (reprinted in his

Philosophical Papers). But he never published an extended discussion of it. There is a letter from Wittgenstein to Moore written in 1944 in which Wittgenstein compliments Moore for a paper he had just given to the Moral Sciences Club about this matter. Could this be the manuscript of this paper? I doubt it – since it presents itself as a response to some remarks of Wittgenstein on this subject. It seems to me more likely that, following Moore's first paper (which is still missing), Wittgenstein gave a paper on the same subject; and then Moore came back to the matter with this paper. Wittgenstein discusses 'Moore's paradox' (the name comes from Wittgenstein) in section x of part II of his *Philosophical Investigations* (Blackwell, Oxford: 1953), which is his selection from the manuscript published as his *Last Writings on the Philosophy of Psychology*, vol. 1 (Blackwell, Oxford: 1982), where there is more discussion of Moore's paradox.

2   'W.' is Wittgenstein.
3   This is the end of page 1. There is no page 2, though there is a page 2a, with four lines of text which have been crossed out and are not reproduced here; the text continues from the top of page 3, which makes perfectly good sense.
4   The numeral '2' here does not succeed an earlier use of '1'; but perhaps one might insert '1' at the start, where Moore says 'I start from this that . . .'.
5   This is the end of page 7 of the manuscript. There is no page 8, and the text which follows comes from page 9.

13

LETTER TO MALCOLM[1]

My dear Malcolm

It is now about a fortnight since I received your very welcome gift of the May *Philosophical Review* containing your article.[2] I read your article through the moment it arrived, and my first feeling about it was that it was a very excellent piece of philosophical writing; but still I was not convinced that you were right as to the main things you wanted to say. On re-reading and reconsideration I have become still more doubtful whether you were right, and since then I have been trying to get as clear as I can as to the reasons for doubting whether you are. Twice already I have begun writing to you about it, but have scrapped what I had written, because it didn't seem to me clear enough as to the main point. I'm now going to make a third attempt.

On p.203 you end your second examples[3] by saying: 'If a doubt remained as to whether it was a real tree *the matter could be finally settled* by approaching nearer to the stage'. Now it seems to me that to say that the matter had been *finally settled* would be merely another way of saying that all the members of the party had come to *know for certain* that the object in question was a real tree: certainly if they all had, it would have been finally settled; and if they hadn't all, it wouldn't. And I think it would clearly be a perfectly natural use of language for one of those who had not been convinced by the one who said 'I saw the leaves move in the breeze', to say, when they had come near enough to settle the question, 'Well, we all know *now* that it's a real tree' or 'Well, it's perfectly certain *now* that it's a real tree'. In other words, I think it is perfectly rational to use such language not only when there *is* a question or a doubt, but also when there *just has been* a question or a doubt, but no longer *is* one because the matter has

213

just been finally settled. This, and not the one you give, is, I think, obviously the right account of the use of the words 'It's perfectly obvious now that it is a tree' in your example on p.215. You say 'The use of the words was to remove the doubt'. But how absurd! It might perfectly well be the case that the doubt had *already* been removed: that the whole party could already see quite clearly that it was a tree: and yet it would be perfectly natural to use the words, just because there *had*, just previously, been a doubt, though there no longer *is* one.

But now, supposing this is the case, *in what sense* would the person who said 'Well, it's perfectly certain now that it's a real tree' be using the expression 'It's perfectly certain that it's a real tree'? What would he be *asserting* by the use of those words? What would be necessary and sufficient to make his assertion *true*? He would be asserting something which had been brought about by a sufficiently close approach to the stage on the part of the whole party – namely that they all, at the moment at which he was speaking, knew for certain that the object in question was a real tree. And though the words he used, particularly the emphatic use of 'now' (as is also the case, though you don't seem to have noticed it, in the case of your 'It's perfectly obvious *now* that it's a tree' on p.215), can, in a good sense, be said to have *implied* that, just previously, they didn't know this for certain, yet I think it is certain that this is no part of what he would have been *asserting* – no part of what is necessary to make his assertion *true*.

Whether his assertion is true or not depends solely on what is the case at the moment when he speaks, not at all on what has been the case just before, although it would not have been natural for him to use the expression unless, just before, they had *not* all been in the condition in which they are now. It is something which has been brought about by the nearer approach, which makes his assertion true; and this, which has been brought about by the nearer approach, and which is rightly called in the case of each of the party 'knowing for certain that' the object in question 'is a real tree', is identical with what was the case with me (and with you), when, sitting in my garden two years ago, I pointed or nodded at the young walnut-tree and said 'I know that that is a tree'. You wanted then, and want now, to say that my use of that expression was a 'misuse' and 'incorrect'; but the only reason you give for saying so is that I

214

used it *under circumstances* under which it would not ordinarily be used, e.g., under the circumstances that there neither was at the moment nor *had been just previously* any doubt whether it was a tree or not. But that I used it *under circumstances* under which it would not ordinarily be used is no reason at all for saying that I misused it or used it incorrectly, if, though this was so, I was using it *in the sense* in which it is ordinarily used – was using it to make *the assertion* which it is ordinarily used to make; and the argument I've just given is an argument designed to shew that I was using it in the ordinary *sense*, though not under any ordinary circumstances. It would, it seems to me, be used in exactly the *sense* in which I was using it by anyone who said, on a sufficiently near approach to the stage in your example, 'Now I know for certain that it is a real tree'; the only difference being that in my case the use of the words was not preceded by a doubt, whereas in the other it was so. If so, it follows that you were wrong not only in saying that mine was a misuse and incorrect, but also in saying that I was using the words in such a way that they 'did not make sense'. It seems to me you have been misled into saying this latter partly at least through having failed to notice an ambiguity in our use of 'senseless'. If a person, under circumstances in which everybody would see quite clearly that a certain object was a tree, were to keep repeatedly pointing at it and saying 'That's a tree' or 'I know that's a tree', we might well say that that was a senseless thing for him to do, and therefore, in a sense, a senseless thing for him to say; and even if he said it only once, under such circumstances, we might well say that it was a senseless thing for him to do – meaning, in all these cases, that it was the sort of thing which a sensible person wouldn't do, because, under those circumstances, it could serve no useful purpose to say those words (in your rather pompous language on p.216 'it has no function'). But this is an entirely different thing from saying that the words in question don't, on that occasion, 'make sense', if by this is meant something which would follow from the proposition that they were not being used in their ordinary sense. It is perfectly possible that a person who uses them senselessly, in the sense that he uses them where no sensible person would use them because, under those circumstances, they serve no useful purpose, should be using them *in their usual sense*, and that what he asserts by so using them should be *true*. Of course, in my case, I was using them with a purpose – the purpose of disproving a general proposition which many philosophers have made; so that I was not only using them in their usual sense, but also under circumstances where they might possibly serve a useful purpose, though not a purpose for which they would commonly be used. It seems to me absurd that you should say that my usage was a 'misuse' and 'incorrect', merely because I used them under circumstances under which they would not commonly be used, when in fact I used them in exactly *the same sense* in which they are commonly used.[4]

NOTES

1 This letter (dated 28 June 1949) is preserved, along with others from Moore to Malcolm, in the Library of Trinity College, Cambridge. It is reproduced here with the permission of the Librarian.
2 'Defending Common Sense', *Philosophical Review* 58 (1949), pp.201–20.
3 Malcolm is discussing a case in which a member of the audience at an open-air theatre is wondering whether on the stage there is a real tree, or a painted imitation of one.
4 After this point Moore added later (21 July) a further paragraph which is largely concerned with personal matters and which is not reproduced here.

BIBLIOGRAPHY

MOORE'S PRINCIPAL WRITINGS

G.E. Moore: The Early Essays, ed. T. Regan (Temple University Press, Philadelphia: 1986)
Principia Ethica (Cambridge University Press, Cambridge: 1903)
Philosophical Studies (Routledge & Kegan Paul, London: 1922)
Some Main Problems of Philosophy (George Allen & Unwin, London: 1953)
Philosophical Papers (George Allen & Unwin, London: 1959)
Commonplace Book, ed. C. Lewy (George Allen & Unwin, London: 1962)
Lectures on Philosophy, ed. C. Lewy (George Allen & Unwin, London: 1966)
These volumes do not contain all of Moore's published writings. There is a comprehensive bibliography at the end of *The Philosophy of G.E. Moore*, ed. P.A. Schilpp, which also contains Moore's reply to his critics.

SECONDARY LITERATURE

Critical studies

The Philosophy of G.E. Moore, ed. P.A. Schilpp (Northwestern, Evanston: 1942)
G.E. Moore: Essays in Retrospect, eds A. Ambrose and M. Lazerowitz (George Allen & Unwin, London: 1970)
T. Baldwin, *G.E. Moore* (Routledge, London: 1990)
A. White, *G.E. Moore* (Blackwell, Oxford: 1958)

Biographical

J.M. Keynes, 'My Early Beliefs' in *Two Memoirs* (Hart-Davis, London: 1949)
P. Levy, *Moore: G.E. Moore and the Cambridge Apostles* (Weidenfeld & Nicolson, London: 1979)
L. Woolf, *Sowing* (Hogarth, London: 1960)

INDEX

Made in the USA
Middletown, DE
03 November 2016